FROM PAUPERS
TO PRIME MINISTERS

A LIFE IN DEATH

THE
STORY

Brian McGarry. Fifty years in funeral and cremation services.
May 1, 1962–May 1, 2012.

Jean-Marc Carisse.

FROM PAUPERS
TO PRIME MINISTERS

A LIFE IN DEATH

THE
STORY

BRIAN M^cGARRY

WITH

PAUL MAHAR

GSPH

GENERAL STORE PUBLISHING HOUSE INC.
499 O'Brien Road, Renfrew, Ontario, Canada K7V 3Z3
Telephone 1.613.432.7697 or 1.800.465.6072
www.gsph.com

ISBN 978-1-897508-45-9 (softcover)
ISBN 978-1-926962-49-8 (hardcover)

Design and formatting: Magdalene Carson
Printed by Image Digital Printing Ltd. dba The IDP Group, Renfrew, Ontario
Printed and bound in Canada

Library and Archives Canada Cataloguing in Publication
McGarry, Brian, 1943-
From paupers to prime ministers : a life in death / Brian McGarry ;
as told to Paul Mahar.
Contents: v. 1. The story. v. 2. The album.
ISBN 978-1-897508-45-9 (v. 1 pbk).--ISBN 978-1-926962-49-8 (v. 1 bound)
ISBN 978-1-897508-53-4 (v. 2)
1. McGarry, Brian, 1943-. 2. Hulse, Playfair and McGarry Ltd.--History.
3. McGarry Family Chapels Inc.--History. 4. Funeral homes--Ontario--
Ottawa--History. 5. Death care industry--Ontario--Ottawa--Biography.
I. Mahar, Paul, 1972- II. Title.
HD9999.U54H85 2012   338.7'61363750971384   C2010-905601-9

Cover photographs:
Front:
The casket of John Diefenbaker leaves Parliament Hill, 1979: Rod MacIvor / *Ottawa Citizen.*
Back, from left to right:
Charles Hulse and Keith Playfair: *Yousef Karsh.* Brian McGarry: *Jean-Marc Carisse.*

Dedicated to my children,
Brett, Erin, and Sheetza;
and to my grandchildren,
Bobby and Sacha McGarry;
and
to loyal colleagues who have helped preserve
this family-owned Canadian institution.

All proceeds from this book will be donated
to the Ottawa Regional Cancer Foundation
and the Queensway-Carleton Hospital.

TABLE OF CONTENTS

ACKNOWLEDGEMENTS

The two books that comprise *From Paupers to Prime Ministers—A Life in Death*, *The Story* and *The Album*, began three and a half years ago. What is basically a memoir along with a narrative and visual history of Hulse, Playfair & McGarry, from 1925 to the present, would never have reached completion without the following people working behind the scenes: co-author and researcher Paul Mahar; GSPH senior editor Susan Code McDougall, who kept us focused; GSPH art director Magdalene Carson, who provided creative vision; photo researcher Vivian Bellar-Spruyt, who tracked every photo, seeking out photographers' names with tenacious effort; Donna Richardson and Charlyne McNeil, both of whom kept me organized (a near impossible task) while holding down day jobs on The Hill; Heather Clairoux, my right arm at McGarry Family Chapels; Dorothy Robinson and Pam Heney, who manage our company archives; and finally Tim Gordon, GSPH publisher, who was referred to me by Roy McGregor, a great author. To Roy I will be forever grateful for introducing me to this professional team.

To the many photographers whose work appears in *The Album* and *The Story*, thank you for your professionalism; in particular, Jean-Marc Carisse, as we travel through life, often together, meeting paupers to prime ministers.

On behalf of my family, thank you all.

—Brian McGarry

FOREWORD

by Rabbi Reuven P. Bulka

In truth, I could have written the foreword to Brian McGarry's multi-faceted book, *From Paupers to Prime Ministers—The Story*, without reading it. Here is what I would have said.

It is a real delight to write the foreword to Brian McGarry's book. It is hard to overestimate the contributions Brian has made to our community. His efforts at the school board are well chronicled. He was a true leader who brought wisdom and clarity to a challenging range of issues. And education is the foundation of everything we do.

When the prospect of bringing "back" the Ottawa Senators became a serious contemplation, it was Brian McGarry who was one of the very first to step up to the plate with more than a lip-service endorsement. The modern-day version of the Senators has not yet brought the Stanley Cup to the nation's capital, but they have been winners in every other way, and we as a community are immeasurably enhanced by their presence. In assessing the many factors and persons who made it happen, Brian McGarry's support ranks right at the top.

To this day, Brian is front and centre with the Ottawa Regional Cancer Foundation. He is honorary chair of the Courage Campaign, which raised over $20 million for cancer care and research and is now shooting to raise $50 million. And, as usual with Brian, he led by example. I know how much he meant to the campaign, because I worked with him, in my capacity as the chair of the first phase of the campaign.

You might not expect it from a funeral director, but Brian has always brought cheer and positive thoughts to our seemingly endless number of meetings, as well as great ideas. And he was a team player.

Finally, there was Brian McGarry the funeral director, or, as I prefer to call him, the complete service provider. By way of full disclosure, there were a number of times the service provision was for personal tragedies—the passing of my young son, and then my first wife. Those were times of intense grief.

Looking back, I realize what a difference it made to know that any and every need that would fall under the umbrella of a funeral home was in such good, capable, and understanding hands. I experienced first-hand what so many others dealing with tragedy experience: the comfort that comes from dealing with a caring company, headed by Brian as CEO.

Hulse, Playfair & McGarry, now McGarry Family Chapels, has for years been the major funeral service provider for the Jewish community in Ottawa. It is an unusual partnership, in that certain ritual aspects of the preparation of the deceased are done by Jewish community volunteers who form the *chevra kadisha*, which literally means "sacred group." Preparing the deceased for burial through cleansing and dressing in shrouds is a sacred undertaking, and is carried out with painstaking dedication by these devoted people. The other logistics are entrusted to funeral chapels.

Brian has been in the forefront of assuring these services are carried out with class and efficiency. This he has done for a grateful community for decades. I know from the many funerals at which I have officiated how much the families appreciate the work of Brian and his team.

So, it is with the fullness of gratitude that I share these introductory words with you, the reader. Knowing Brian as I do, I am sure you will thoroughly enjoy his book.

This is the introduction as I would have written it without reading the book.

But I did read the book, from cover to cover, and therefore share with you a few more introductory thoughts.

Be aware that this is not one book. Instead, it is actually a few books within one book. One book is the Brian McGarry story. Another book is the story of Hulse & Playfair, which became Hulse, Playfair & McGarry, and now McGarry Family Chapels.

The books are at once somewhat independent and overlapping, with each containing a remarkable collection of insights. The reader will be drawn into the stories, and at the same time will be reconnected to some of the most memorable persons and events in Canada's history. The view from the inside is fascinating.

A few themes emerge. Brian McGarry the person and Brian McGarry the funeral director / CEO are faced with enormous challenges, which are overcome through unrelenting determination and uncompromising commitment. The two stories are intriguing dramas that become triumphs of the will, and are thereby truly inspirational.

There are parts of the book that are really funny, if not hilarious, and not all of it black humour. But, ultimately, this is a book about dignifying death. The dignity we give to the deceased translates into the dignity we give to life itself. That is the subtle but unmistakable message of this extraordinary book and Brian McGarry's extraordinary life.

Read and enjoy.

Charles Hulse welcomes new partner, Brian McGarry, to Hulse & Playfair's
Central Chapel, McLeod Street, 1972.

Courtesy of the Hulse Family Archives.

CHAPTER 1

A Death in the Family

Charles Hulse was dying. Early in the fall of 1986, his doctor discovered a hard fist of cancer wrapped around his prostate. Charlie knew all too well the battle that he faced. He had watched the quiet devastation of cancer take his first wife and childhood sweetheart, Lillian, when she was still a young woman. This painful experience led him to co-found the Ottawa chapter of the Canadian Cancer Society.

The perseverance that had accompanied him on his journey from Orangeville, a small town northwest of Toronto, to the homes of prime ministers would not abandon him now. He faced the disease with his characteristic good nature and a quiet sense of acceptance.

The treatments started soon after he was diagnosed—chemotherapy and a daily regimen of pills and medications—but by Christmas of 1987, the cancer had spread into his bones. He was eighty-eight years old, a good long life in his own estimation, and even though he was beginning to have difficulty walking, nothing was going to keep him from getting to his sunny winter retreat.

Years before, Charlie had built a home on Anna Maria Island, a white-sand paradise just off the west coast of Florida in the Gulf of Mexico. In the years after he retired in 1964, he and his second wife, Margie, would make their annual journey south, loading up their big Lincoln Continental after the last colourful vestiges of autumn had been swept off the trees. I can remember many times helping to load that car. Sometimes, Charlie and Margie would come back to Ottawa for Christmas, the car loaded with neatly wrapped presents and smelling vaguely of coconut oil, but in his last few years the travelling became too much of a strain, and they stayed in Florida until spring.

Charlie knew his time was running out. His doctors had given him the sombre assessment that he probably had one more year left. He lived without regrets and never gave up the fight, always talking excitedly about new treatments and research and the brilliant minds of those fine young doctors who were working on a cure. Not once did I hear him bemoan his condition.

Charlie had his religion, raised in a strict Anglican family, but I wouldn't say his faith was his anchor. He was very matter-of-fact about his own impending mortality, and his stoic acceptance was both inspiring and comforting to see. Of course, he had been involved with thousands of funerals over the course of his career, and no doubt all of those experiences had given him a unique perspective. The tenuous fragility of life becomes very clear when you deal with death on a daily basis.

I often called Charlie in Florida to chat, never tiring of the stories he would tell about his early years working in Orangeville at his uncle's funeral home where he had learned to handle a team of horses, carefully guiding them as they pulled the hearse over bumpy dirt roads and down long country lanes. Charlie also liked to reminisce about the years he spent working as a travelling casket salesman for Dominion Manufacturers, crisscrossing southern Ontario more times than he could count and making friends in every town along the way.

Right up until the end of his life, Charlie was interested in hearing about what was going on with the business he had founded on luck and determination, and then built into one of the most respected funeral homes in Canada. He would listen carefully as I related news of the funeral home, and then offer suggestions or impart an anecdote of a similar experience. Even after I became a senior partner, I often called him for advice. He was an icon in funeral service and I was grateful for his direction. I can hear his voice clearly in my memories even now:

"When are you going to build a new funeral home?"

"Remember to give back to the community."

"You have to do more than put up new wallpaper and a coat of paint. You have to think ahead."

Even after he officially retired, Charlie remained involved with the business on a professional level as chairman of the board, a position he held until he died. He was a valued adviser to the firm, but he was also a good friend.

On one particular day in the middle of a bleak winter afternoon in 1987, I sat in my office, staring down at the phone in dismay. I had been putting off the call I knew I had to make. I had just been betrayed by a business partner and, as a result, one of the large funeral conglomerates was going to get a major foothold in Hulse, Playfair & McGarry, and there was nothing I could do to stop them. I was calling Charlie to tell him that the company that he had founded sixty-two years earlier was in danger of losing the independence that he had been so proud of. It felt like I had lost the keys to the castle.

Years before, when the conglomerates began absorbing funeral homes across North America, the biggest of these companies, Service Corporation International (SCI), of Houston, Texas, made Charlie a lucrative offer to buy his business. He turned them down flat. Swelling with overconfidence, the representatives from SCI told Charlie he wouldn't be able to compete, that he was clinging to an old, outdated business model and would eventually have no choice but to sell, if not to SCI, then to another conglomerate. In their minds, it was only a matter of time. Of course, bombastic threats only served to strengthen Charlie's resolve, and he began thinking of ways he could work around the corporate giants. It would be an uphill battle. Charlie could see that the conglomerates were getting stronger, and pressure was increasing steadily on smaller, family-run businesses.

As part of their business strategy, corporate funeral service operators buy up small family firms, and then make deals with suppliers who lower their prices in order to get the business. Because of this arrangement, the conglomerates can pressure their suppliers to maintain higher prices for small independent funeral homes.

Charlie knew a handful of small business owners who had retired and sold their stores to their employees, but this was unheard of for a larger business like his. Nevertheless, it prompted Charlie to ask the question: Could the same strategy work for Hulse & Playfair?

After going over the numbers with his senior staff and accountants, Charlie decided to try it. He opened the door to trusted employees and invited them to buy a share of the business and become partners. If the arrangement worked, and if the tradition was continued, there was no reason why the funeral home could not maintain its independence indefinitely. As it turned out, Charlie was one of the first bigger business owners in Canada to employ this strategy. I remember clearly the meeting we had where Charlie stood up to explain the plan.

"You know," he said, "if it was all about money, I wouldn't be here with you right now." He looked around the room, "This business is not about money, it's about serving the families who put their trust and faith in us."

It was a significant lesson, one that I never forgot. Charlie believed strongly that the first and most important reason we are funeral directors is to help people. A few days later, during the trip back to the funeral home after a service, he explained his rationale.

"It's only right that we give back to the folks who support us locally. How can these conglomerates be involved in the community in Ottawa when their office is in Texas?"

I drove and listened.

"You know, Brian, someday you might be asked to become a partner in this firm, and if that happens, you have to promise me one thing."

"What's that, Mr. Hulse?"

"That you will never sell out."

I promised, and eight years later I became a partner.

Charlie knew "Tricky Dickie" by reputation, and had warned me to be cautious a few months earlier when I explained the plan to bring Dickie in as a partner. Dickie had earned his reputation by buying funeral homes and then quickly turning them over for a profit. Many people saw him as an astute businessman, and I found this to be true. I also found him to be a very intelligent man, ahead of the curve in funeral service in many ways. He had helped me immeasurably by putting together the deal that would allow me to buy out my senior partners, who were all approaching retirement. Because most of the other staff members were too young to be able to buy in, and I didn't have the resources to buy the whole firm, Dickie agreed to sign on as an equal partner. As part of this agreement, he promised to stay for at least five years, which would give me enough time to bring in other partners from within the firm to buy him out. It seemed like a perfect solution to the problem.

While Dickie had arrived under the guise that he could help me out of a bind, I'm not sure that was ever his intention. In retrospect, I think he was there purely to help himself. The ink wasn't dry on the initial agreement when he started shopping his shares across North America to anyone who might be interested. Our partnership, which had seemed so promising at the beginning, would last less than eight months.

Charlie listened carefully as I explained the details to him over the phone. He was bedridden by this point, and I could hear his laboured breathing.

"I don't think I can keep the conglomerates out, Mr. Hulse."

There was a pause.

"Well, it's a changing world out there, Brian, and not everybody is of their word." His voice was weak and strained. "Are you and Sharon going to sell your shares?"

"No. We're doing all we can to maintain control."

"That's good. You've certainly had your hands full with Dickie . . ."

He was right. It had been a trying and stressful few months. I was doing all I could to convince Tricky Dickie to sell an extra 3 percent to my wife Sharon and me, which would put us at 53 percent, a small majority, but enough to keep control of the firm. The problem was that when Dickie offered his shares for sale, he had sparked a bidding war among the three largest conglomerates in the funeral business, and the price of the shares had doubled overnight. Sharon and I had stretched ourselves financially just to purchase the initial 50 percent, mortgaging our home in the process, so even if we could convince Dickie to sell the extra shares to us, we weren't exactly sure how we were going to pay for them. Our resources were running out. I knew one thing, though; I was determined to keep my promise to Charlie and I just needed to find a way to do it.

Charlie and I talked some more, and at the end of the conversation, he asked me to come down to Florida to see him. I told him I'd make arrangements to get down there before spring.

"Don't worry, Brian. I'll be home soon enough, and I'll have a chat with this Dickie fellow."

We said our goodbyes, but Charlie stopped me right before I hung up. "Brian," he said, "I knew you'd make the right choice when it came right down to it."

I was relieved that he hadn't felt let down and that he was confident the firm was in good hands. It strengthened my resolve to keep pushing for control. I knew we were in for a battle, but Sharon and I were determined that we would not sell out.

A few days later in the early afternoon of Thursday, March 12, 1987, I was at a military funeral at Uplands air force base. Two officers had been killed in a Hercules crash, and we were handling one of the funerals. The officer had a young family, so it was a very emotional ceremony. My cell phone rang, and I excused myself from the service in order to answer it. It was Laird Barclay, one of our most senior staff members and a partner.

"Charlie's gone . . ."

The words rang through my mind like a bell. I was moved. Charlie had been my mentor at the funeral home, teaching me all he had learned about business, but he was also like a father to me. Even though we all knew he was ill, the news of his death still came as a shock. It was the beginning of March, and he would have been returning to Ottawa in only a few weeks. Everyone expected him to make it home.

It's very rare for me to leave a funeral, but in this instance I just couldn't stay. I was struck emotionally, and I knew that it would be impossible for me to concentrate on the proceedings at hand. We had enough staff members at Uplands to handle the rest of the service, so I left and made my way to the office. Charlie's wife, Margaret, had phoned us right away. She and their daughter Helen had been with Charlie when he passed away, and their other daughter Phyllis had just left his bedside to go back to Toronto. His body was still at the house, and we made arrangements with the Griffith-Cline Funeral Home in Florida, which is on the mainland near the causeway leading to Anna Maria Island. We had used this same funeral home ten years before when Keith Playfair had died at his winter home. Even in retirement the two former partners were only a stone's throw from each other.

Arbor, the funeral conglomerate that was about to become my unwanted partner, had a branch in Florida. It ran through my mind to call on them to remove Charlie's body and do the initial preparation, but I was so angry that we were being forced into a partnership that I decided to call the independent funeral home that had served us so well before. Laird began to make arrangements with Griffith-Cline, and I called Margaret.

"Hello, Brian . . . What should I do?"

It was telling that she was asking me this. While she had never worked at the funeral home, she had become well acquainted with most aspects of the funeral business over the years.

"What would you like to do, Margaret?"

"I . . . I just don't know."

"Would you like to have a viewing in Florida for your friends there?"

"No. I think I would like to get back to Ottawa as soon as possible. That's what Charlie would have wanted."

"That's fine, Margaret. We'll take care of everything."

We arranged for her airline ticket, and she flew home the next day. We had all the information we needed to transfer Charlie's body across the border, and we signed all the paperwork on Margaret's behalf.

The Griffith-Cline Funeral Home in Florida was very good; they remembered Keith Playfair and knew about our firm. Everything was done professionally, and Charlie would have been pleased. As a sign of respect, Griffith-Cline did most of the work free of charge, even providing a shipping container at no cost. According to American law, any remains that are to be shipped outside of the country must first be embalmed, but I asked them not to apply any cosmetology. We knew Charlie so well that we could take care of that aspect when he arrived home. Of course, they understood completely. There was no autopsy performed, which is normal if the deceased had been undergoing treatment for cancer or any other terminal disease. Charlie wouldn't have wanted an autopsy done.

The good folks at Griffith-Cline did all the necessary preparation quickly, and Charlie's body arrived in Ottawa a day later. A couple of the other senior colleagues and I drove to the airport to pick Charlie up. I felt very strongly that I should be there; it was an emotional event.

We are not allowed to remove remains from the aircraft ourselves. It sounds crude, but the shipping container comes down on a conveyer belt. Airport personnel then place it on a trolley and bring it out to the holding area. From there, we move it into our hearse.

Later that afternoon I had a meeting with Margaret. There wasn't much to consider, as far as preparations. Charlie had already picked out the suit that he wanted to wear and had preplanned most of the other arrangements. Our technicians applied the cosmetics, and they did a fine job. Charlie looked like himself, which of course is the highest compliment you can get as a cosmetologist. Typical of Charlie, he had decided on a top-quality casket, requesting that it be open for the viewing. I often heard him say, "There is a sense of closure when you have an open casket."

It gives friends and family a chance to say goodbye, face to face. But I think Charlie believed that by seeing the deceased, it also allowed a person to fully accept the loss. Not as a way of taking away the pain, but to reach the bottom of that sadness so that the healing process can begin.

In some ways, Charlie lived beyond his means. I remember one story George Schaef, our secretary-treasurer, used to tell. One summer day, Senator Norman Paterson was to attend a service at our funeral home. Parliament had called us in advance to let us know the time of the senator's arrival, so Charlie and George were waiting outside to greet him. At the appointed time, a beautiful Silver Cloud Rolls-Royce pulled up to the front door. The driver emerged to walk around to the back of the car and open the door. Out stepped Senator Paterson. Charlie, obviously impressed by the sleek car and driver, turned to George and quietly remarked, "I'll have one of those some day."

Without missing a beat, George, privy to Charlie's finances, looked over at his boss and remarked wryly, "Oh, no you won't!"

Though he lived an extravagant life, Charlie didn't die a wealthy man. He always said that he was going to spend everything he had, and that's exactly what he did. His two daughters were very successful in their own right, and I remember him saying, "The girls are independent and doing well, why should I leave a big estate?"

So he didn't. It was kind of amazing, really. He seemed to have it timed right up until his last day. It reminded me of that old saying: "The Brink's truck doesn't follow the hearse on the day of your funeral!"

Charlie was a great traditionalist, so in typical Charlie Hulse style, he had chosen a solid mahogany casket—and we paid for it. In fact, we paid for the entire funeral, and I was happy to do so. Some people at the firm would sometimes complain that Charlie spent too much money, but I would always remind them to think about the money he made for other people, and the opportunities he gave his employees. I never criticized him for his extravagant style when he was alive, and I wasn't about to criticize him in death.

"A solid mahogany casket?"

"That's what's on his prearrangement."

"Well, he didn't prepay it."

"But none of us would have jobs if it weren't for Charles Hulse."

Taking care of the expense of the funeral was the least we could do, as far as I was concerned.

To the casual observer, it might look as if Charlie was preoccupied with money. But when you got to know him, you found out that money really meant nothing to him—it was simply a means to an end. He liked fine things, but he wasn't obsessed with them. When he had money, he spent it, and when he didn't have it, he still spent it.

I took some private time in the visitation room before it was opened to the public. Charlie had taken me under his wing when I was seventeen, and had guided me to where I was now. He had always pushed me to take more control and to keep building the business. I owed him a debt for that, and I wasn't too sure how I was going to repay it. As I stood there, looking at him lying in his casket, I couldn't help feeling alone. I was in danger of losing a grip on the firm that he had built up over a lifetime.

There was a lot of pressure from my former partners and my employees to find a solution to the corporate conundrum, and here, lying in a casket, was the one man I would have gone to for advice. As I stood there reflecting on all my memories of this great man, one question kept running through my mind: "What would you do, Charlie?"

Tricky Dickie wanted to be front row centre at Charlie's funeral. We argued about it, and I had to strain to control the anger in my voice. "Don't you come to this funeral. It's not appropriate. There will be a lot of people there who are very proud of what we have accomplished here, and you're not part of it."

Those were the kinds of conversations we were having by that point.

"Well, I'm still a partner."

"In name only. The Hulse family doesn't want to see you. Mrs. Playfair doesn't want you there. You are not welcome."

Begrudgingly, he respected my request and made himself scarce on the day of Charlie's funeral.

Charlie's obituary appeared in the *Globe and Mail*, and there were great accolades for him from across Canada. The *Ottawa Citizen* published an article recounting his life and many achievements, and there was local television coverage of his funeral. He had touched the lives of so many people, helping them to deal with the death of their loved ones. In particular, he had spent a good part of his life working to improve the education system, an issue he was passionate about. Charlie served thirty-one years on the school board, eight as chairman. He was also a governor of Carleton University, helping to raise money for the school when it was a fledgling organization housed in a collection of small buildings on First Avenue in the Glebe. In recognition of this dedication, there's a public school named after him in Ottawa.

In short, he was a well known man around town, and I expected a large number of people to attend the funeral. In fact, I was worried there wouldn't be enough room in our chapel, so I discussed it with Margie.

"Do you think we should have the service at St. John's or St. Luke's?" Both churches are much larger than our chapel.

"You know, Brian, we've been in Florida six or seven months of the year for a lot of years now. I think the chapel at the funeral home will do nicely. Charlie was so proud of that chapel."

We had three visitations scheduled: an afternoon, an evening, and one the following day before the service at two o'clock. I was a little surprised at the number of people who came to the visitation. I thought there might have been more, but Margaret had been right. Charlie had been out of social circulation for some time, and at the age of eighty-eight, many of his friends had predeceased him. If it had been ten or fifteen years earlier, I'm sure the chapel wouldn't have been large enough. With that being said, funeral directors from homes all over the province came to pay their respects and to retell old stories through smiles and tears.

I've often thought a funeral service takes on the personality of the deceased; it's as if a person's character is actually bigger than the physical confines of his or her body. Charlie's funeral was no exception. His love of life and vitality was very much present that day. It was an Anglican service and Archdeacon Doug Christie, a contemporary of Charlie's, conducted the service. The two men had been good friends. Charlie was a devout Anglican, although I can't say that he attended church often in his latter years. There weren't a lot of things said by friends at the service. I didn't speak, and neither did any of the other partners. While Charlie wouldn't have minded being eulogized, Margaret preferred a different approach. Although she was a prominent figure in the community in her own right, she was more low-key than her husband, so speeches were kept to a minimum.

After the service, we brought Charlie to Beechwood Cemetery. There were three limousines for the family, cars for all the visiting funeral directors and the clergy, and a flower car. It was quite a procession. The chief of police had phoned earlier in the day to tell us that they wanted to provide an escort for the cortege, a gesture we accepted with quiet pride. So, with four officers on motorcycles leapfrogging down the street to stop traffic, we made our way to the cemetery. Charlie would have loved every moment.

When we got to the gravesite, I saw the big vault Charlie had picked out. That was Charlie, going out in style. In his prearrangement, he had chosen a Victoriaville 95 casket, mahogany, made in Quebec, the same model that Prime Minister John Diefenbaker was buried in. Similar also to Mr. Diefenbaker, Charlie had requested a vault. Both of these choices were reflective of a different time. A vault is used to keep the casket from caving in under the pressure from the earth on top of it. There are various kinds, and the one Charlie had chosen is called an "open end" vault. It looks like a big, steel mailbox. On one end there's a flap, which opens up and flips onto the top. The casket is placed in the opening, pushed inside, then the flap is brought down and sealed. Once this is done, the vault and casket are lowered into the grave. With the growing prevalence of cremation these days, vaults are becoming increasingly rare, a relic from a bygone era, but Charlie liked them. After he retired, Charlie would sometimes sit in on an arrangement if he knew the family, or if it was the funeral of a friend. He would listen quietly and occasionally offer suggestions. On more than one occasion he would say, "The firm should give them a vault."

A vault is not an inexpensive option, but he was the boss, so there was no room for discussion. "Would you accept a vault on behalf of Mr. Hulse?" I would then ask.

"Well, sure. That's very nice of you, Charlie."

Typical of Charlie, he wanted to give something to someone. Make it a bit more special. He loved to do that, even when it wasn't his money! Our treasurer George Schaef used to say to me that the way Charlie spent money, all he could do was to look at the pile of bills that would arrive on his desk almost daily, take the one on the bottom, and pay it. If he ever made it through one pile of bills, there would inevitably be another stack waiting to be brought in, all with Charlie's signature on them.

This thought brought a smile to my face as I watched Charlie's casket being placed into the vault. There was a brief prayer, then it was lowered into the ground.

After the funeral, a reception was held at the Laurentian Club, where Charlie had been a long-time member. As a younger man, he had tried to get into the Rideau Club, which, in those days, was seen as the premier men's club in Ottawa, but had been rejected, a sore spot for Charlie. "I guess they don't want a lowly undertaker."

It was true, but that was a different era, a time when women were not accepted into the club, and Charlie's friend Lawrence Freiman was refused because he was Jewish. All of this, of course, has since changed and the Rideau Club of today is a progressive institution.

The reception is such an important part of funerals now. It allows people to take a breath after the emotional events of the service and burial, to ease back into the world of the living. Of course, keeping with the typical club atmosphere, Charlie had made sure there were drinks available at his reception. It was a convivial event attended by many prominent Ottawa figures from Charlie's past.

After a couple of hours, everyone said their goodbyes and made their way home. The club is only a short distance from the funeral home and the upstairs apartment where my family and I were living at the time, and where Charlie's family had lived before us (in fact, we always referred to it as "Charlie's apartment"). So, I decided to walk. The events of the previous few days had been busy, and as I made my way down the street I realized that at some point during the planning and funeral, I had slipped into work mode, allowing myself to become emotionally distanced. I think this happened partly out of reflex, but I suppose it was also a way of dealing with my painful loss, putting off having to accept Charlie's passing. It's a defence mechanism that I have often noticed in others, sometimes exhibited by throwing themselves into work or a favourite hobby. I walked down the street with my hands buried in my overcoat. The dull grey clouds that had been hanging in the sky all week had given way to a starry night that was all too indifferent to the loneliness I felt. I was truly on my own.

We have one employee who swears to this day that, on occasion, when he walks through the funeral home in the evening turning off the lights, he catches a glimpse of Charlie in the chapel. I haven't seen Charlie's ghost, yet, but I do know that his spirit is alive and well in the firm.

Brian's father, William McGarry, weeks before his death in a
mining accident, with his daughter Mary-Ellen, age two, and
sons Brian, age ten, and David, age thirteen. 1953.

Courtesy of the McGarry Family Archives.

CHAPTER 2

The Long Road to Ottawa

There's an old steam train that chugs through the picturesque landscape of the Gatineau Hills on its way from Ottawa to Wakefield, Quebec. These days, its cargo is made up of summer tourists and families eager to experience a bygone era, but until the early 1960s, the train was a vital lifeline for residents of the small west Quebec farming communities scattered between Ottawa and Maniwaki. The train brought people and manufactured goods from the city and returned with produce from local farmers and raw minerals from the area's quarries and mines.

One sunny June evening in 1911, among the passengers was a young doctor who had recently graduated from McGill medical school. Originally from Quebec City, he had decided to set up his new practice in Wakefield. As the train made its regular stop at Farm Point, just south of Wakefield, the conductor hurriedly walked down the aisle looking for the doctor. When he found the right compartment, he breathlessly explained that there was a medical emergency—a woman was in labour at a nearby farm. Of course, small towns being what they are, everyone knew that the new physician was arriving that day. A family member was waiting on the platform when the train pulled in and had asked the conductor to speak to the doctor to see if he could help. The good doctor accepted, got off the train, and was taken to the farm by horse-drawn carriage.

The woman in labour was my grandmother, and she was about to give birth to my mother. The young physician who was starting his new job a little earlier than he expected was Dr. Harold Geggie, a man who would come to play a major part in my family and my life. The delivery was successful, and years later, Dr. Geggie would joke with my mother, "I know exactly how old you are, Lyla!"

My mother's family, the Crosses, were well established and prosperous farmers in Farm Point, Quebec, and owned quite a lot of land. My grandfather and his four brothers were not highly educated, but in Wakefield at that time, the most practical education came from working on the family farm.

The Crosses employed seasonal workers in the spring during the planting season and in the fall when there was thrashing and other farm work to be done. One of the young men who worked for them was my father, Bill McGarry.

The McGarrys and the Crosses couldn't have been more different. My dad's side of the family was known to be hard workers and labourers, but they didn't have a knack for business. This fact didn't seem to bother them much, though, and didn't stop them from enjoying life. By all accounts, they were a convivial group, and you wouldn't be in a McGarry home for any length of time before someone would sit down at the piano and start plunking away. Before long there would be people gathered around, singing and playing the fiddle and spoons. My father had eleven brothers and sisters (one died as an infant), and all were very musical. On occasion, a little too much liquor would be involved, and one story often retold involved a party near Mont Cascade, where a fiddler was having such a good time that he fell off his chair. As the story goes, he was quickly propped back up and continued playing without missing a beat.

My mother's family was more staid and focused on business, working hard to make sure the farm was prosperous. Over time, they were able to expand, eventually buying real estate in the Gatineau Hills. We would often go over to my grandparents' home for Sunday dinner, and I remember seeing my grandfather on humid summer evenings dressed in a suit and tie. As a church-going family, Sunday was a day of rest and respect, and for my grandfather that meant all day.

The Crosses and the McGarrys didn't interact very often socially, and the Crosses were seen in the community as more refined than the McGarrys. Nevertheless, one spring day during the planting season, my father caught the eye of young Lyla Cross. Later that summer, they saw each other again at a place called the Tip Top, a dance hall built on top of a hill in Cascades, Quebec, popular with young people in the area. My mother was dating another fellow at the time, but my father swept her off her feet. Their relationship was cautiously accepted by the Cross family, but viewed as a bit unequal in the social strata of village life. My father was seen as being from the wrong side of the tracks, a label that followed him for the rest of his life.

Even as a child I could sense that my grandfather looked down on my dad somewhat. He would never say it out loud, but I could feel it. Every Christmas, my grandfather would give my mother a box of Laura Secord chocolates with

$500 cash inside. Even though it looked like a box of chocolates, everyone knew what it was. That was a lot of money back in those days, but it always bothered me because it was only ever addressed "To Lyla," never "Bill and Lyla." My brother David and I would hand out the presents, and we would always save the box of chocolates for last. The Crosses liked my dad, so I don't think this gift was mean-spirited on my grandfather's part, but I don't think they took the McGarrys very seriously. They were thought of as fun-loving, happy-go-lucky people, as opposed to the more serious and accomplished Cross clan.

After my parents were married in 1937, Grandfather Cross helped them buy their house, a two-storey home alongside La Pêche Creek, just outside Wakefield, Quebec. The newlyweds had no money at all at that time. Dad could hardly read or write, but Mom would eventually teach him to do both. They would sit together at the kitchen table every night with a copy of the *Ottawa Journal* spread out in front of them. Mom would read aloud, tracing the words with her fingers until Dad was reading on his own.

I was born in 1943 in that house, delivered by Dr. Geggie, as were both my brother, David, and my sister, Mary-Ellen. Upstream from us there was a gristmill. On Saturday mornings during the autumn, Mom and Dad would take us there to watch the farmers bringing in their grain to be ground up. I was amazed to see these great, noisy, wooden wheels and thick leather belts driven using only the flow of the water for power.

Dad worked hard to support his young family. Like many of the men in Wakefield at that time, autumn meant a trip down to southern Ontario for the tobacco harvest. It was gruelling work, but it paid well, and in the two months he was away, he could earn enough money to get us through the winter. There was never a shortage of things to do around the house, and when work was slow, you could find Dad outside cutting firewood for the wood furnace in the basement. Eventually, Dad went on to find more stable employment closer to home at Morrison's Quarry, which was at that time owned by the Aluminum Company of Canada. They mined raw bauxite, which was sent off to be processed into aluminum. It was hard work, but steady, and eventually Dad was promoted to foreman.

During the week, Dad would leave for work very early in the morning, but if it was cold outside, he would first go down to the basement and put some wood in the furnace. You could hear the big iron door creaking open and the wood being thrown in, then he would come back upstairs, his heavy work boots clunking up the wooden steps. He would walk by our bedrooms, looking in on David, Mary-Ellen, and me, and say goodbye to us before leaving for the day.

I was always close to my dad. Wherever he was, I wanted to be. I used to love watching him shave in the mornings before he went to work. He would sit me on the edge of the sink, so I could watch him as he stirred up the water and shaving cream in a wooden cup, and then brushed it onto his face. He always used a straight razor. In the evenings, I would wait by the front window and watch for him to arrive home from work. Dad had a car, but he never took it to the quarry, always getting a ride with some of the other workers from town. He'd be dropped off at the corner and walk up La Pêche Road to our house. As soon as I saw him coming up the lane, I would run out to greet him and he'd pick me up and throw me over his shoulder. Even now, years later, I can still remember how he smelt—the smell of sweat and dust and hard work—and it always comforted me. After putting me down, he would open his lunch box. Every day he saved me a sandwich, and even if it was soggy and warm, I would gobble it down. It always tasted good.

Ours was a good home, filled with love. We didn't have much money, but we had each other, and we made our own fun.

In the summer, Dad would take David and me down to the village every weekend. He'd pick up some groceries, do his banking, and then take us to the ice cream parlour, where my brother and I would climb up onto the stools on either side of him. I used to imagine that I was in an old Western saloon, like the ones in the comics I read. David and I read comic books voraciously, although he was more interested in science fiction, whereas I went for the cowboy stories—Roy Rogers, Trigger, and Gabby Hayes. Dad would order us buttermilk and, going along with my Western daydream, he'd slide the glass across the counter in front of me and say gruffly, "Here, boy, have a drink," and I'd pretend I was drinking beer. He would add salt to his, so David and I would add salt to ours. The owner of the parlour, Elmer Wills, would come over to talk with my dad about local news and gossip. Dad was a very social person and he always had a new joke or story to tell. I have a lot of good memories of the ice cream parlour, all of them filled with laughter.

Occasionally, Dad would find his way over to the real bar, which was in the Château Diotte hotel. The building is still there today, but it's now called the

Black Sheep Inn and is a popular spot for listening to live music. When it was the Château Diotte, occasionally a country and western band might blow through town, but for the most part it was a watering hole, pure and simple. It was generally frowned upon for men to go to the bar—times were different then—and on Sunday mornings, it wasn't unusual to hear the clergyman sermonizing about the evils of liquor. Dad wasn't a heavy drinker by any means, but we only lived about three hundred yards from the bar, so occasionally he'd wink at me and say, "Brian, I'm just going down to the corner," which meant that he was going down to the bar to have a few beers with the guys. I know Mom didn't like it, as she was very much against any kind of drinking. She would have a glass of wine now and again, but aside from that, she was a teetotaller. She wouldn't say anything in front of my brother and me, but Dad's trips to the bar led to a few serious discussions in hushed tones in the kitchen.

Dad loved all sports, but was especially fond of baseball and hockey. While he never played, he was a top-notch spectator, and whenever he could afford it, he would take me into Ottawa to see a game. I don't ever remember David coming on these trips; he preferred books to sports and would spend most of his free time reading. In the winter, Dad would bundle me up and we'd go over to pick up John Caves, a friend of his from the Aluminum Company, and the three of us would head into town. Back in those days, a hockey game was a big event, and I can remember Dad putting on a shirt, tie, and fedora before leaving for the game.

Dad only had two cars in his life. The first was an old black Dodge that he got in the 1940s, but the one I most remember was his second car, a pea-soup green 1951 Plymouth. I thought the colour was awful, but my mother liked it, so I never said a word. I would sit in the back seat as we made the bumpy trip into Ottawa. Back then, it was a dirt road until you got to Chelsea, so the drive took almost an hour. I remember Dad looking back, smiling, and telling me to "sit heavy," to help us get up the big hill that led out of the village.

On the way to the hockey game, Dad would say, "Now, Brian, John and I are going to have a little drink, but you can't tell your mom." They would get two bottles of Orange Crush, likely chosen because the bottles were made of dark brown glass with perpendicular grooves all around the outside. They'd take a couple of sips of Crush and then pour in some vodka. I never told a soul, mainly because I wanted to keep going to games, but it also made me feel like a grown-up, like I was being accepted into some secret club.

We would drive into the city to the old Ottawa Auditorium on the corner of O'Connor and Argyle Streets, just one block south from where Hulse & Playfair is located on McLeod Street. We would drive by the funeral home on the way, and if there weren't any cars in the lot, we would sometimes sneak a parking spot there. I'm sure Mr. Hulse noticed that we were in his lot, but we never got disciplined for it or returned to find a note on the car. Little did I know that it would some day be my place of work.

The Auditorium was a grand old spot. A wooden structure built in 1923, it was the only arena in Ottawa at the time and held about 10,000 people. All around the inside of the building there were large support beams holding up the roof; the seats were cheaper around these, and that's where we sat, usually behind the visitors' goal. You were always sort of leaning to one side or the other to try and see around those damn beams, and if the angle was bad, you might miss a play or even a goal. I never remember it bothering me that much; I was excited just to be there. There were people walking around carrying trays with popcorn, Pepsi, and hot dogs, and that was usually our dinner. It was a noisy, boisterous place filled with cigarette smoke, talking, and occasionally the sound of someone heckling a player. For me, coming in from the country, it felt like I was going to Madison Square Garden.

We would go watch the old Ottawa Senior Senators, a semi-professional team that came to town after the original Senators of the National Hockey League moved to St. Louis in 1934. This was in the early '50s, and the Senior Senators were playing in the Quebec Senior Hockey League, a rough and tumble stepping stone to the big league. I don't know how Dad managed to do it, but somehow he got me signed pictures of all the players I liked. I've still got a couple of them framed at home. My two favourite players in those days were Butch Stahan and "Legs" Frazier. Butch was a fierce defenceman who would later come close to buying the Wakefield Inn. Frazier was a goalie whose style I would compare to Dominik Hasek—sprawled out all over the ice and practically standing on his head to stop the puck. Of course the players didn't wear helmets or face masks in those days, but there weren't any slap shots, either.

When spring came, so did baseball. The local team back then was called the Ottawa Athletics, or Ottawa A's for short. They were a triple A farm team and would play at Lansdowne Park, which was a bit different back then. Where the south side stands are today, there was a fence marking the perimeter of the baseball field. All the seats were on the north side behind home plate.

When Dad started working at the mine, he worked six days a week, but after a while that was reduced to five-and-a-half days, and he would be done on Saturday afternoon. He was proud of the fact that he had earned this extra time off. Saturday night was always something special; we'd go to the clubhouse up on a hill behind the old hospital, now a seniors' residence. There was a band playing most weekends and people would go to square dance, which my dad loved, and he and Mom would often take us along.

Sundays were usually reserved for church and then family dinner. Mother didn't like us attending softball games on Sunday afternoons. She believed, like my grandfather, that it should be a day of rest, but Dad and I enjoyed the games so much that she allowed it.

It was Victoria Day, the holiday Monday, in May 1953. It was early afternoon and the weather was beautiful and sunny. Spring had finally arrived. David and I were in the small building next to our house that served as a garage on one side, and my dad's workshop on the other. We were using a coping saw to make little ornaments for the lawn, carefully cutting around a pattern for a little Dutch girl. You don't see these kinds of lawn ornaments so much anymore, but back then, everyone seemed to have one in their front yard. I was just about finished when I looked down the driveway and saw a group of people walking toward the house. For some reason, they had parked their cars further down the road. The entourage was made up of my uncle, Jack McGarry, and his wife, Lily; another uncle, Howard McGarry, and his wife, Dorothy; and more oddly, the president of the Aluminum Company. When they got a bit closer to the house, they cut across the lawn toward the front porch. This all seemed very strange; even the way they were walking seemed odd. It was like they were carrying some unseen weight on their shoulders.

I had been excited all day, because Dad had promised to take me to a baseball game that evening. Although he was supposed to have the day off, he had gone to the quarry in the morning. Some of the men had decided to go in on the holiday, because they were preparing to open a new area of the pit, but one of the fellows, a bulldozer operator, didn't make it in, so they called my dad. Dad had been a bulldozer operator when he first started at the quarry and was well acquainted with the machine.

After noticing the odd group of people making their way across the lawn, David and I went into the house through the back door and made our way to the front porch. In the little time it took us to get there, our whole world turned upside down. Our two-year-old sister, Mary-Ellen, was having her afternoon nap upstairs, but Mother was sitting with her head in her hands, weeping. I don't know if I had ever seen her cry before that. My uncle came over and knelt down in front of my brother and me. In a soft voice, he told us that Dad had been moving the bulldozer when the ramp he was on collapsed. The machine had rolled down the rock wall into the pit. Dad wasn't able to jump clear and had been killed instantly.

I went over and sat down beside Mother; David ran out the door. I remember watching him and wondering where he was going. He ran across the lawn and jumped over the little fence to the Vaillancourts' house. They were good friends of ours and, for whatever reason, David wanted to tell them Dad had been killed. Leger and Nellie Vaillancourt brought him back right away, walking around the fence and sitting with us. David was speechless, and stayed silent throughout the entire event. In the months that followed, people would sometimes say to him, "You're the man of the house, now." How scary is that for a thirteen-year-old?

My mother was devastated. In an instant, she had become a widow with a young family and no life insurance. The next few hours were blurry with grief and shock. Dozens of people arrived, family, friends, and neighbours. Some brought food, others sat with my mother offering quiet support. That's the way rural people react to a death in their community. Grief gave way to whispered anger over the idea that none of the men should have been at the quarry to begin with, because it was a holiday.

I remember our clergyman arriving. He was a young man, awkward at the best of times, and there we were, a little family waiting for the comfort of the church. He was perspiring heavily as he stood in front of us, rocking from one foot to the other, and he spoke in a shaky voice, "I don't know what to say . . ."

Clarence Smith, one of my dad's best friends, happened to be there at the time. He was growing more bitter with each passing moment, and he scowled at the minister, "Well, if you don't know what to say, we sure as hell don't know what to say."

The clergyman stood silent in the middle of the room. I had never heard anyone speak to a minister that way before.

Grandfather Cross immediately took charge of all the funeral arrangements, gently talking things over with my mother. She wanted my dad brought home one last time. My grandfather made the arrangements with the local funeral director, Mr. Ross Shouldice, and arranged for the wake to be held in our house.

In those days, except in extreme circumstances, having a closed casket was not done. It was probably considered in my dad's case, because his body was damaged, but in the end the decision was made to have the casket open. Preparing my dad's body for viewing was beyond Mr. Shouldice's abilities, so he arranged for Dad to be sent to Hulse & Playfair in Ottawa. He explained that there were experts there who could do the necessary work. The funeral arrangements cost more than $800, which was a high price for the time, but my grandfather paid it. He wouldn't let my mom pay for anything.

A couple of days later, Dad was brought home. I remember his casket; in fact, the model is still available today. A different company makes it now, but the style is the same. The only difference is that, back then, it was called Dominion Birch Mahogany, and now it's called Northern Birch Mahogany. Funny how small details like that can stick in your memory.

I can't say that it did me any harm seeing Dad's body. My brother and I had attended funerals from a young age; my family had always felt it was better to include children in the ritual, rather than try to explain the inevitable empty chair at family dinners.

There were two nights of visitation, my brother and I watching friends and family file slowly past my dad's casket. The first night after everyone left, I stood in the living room looking down at my dad and talking to him, telling him that I loved him and missed him. I could see where there had been work done by the technician; he was an expert in his trade, which allowed us to see Dad one last time.

Those nights David and I sat together in our room, listening to the hushed conversations in the kitchen after Mother had gone to bed. There was resentment about the men having to work on the holiday and whether or not Dad should have been on that particular road. Someone commented that he should have known better, and one person even wondered aloud if Dad had planned to take his own life. Of course this wasn't the case, but still, the thought that my father might have committed suicide hurt me deeply. Someone else said, "It must be in God's plan," and this bothered me as well. I'm still a member of the United Church, although I'm not as active as I once was, but I've always felt that there is some greater influence in our lives, whether you call it God or the power of goodness and honesty. However, even at ten years of age, I couldn't accept a god that would conspire to take my dad away. "He's probably better off where he is now." Well, why would he be better off away from us?

Over the next few days, David and I talked about everything we had heard and we agreed that none of it was true.

The funeral was held at St. Andrew's United, and the community really came out to support us. I remember walking through the tall wooden doors at the front of the church and that there were so many people inside it was difficult to get into the sanctuary. In fact, the Sunday school was opened to make additional space.

The service was a blur, and before I knew it, we were standing on the steps outside watching as my dad's casket was placed into the back of the hearse. I rode in the limousine to the cemetery, and as we drove up the hill out of the village, I looked back. There, as far as I could see, was a line of cars behind us. I thought it was an amazing tribute to my dad. As it turned out, it was the largest funeral that had been held in Wakefield up to that time.

The Aluminum Company gave my mother a small benefit and offered a huge quarry rock as a headstone. It was going to be polished on one side with Dad's name inscribed on it, but my mother refused. Even though she had no money, she turned the company's offer down because, in a sense, the quarry had killed him. She didn't want to be reminded of that every time she went to his grave, which she would take care of faithfully until the end of her life. More fittingly, the local hockey league named their trophy after him, the McGarry Memorial Cup. The team I was on even won it one year, and it was a very proud and emotional moment for me.

Over the years, I've tried to analyze what influenced me to go into the funeral business, and I think my dad's death and funeral had a direct impact. At a young age, death was brought right into our home.

My uncles, Jack and Howard McGarry, helped us out quite often over the years after my father passed away. Both had worked at the quarry with my dad, and they had been very close. Dr. Geggie was also a strong presence in those years and quickly became my mentor.

The first year after my dad's death was a tumultuous time for me. I was in grade five, not quite eleven years old, and I almost failed my year at school. My teacher, Louisa Wills, was an imposing figure, probably close to six feet tall, statuesque, and strict. Today, we have a better understanding of tragedy and grief and how it can affect people, especially children, but back then, feelings and emotions weren't discussed and you were expected to be stoic and carry on. The experience had changed me, and I was never the same afterwards. One particular day in class I wasn't paying attention at all, and it was obvious. On top of that, I had stopped doing any schoolwork. Mrs. Wills stopped what she was doing and addressed me directly, "What are you doing here, Brian?"

I looked up and said, "I guess I'm just occupying a seat." My classmates erupted in laughter, but Mrs. Wills didn't find it amusing at all and my mother was called. After a few serious discussions with my mother and Dr. Geggie, and likely some leniency from Mrs. Wills, I managed to get through the worst of it and salvage my year. The following year was much better, and I was able to get back on track.

Dr. Geggie became an integral part of the community in Wakefield. He held education in a high regard, and helped to develop and build the first library in town. He also worked hard to make sure that Wakefield had its own fire station and hospital. He was a true general practitioner, treating people for just about every kind of ailment, and he was good at his job.

I remember being somewhat surprised to find out that he was a churchgoing man. I suppose I had always thought of him as a man of science and, as such, I assumed that he wouldn't be involved in religion. Dr. Geggie went to church every week, but it was on his own terms. He would arrive late every Sunday, although I suppose you can only say that about someone whose intention is to be on time. The doctor would arrive and take a seat just in time to hear the minister's sermon, and then he'd be gone as soon as it was over. He had it timed perfectly. One time I asked him why he always arrived at 11:30 for the 11 o'clock service. He told me that he didn't like the pomp and ceremony surrounding much of the ritual, but that he did enjoy the message. "I don't always agree with what the minister says, but I do enjoy it." Not surprisingly, he influenced my views on spirituality and never shied away from the topic. He often told me to remember that God was bigger than any one religion, and wasn't confined to the church. The common sense and simplicity of his philosophy has stayed with me ever since. Years later, his funeral reflected these views; it was a very plain service without any extravagances.

Dr. Harold, as we called him, would often come by our house and pick me up on Saturday mornings before making his weekly round of house calls. We would usually spend the day visiting people in Wakefield's French community. He saw a need for a male role model in my life and took up the job; he was good at it. For example, Mom would make porridge every morning enriched with vitamin B. My brother liked it, but I couldn't stand the taste. More than once on a Saturday morning, Dr. Harold would arrive to pick me up for our day and I'd still be sitting at the kitchen table with a full bowl of porridge in front of me. He would look down at me and ask, "Well, Brian, are we going?"

I'd say, "I don't want to finish my porridge."

Mother, who would usually be washing up the breakfast dishes, would then chime in, "He has to finish his porridge. It's good for him."

That's when Dr. Harold would lean in close to me and say in a low, serious voice, "Eat your porridge."

I tell you, I'd have the bowl finished in five or six spoonfuls.

I enjoyed these weekly adventures. It was a real life experience going to people's homes and meeting these warm French-Canadian families, who always seemed to be gathered in their kitchens. Dr. Geggie was serious about his work. One morning we arrived at a house that had a radio on in the room. He was there to work, and I guess the noise was intruding on his thoughts, because he went over and impatiently slammed it off. He was a well-respected man in town, not arrogant, but at times his behaviour might have made it seem like he was ill-tempered, but I think he was really just assertive. Nevertheless, no one would ever question him.

Dr. Geggie helped David and me get jobs in the summer months. He knew we needed the money and was very good to us, paying us well. I think we must have painted every inch of the hospital, inside and out, whether it needed it or not.

Dr. Harold was a stickler for the rules, but he wasn't without a sense of humour. Back then, hospital visiting hours were strictly kept. One summer day we were walking together down a hallway in the maternity ward, so he could show me what I was to paint that day. The hospital had a rule that when a woman had a baby, only her husband was allowed to visit for the first few days. As we walked past one room, we saw it was occupied by a woman in bed holding her newborn child and two men sitting in chairs next to her. Dr. Harold stopped in his tracks, walked into the room and said, "Our policy here is that the husband comes to visit the wife and child, so why are there two of you here?"

One of the men piped up, "I'm the husband," and without missing a beat, the other man added, "And I'm the father."

Dr. Geggie appraised them for a moment with a furrowed brow, and then, without saying another word, turned around and walked out. We hadn't gone more than a few feet down the hall before I burst out laughing. Dr. Geggie didn't laugh, but a smile did stretch from ear to ear.

Over the years, Dr. Harold and I became close friends. I enjoyed spending time with him, and was never bothered by his grumpiness; in fact, I found it endearing.

In the summertime, Dr. Harold would often invite us up to his cottage on Wolf Lake. We never had much money, and this was a luxury we were very grateful to be able to enjoy. We'd go to the lake after church on Sunday, have lunch, and then spend the rest of the day swimming and fishing. My brother and I certainly enjoyed it, and I'm sure my mother appreciated the break.

Dr. Harold became a father figure to me in many ways. He would sit down with me and we'd discuss the future. He didn't just want to know what I wanted to be when I grew up; he wanted me to really think about the direction I was going. He would listen to my answers, then ask more detailed questions. He was also a patient listener and would answer any questions I had. Our conversations were a way of preparing me for the responsibilities of adulthood.

Mom eventually went to the Willis Business School in Ottawa to learn bookkeeping and other clerical skills. She did well in her studies, and as soon as the course was finished, the Aluminum Company offered her a job in their office. I know she found it difficult seeing all of my dad's old friends; it was a constant reminder that Dad was gone. Eight months later, she left the Aluminum Company to take a job at the post office in Wakefield, where she became the assistant postmistress. She was very happy in her new job and stayed there until she retired.

To further supplement our income, Mom began renting out a room in our house to a boarder. During the winter months, the room was usually rented by one of the young teachers at the local public school. For many years in the summer months, the room was taken by a friendly retired barber named Mr. Gordon from Huntington, Quebec. Mr. Gordon liked Wakefield and knew quite a few people in town. He would always cut hair at the local barbershop to give the regular barber a break. As a favour to our mother he would cut our hair for free. This would have been great if it weren't for the fact that Mr. Gordon seemed to be familiar with only one style of haircut, and it was about twenty years out of date. The haircuts were awful. My friends and I wanted to look like Elvis, with greased-back ducktails, but after Mr. Gordon was finished snipping away, it looked like you had a bowl on your head.

The last summer Mr. Gordon stayed with us, he became very ill. He was a very religious man, and every day that summer my brother would go into his room, sit down next to his bed, and read him passages from the Bible. One morning, my mother brought breakfast to his room, but there was no answer when she knocked on his door so she let herself in only to discover that Mr. Gordon had passed away during the night. Mom came down to the kitchen and called Hulse & Playfair, and they made arrangements to have Mr. Gordon's body transported back to Huntington on the train. I remember thinking that he was going on one last trip, because back in those days, the fastest way to get back East was to cross the border and travel through the northeastern United States.

The Vaillancourts had been our next-door neighbours in Wakefield since my parents had moved in. One of their sons, Hector, studied to become a funeral director. After graduating, he got a job working at Shouldice's in Wakefield, then went on to work at Hulse & Playfair and finally at McEvoy-Shields in Ottawa, where he became a partner. Hector was about twelve years older than me, and I would see him arriving home from work in one of their nice company cars. I remember noticing that he was always well-dressed. This impressed me greatly, because I had only one hand-me-down suit, which I wore to church on Sunday. One day I was out in the yard when Hector arrived home, and I decided to go over and ask him about his job. He looked at me a little curiously before saying, "You have to understand, Brian, that as a funeral director, you work twenty-four hours a day, seven days a week. If a family calls you, you can't tell them that you've just packed the car to go on a vacation—you unpack the car."

He went on to tell me that as much as he loved his job and appreciated helping people, sometimes he would have to work on Christmas Day and other holidays, since people don't schedule their final hours around the holidays.

Despite the strange hours and the sacrifices that would sometimes be necessary, I was still intrigued.

By that time, my brother David was attending the Eastern Ontario Institute of Technology in Ottawa and I was enrolled at the Ottawa Technical High School, which was within walking distance of McEvoy-Shields. We began stopping by the funeral home after school in the afternoons to visit with Hector. After my third or fourth visit, he showed me around. Hector never betrayed a family by taking me into the preparation room when there were human remains present, but on a day that wasn't busy, he took me in to show me all the equipment they used. I was fascinated by all the odd-looking steel instruments.

Every so often I would ask Hector if they had any positions open at McEvoy's, and he would tell me to finish school first before I even considered it. My interest had surprised Hector at first, but a few months later when I was still coming by the funeral home, he began to give me a more detailed introduction into what the job was all about.

I was bored with school at this point, but I always passed my courses. However, I think I could have done better, as I was a rather lazy student. My friend Barry Craig was a little bit older than me and he had joined the navy. When he was discharged, he came home and told me that he planned to sign up with the Merchant Marines and work the shipping lanes on the Great Lakes. He told me a few sea tales and asked me if I wanted to go with him on the adventure. It seemed like an exciting idea, and the pay was quite good, but it would also be a tough life. When my mother heard this idea, it was the last straw. There was no way her son was going to be joining the Merchant Marines. Mom was determined that I would finish high school and go on to university. She was a fierce lady, a wonderful person, but she had her standards and it's a good thing. If it weren't for my mother, I don't know where I'd be today.

Dr. Geggie offered to pay for my university education. He encouraged me to take medicine at McGill, which was where he, his sons, and later one of his grandsons studied, but I wasn't sure about a career in medicine. I mentioned that I was interested in the funeral business. By that time it had been in the back of my mind for about five or six years, and Hector was quite used to seeing me at the funeral home.

Dr. Geggie didn't understand my interest in funeral service, as he didn't think much of the funeral business and wasn't afraid to say so. I eventually discovered that this sentiment isn't unusual among physicians, and I've met other doctors who feel the same way. Perhaps it's because a doctor's job is to preserve life, so death becomes synonymous with failure. Dr. Harold would attend funerals, but it was one of the few places where he seemed uncomfortable.

Dr. Geggie tried several times to change my mind, but I kept insisting that I was interested in a career in funeral service. Finally he said, "Well, if you have to do this damn thing, then you need to go and have a talk with Charlie Hulse."

So, that's what I did.

I phoned Hulse & Playfair and asked the secretary if they were hiring. She replied, "No," and that was the end of the conversation. Next I went over to Tubman's funeral home, where I was able to meet with Joe Tubman, and he, very kindly, took me on as a part-time employee. I was thrilled to get the job, and it allowed me to have a good look at the business. I was determined to continue working and learning, and I think Mr. Tubman found it interesting and perhaps a little quirky for someone so young to be so interested in the business. I suppose there aren't many seventeen-year-olds who know that they want to work in a funeral home.

I worked at Tubman's for only a short time, but considering my interest, Joe decided that I should see everything, and I was invited to observe an embalming. This is not usually done with untrained newcomers, but I guess he saw in me a spark of something that told him the job was a good fit for me. One afternoon I arrived at work and, after greeting me, Mr. Tubman said, "Now, Brian, I'm going to take you into a private area. If you're thinking seriously about this profession, then you need to see this procedure."

It was a normal embalming, but still, there are incisions made and fluids removed. I stood next to Mr. Tubman the whole time. I've never been squeamish, and I think the summers I spent working at the hospital may have been partly responsible. I had seen human remains being removed and, of course, I had also seen death firsthand in our family's house.

Tubman's was still a small family firm in those days, and Mr. Tubman suggested I try to get on at Hulse & Playfair, to get more experience.

"I respect my own place very much, Brian, but if you're serious about being trained, you should talk to Charlie Hulse; he's an icon in funeral service."

I mentioned this to Dr. Geggie, and it just so happened that he sat on the board of the National Capital Commission with Charlie Hulse. Dr. Harold was still downhearted by my decision not to go to medical school, but he held Mr. Hulse in high regard and was willing to help me out, if that's what I really wanted. However, never one to give up easily, he also added, "If you change your mind, we can still get you into McGill."

But the thought never really crossed my mind. Dr. Geggie must have spoken to Charlie on my behalf, because a few weeks later, I received a call from Hulse & Playfair inviting me to come in for an interview. I was to meet with George Schaef, who was the secretary-treasurer at the time.

The day of my interview arrived, and I put on the only suit I owned. It was my Sunday best, but still quite ordinary. My family wasn't poor, but we certainly weren't wealthy, either, and I suppose there wasn't really a need for me to have more than one suit, anyway. Joe Tubman drove me over to Hulse & Playfair, and I was nervous. Everyone had told me so much about this great funeral home, and there was a real sense that it was the best in town. Mr. Tubman picked up on my nervousness, and as he parked the car in front of the funeral home's elegant stone building, he turned to give me some parting advice. "You're a good worker, Brian, and one thing to remember is that the most valuable trait to have in the funeral business is dedication. If you're truly committed to the job and the people you work for, you will be successful."

Joe dropped me off and I walked up to the front entrance. The door was opened for me before I even had a chance to knock, and Charlie Wellington ushered me inside. I told him I had an appointment with Mr. Schaef, and he nodded and disappeared down a hallway. He returned a few moments later to inform me that Mr. Schaef was still in a meeting, but that I could stay with him if I liked. He had been arranging the names of all the funerals taking place that day on the announcement board near the front entrance. The board was full, with ten names or so, which was a lot. I looked over the list.

"Are you always this busy?" I asked.

"No, not always, but often. What are you here for?"

"I'm hoping to get a job."

"Well, it must be serious because Mr. Schaef does all the hiring and firing."

"My God, I'm going to get fired before I'm even hired!" I thought.

Mr. Wellington and I chatted a little while longer until I was led into the back office. George Schaef was sitting behind his desk, and he smiled warmly as I walked in. He had a German background, a little moustache, and was direct and to the point. He stood up to shake my hand, inviting me to sit in one of the leather-backed chairs across from his desk. He took a long look at me, then said, "Well, if you're going to work here, you're going to have to get rid of that." He pointed toward my hair, which I had styled into a ducktail.

"Oh, of course, sir." I had actually gotten my hair cut the day before the interview, but I guess it wasn't quite short enough.

"No hair over your ears, no hair below your collar, and no ducktails."

The interview continued, and he asked me about my experience at Tubman's and about my family. I told him that I had been thinking about working in the funeral service since I was about twelve or thirteen. He seemed a little surprised by this, then asked, "What do you think is the most important thing about working in this business?"

Joe Tubman's words rang out in my mind. "Well, sir, I think one of the most valuable traits to have in the funeral business is dedication."

Mr. Schaef smiled broadly. "That's right! And believe me, you'll find out the true meaning of the word when you're up at three in the morning making a removal from a house. Do you think you can be dedicated at three in the morning, as well as three in the afternoon?"

"Yes, sir, I would hope I would."

This seemed to satisfy him, and we continued talking a bit more informally. I told him that I knew Hector Vaillancourt, who had worked at Hulse & Playfair at one time, and he said that Hector had been a great employee and they were sorry to lose him. I also mentioned that I knew Dr. Harold Geggie, and Mr. Schaef said that they knew Dr. Geggie well; Charles Hulse and he were friends.

"You'll meet Mr. Hulse one of these days."

The interview lasted about forty-five minutes, as George went on to explain some of the firm's details and policies.

Finally, he asked me if I had any questions for him, and I said I didn't.

"Well, Brian, I think we're going to take you on. Your pay will be $40 a week, and you can start next Monday."

"Thank you, but I'll have to give my notice at Tubman's . . ."

"Actually, I've already spoken with Joe about it, and he said it would be fine."

I couldn't believe it; Mr. Schaef had hired me right on the spot. As I walked out, he said, "Now, remember to go and get yourself a haircut. We don't have

THE LONG ROAD TO OTTAWA

anyone here with a ducktail."

"I noticed that, sir."

"And you'll need to get yourself a new suit. We'll pay for it in a few months after your probationary period is finished."

"Yes, sir."

"Good. We'll see you on Monday at 8:30 a.m."

I nodded, even though I wasn't sure exactly how I was going to get into Ottawa from Wakefield that early in the morning, but it didn't matter. All I knew was that I had just gotten a job.

After my interview, I went back to Tubman's. I've always been grateful to Joe Tubman for taking me on. He hadn't needed another employee, but wanted to give me a good introduction to the business. I wouldn't be where I am today if it weren't for his help.

During the next week I got organized. With my mother's help, I found a nice dark suit and made a second trip to the barbershop. Sitting there watching as my ducktail succumbed to the barber's scissors, I wondered what the future had in store for me.

Charles Hulse

Yousef Karsh

Keith Playfair

Yousef Karsh

CHAPTER 3

Hulse & Playfair

In some ways, Charles Hulse was destined to become an icon of funeral service in Canada. Even though the drive and determination that came naturally to him would have likely meant success in any field he chose, fate conspired to lead him into the funeral business. Charlie was born in 1899, in Schomburg, Ontario, a small, rural community nestled in the rich farmland of the Holland River Valley, just north of that great green strip of wilderness known as the Oak Ridge Moraine, which runs from the Niagara Escarpment down to Rice Lake. Charlie had a happy childhood there, but his father worried that Charlie's future was limited by the small farming community.

When Charlie turned fifteen, he was sent to live with his uncle Joseph, who lived in the larger town of Orangeville and was the community's funeral director. It was a mutually beneficial move. Charlie would have the opportunity to learn a profession, and Joseph, who had no children of his own, would get an assistant. For the next four years, Charlie finished high school, working at the funeral home on weekends and during the summer. Equipment and embalming instruments would be loaded into the back of a horse-drawn buggy in the summer months, and when winter arrived, a sleigh was used to get to the homes of the recently departed. From the beginning of these early funeral service experiences, Charlie was intrigued by the business. Years later, the memory of watching his uncle perform an embalming in front of him for the first time was still vivid in his mind. "It's as if he were here beside me. I was seventeen years old."

Joseph Hulse was skilled at his job, and the education he provided Charlie was invaluable. The work so captivated him that by 1916 Charlie told his girlfriend (who would later become his wife) of his ambition. "I intend to one day own the finest funeral homes in the entire Dominion of Canada."

After graduating from high school, Charlie enrolled at the University of Toronto to get his funeral director's license. For a year, he travelled back and forth from the city, studying anatomy and embalming during the week and returning to Orangeville on the weekends to help his uncle.

After passing his final exams in 1918, Charlie made the difficult decision to leave his uncle's business. He knew he needed more experience and decided the best way to do this was to get a job in one of Toronto's big funeral homes. Naturally, Joseph wanted Charlie to stay with him, but could see that his nephew's ambition was going to prevail. Joseph wished Charlie luck and sent him on his way. Charlie packed up his things and moved to the big city. His dream of working in one of the esteemed funeral homes in Toronto was not so quickly realized, and he initially settled for a job in a small funeral home on Dovercourt Road in Toronto's west side. As the newest employee, he was required to work seven days a week, a gruelling schedule that brought him only $20 a month. He soon moved to another establishment where he earned more money and worked fewer hours.

By 1922, Charlie was ready to expand his horizons again, so he took a job with Dominion Manufacturers, one of the biggest suppliers of caskets in Canada at that time. His gregarious personality and experience landed him in their sales department. Charlie's territory was broad, extending to every small town and village in southern Ontario. He was good at his job and quickly became popular with customers, earning the respect of his employer, so much so that his sales manager, D.M. Andrews, treated him like a son.

In 1925, one of Dominion's customers, a small funeral home in Ottawa, got into debt trouble. Charlie was sent up to see if there was anything he could do to solve the problem. Charlie made the seven-hour journey by train, taking a room at the regal Château Laurier Hotel upon his arrival. For three weeks, Charlie worked with the owners of the modest funeral home at 315 McLeod Street. He soon discovered the core of the problem lay in the fact that the owners had grown tired of the business and wanted to get out of it entirely. They told Charlie that, if the opportunity arose, they would sell without hesitation. Charlie realized that this was a chance to go into business for himself. Excitedly, he called his brother Percy, who had followed Charlie into the funeral business and was working in Toronto at the time. He told Percy about the opportunity in Ottawa and asked him to be his partner. Percy accepted immediately. Neither brother had much money, but they borrowed from friends and family, and in the months that followed, they managed to scrape together enough for a small down payment, which they took with them to the owners of the Ottawa funeral home with their offer. Shortly afterwards, the paperwork was signed and the Hulse Brothers' funeral home was born. Of course, when they took over the business, they also took over the debt, but Charlie's excellent relationship with Dominion Manufacturers stood him in good stead, and the casket company agreed to hold off on debt collection until the two brothers could establish themselves.

The first few months of operation were difficult, and after the first year in business, the brothers sat down to evaluate their situation. They had done fewer funeral services than any other funeral home in the city and were barely breaking even. They came to the painful realization that the business was not able to support both of their families. After discussing the matter for several days, and mulling over every possible solution, they realized that one of them would have to move on. Unable to decide who should go, they finally settled the matter with a coin toss, each man agreeing that he would leave graciously if he lost. A penny was flipped into the air, spinning for what must have felt like an eternity until it landed, fatefully, on heads. Charlie would be staying. Keeping his word, Percy shook his brother's hand, smiled sadly, and went to tell his wife the news. He would eventually find his way to St. Catharines, and success in a funeral home of his own.

With Percy gone, Charlie took on a tremendous workload, handling all aspects of the job himself as a way to try and save money. Still, he struggled to keep the business afloat in those early years, never losing his determination. He was fortunate, however, to have two benefactors who strongly believed in him, his former boss at Dominion Manufacturers, D.M. Andrews, and a local accountant named Ed Holcomb, and a natural business acumen. Both men helped Charlie through those difficult early years with advice and credit; their good will was a kindness that Charlie never forgot.

Over the next ten years, the funeral home began to grow and flourish. Charlie had a knack for seeing potential where others did not. One such decision involved the purchase of a new Dodge ambulance. At that time, the hearse and the ambulance were usually one and the same, and Charlie was the first in Ottawa to have a vehicle that was used exclusively as an ambulance, a service that earned him $2 for every trip to the hospital. Charlie's ambulance was outfitted with modern equipment, and it soon became the talk of the town, which likely explains why Charlie was asked to bring his new vehicle to Uplands Airfield on the day the famous American aviator, Charles Lindbergh, was to fly in. This would turn out to be a twist of fate, which would open the door for Charlie's future involvement in state funerals (see Chapter 5, State Funerals).

By 1931, Hulse Brothers funeral home was flourishing (although Percy had left the firm, the name remained unchanged), and Charlie realized he needed a partner to help with the workload and keep up his high standards of service. Naturally, the first person he called on was his brother, but by that time Percy had established himself as a funeral director in St. Catharines and politely declined Charlie's offer.

Not long after, on a sunny summer's day, Charlie was sitting in his favourite barbershop waiting to get a haircut and no doubt contemplating his dilemma, when in walked one of his competitors, Keith Playfair, who took off his hat and sat in the chair next to Charlie. The two men struck up a conversation. Keith was a highly respected man in Ottawa society and had been employed for several years as the manager of the George B. Burney and Son funeral home. During the course of their conversation, Charlie realized that he had found in Keith the ideal candidate for a business partner.

Knowing that Keith was unlikely to be invited to become a partner at Burney's, Charlie quietly suggested that it might be beneficial for both of them if Keith dropped by to discuss possible opportunities at Hulse Brothers. A few days later, Keith and Charlie met. Keith listened as Charlie talked about how his business was growing and how he was in need of a partner. Getting straight to the point, Charlie told Keith he could offer him a senior position at the firm with the understanding that, if the partnership worked well, Keith would be made a full partner within five years. By the end of the week, Keith accepted the offer and their partnership was born.

Charlie's initial feelings about Keith proved to be true, and the two men worked well together. Where Playfair was social and innovative, Hulse was reserved and detail-oriented; however, they both shared a similar work ethic and were dedicated to providing the best service possible for the families who came to them. Business continued to grow and the two men got along famously. True to his word, in 1936 Charlie made Keith a full partner and to honour this, the name of the firm was officially changed from Hulse Brothers to Hulse & Playfair Limited.

Charlie and Keith began to reinvest in the funeral home, renovating the once shabby building, and in 1937, Charlie suggested that they build a chapel adjoining their funeral home. Keith agreed and they further decided that, in order not to exclude anyone, the chapel would be non-denominational, making it open for anyone of any religious faith to use. This turned out to be a historic decision, as it was the first non-denominational chapel to be built by a funeral home in Canada. Two years later, construction was finished. To give people a chance to see their new building, Charlie and Keith decided to present a series of free organ recitals on Sunday afternoons, but with opening day fast approaching there was a problem—they couldn't find a clergyman who would agree to bless the chapel. Even though Charlie was very active in his church, he was openly criticized by members of his own parish and others throughout the city for building a chapel that was not attached to any one spiritual faith. The prevailing thought of the day was that the only place you should conduct a funeral was in a "proper" church, and how could this so-called "non-denominational" chapel be even considered as such? It was nearly sacrilegious. Finally, the Very Reverend J.W. Woodside, moderator of the United Church of Canada, agreed to perform the dedication ceremony and the whole controversy was quickly forgotten. The free recitals went on to become very popular.

Ottawa's Jewish community was among the first to support Charlie's non-denominational concept, which opened the doors to a strong, warm relationship between us, which we enjoy to this day.

In the years following, more renovations were made to the funeral home. Charlie wanted the building to reflect the high quality of service that was offered, and by 1964, Hulse & Playfair bore little resemblance to the little funeral home that Charlie had purchased forty years earlier. Hulse & Playfair had become one of the premier funeral providers in Canada, and well known for its dedication to professional and high quality service.

Charlie and Keith continued to be innovators in the funeral business. In the '40s, one of their employees, Keith Shaver, contracted tuberculosis, which meant that he would not be able to work for the better part of a year. It was a time when there were no medical plans and an employee unlucky enough to get sick was often let go. Knowing that Keith was a hard worker and a trusted employee, Charlie assured him that his job would be waiting for him when he was well enough to return to work. Furthermore, he made sure that Keith was paid a portion of his salary for the duration of his illness. Both of these actions marked one of the first times that this type of employee support had ever happened in Canada. Subsequently, Hulse & Playfair became one of the first firms in our nation to institute health benefits for all its employees. Keith Shaver eventually regained his health and was able to return to work. Years later he would become president of the firm; he never forgot Charlie's decision to remain true to his personal ethics, even though it meant going against conventional wisdom.

This kind of logic carried over into other aspects of Charlie's life as well. It was important to him to help and support the community as much as he could, because that support would eventually come back to you.

Over the years, Charlie became a great supporter of the arts and education. His philanthropic efforts did not go unnoticed, and Charlie soon found himself to be a highly respected member of Ottawa society. His achievements and efforts were recognized by the Jewish community, who named him the B'nai B'rith "Man of the Year" in 1965. (I received this same award in 1991; people of the Jewish faith have been kind to both of us.) When Charlie received the award, he humbly remembered all those who had helped and believed in him when he was first starting out, and noted his philanthropy was a way to repay that debt.

By 1964, Charlie had achieved all he had set out to do, and both he and Keith felt that they could retire. Before this could happen, however, they had one last innovation to implement. Over the years, as "corporate" principles began to mark the funeral business, and offers started to come in to buy the firm, Charlie and Keith were quick to see that the personal touch would be lost if they sold to a conglomerate. They believed that a big part of what had made their funeral home so successful was the close personal ties the business and its employees had with the community. Losing these ties would mean losing their identity. Charlie and Keith decided the best way to continue in the tradition they had started was, upon their retirement, to sell the company to their employees.

Since the beginning, they had been very careful to select employees based on their sincerity and compassion. Charlie and Keith trusted their employees implicitly, and knew that the firm's reputation would be safe in their hands. At the time, this type of business model was unheard of for a firm of their size. Unafraid of breaking new ground one last time, the sale was arranged, and the echoes of this decision can still be seen in the firm's continued dedication to the principles of independent, local ownership. With the firm's future in good hands, the two partners retired from active duty, although they continued to exert a strong presence in the business for the rest of their lives, working tirelessly as chairmen of the board, trusted advisers, and friends.

Duck-tailed Brian driving his mom's '57 Chevy, equipped with
fender skirts and bug screen. Mom was not amused. 1960.

Courtesy of the McGarry Family Archives.

CHAPTER 4

Milk and Flowers

On May 1, 1962, a week after my interview with George Schaef, I started working at the funeral home. To get from Wakefield to Ottawa, my mother suggested I call Doug Brown, who lived on a farm outside the village and was a friend of the family. Doug worked for the Sealtest Dairy on Kent Street in Ottawa, driving a delivery truck. His job was to bring larger jugs of milk to restaurants and hotels, and the dairy let him take the truck home at night so he could get back and forth easily. Every morning during the week, he made the forty-five-minute drive into town, returning after work in the evenings.

"Hello, Doug, this is Brian McGarry."

"Hi, Brian."

"I've got myself a job in Ottawa at Hulse & Playfair, and I was wondering if I might be able to hitch a ride with you in the mornings?"

"Sure, I'd love the company, but it's an early start. I get to Wakefield around quarter to six, then I've got to go straight to the dairy. You can jump out then, but if you don't mind waiting while I load the truck, then I can drop you off at the front door of the funeral home."

"That sounds fine, Doug. I'll see you Monday morning."

So I had my transportation, and even though I'd be arriving at work a bit early, it was a small price to pay. Since I lived just outside of town, Doug and I agreed to meet at the corner of Highway 11 and Mill Road. It was a little less than a kilometre's walk. Mom made sure I was up and out the door with plenty of time to spare, since Doug was on a tight schedule and wouldn't be able to wait for me if I was late.

On Monday morning, I stood on the side of the road and waited for his truck to wind through the village to the highway. It was a big, flat-nosed contraption, green and white, with the diesel engine chugging away under the front seat. The truck pulled up, and Doug opened the passenger door to greet me with a wide grin.

"Well, you're looking spic and span!"

I was wearing the new suit that my mother had helped me pick out at a local shop. I climbed into the truck and off we went. Doug was a talkative man, and there was never a lack of good conversation on the way to town. Ottawa was a much smaller community in those days, and he seemed to know a lot about most of the local businesses, including Hulse & Playfair. He told me stories about George Schaef and Laird Barclay, and some of the other people I'd be working with. After making his stop at the dairy, Doug drove me over to the funeral home and pulled up to the front door. I thanked him as I jumped out.

"Good luck!" he said, as he drove off. It was still well before 7:00 a.m.

I walked up to the big wooden door at the front of the funeral home and pressed the doorbell. A few minutes went by, and I began to wonder if the bell was broken. I pressed it again, this time holding it for a few seconds, just in case. I was just about to try it a third time when a squinty-eyed face appeared in the window. The door opened, and I found myself standing before a man wearing a bathrobe and slippers, and whose hair was slightly askew. This was Laird Barclay. In those days, the funeral home provided accommodations for employees working the overnight shift, and Laird had been working that night. Charles Hulse also lived in the building at that time, but of course the doorbell only rang in the staff quarters. Laird was cautious at first, perhaps thinking that I might have suffered a death in the family. Back in those days, people would sometimes come to the funeral home directly from the hospital after a death had occurred. But as soon as he got a look at me with my new haircut and an ill-fitting suit, he knew I wasn't there to arrange a funeral. He cleared his throat. "Who are you and why do you have your finger stuck on the doorbell?"

"I'm Brian McGarry, sir."

"I'm sure you are. And to what do I owe this pleasure, Mr. McGarry?"

I guess I sort of thought everyone would be expecting me.

"I'm starting work today."

"And who told you to arrive before 7:00 a.m.?"

"Nobody, sir. I just thought . . . I got a ride and . . ."

"You're very early."

I must have looked terrified because Laird softened. "It's all right, Brian, come in."

He didn't seem angry, but he was direct. He pointed to the clergy office. "Go and have a seat in there. I'll be down in a little while. I'm just getting ready for the day."

And with that he disappeared around a corner. I walked into the nicely appointed wood-panelled room and sat in one of the big, red leather chairs that faced the desk. I was about two hours early, but I remember thinking, "This guy's not going to be too easy to work with." I never would have guessed it at the time, but Laird and I would go on to become good friends.

After a while, he came back downstairs; it was still well before 8:30. By that time, the maintenance staff started to arrive and word quickly spread that there was a new employee, so everyone was peeking in to take a look at me. Over the next little while, most of the employees arrived, and I watched as the funeral home slowly came to life. Eventually, Laird came back into the office and looked at me appraisingly for a moment.

"Well, there's a coffee machine down the hall. It'll be a while yet before Mr. Hulse arrives and we can figure out what to do with you."

I found the coffeepot, and even though I wasn't a coffee drinker, I poured myself a mug. I wasn't sure where I should go. All I knew was that I didn't want to be in Laird's way. In any event, I decided to do some exploring on my own. I opened one door and found myself in the garage, where a short, almost bald man was organizing a long shelf filled with soaps, polish, and shammy cloths. My eyes were drawn to the sleek black hearse that was parked there, a vehicle that I had often seen in Wakefield. The man was Joe Becker, and as the car-washer, his job was to make sure all the vehicles the funeral home used were kept in pristine condition. He took pride in his work. Joe was a brusque German fellow, nice, but, like George Schaef, was very direct. He turned around and looked at me. "Hello. Who are you?" he asked.

"Brian McGarry, sir. Today's my first day."

"A helper! That's good. Do you know how to wash a car?"

"Sure."

He smiled. "No, no, do you know how to wash a car *properly*?"

"I wash my mom's car every weekend in the summertime."

"Well, that's a start. Let's see what you can do."

I walked over to the bucket next to the hearse and looked down at the soapy water.

"You might want to take off your suit jacket before you get started," he advised.

I did, and also rolled up my sleeves. Then Joe walked over, reached into the bucket, pulled out a sponge, and handed it to me. "We make them shine, yes?"

"Yes."

And that's how I started my first day, elbows deep in soapy water, learning the secret art of car washing. I have to say it was satisfying to buff the last bit of turtle wax over the hood and then stand back and look at the hearse, gleaming under the garage lights.

Not long after I heard the unmistakable sound of a car pulling up and idling outside the garage door. I was about to mention it to Joe, when I was cut off by two blasts of a horn. Becker's eyes darted to the door. "Damn, Hulse!" he muttered.

Quickly, he moved to the front of the garage and began pulling on the chain that opened the big wooden door. As soon as it was up, a '62 Lincoln wheeled in and parked next to the hearse. A regal looking man stepped out of the car wearing a short-sleeved shirt and a fedora tilted to one side of his head, his moustache perfectly trimmed. This was the famous Charles Hulse that I had heard so much about. He'd been at his cottage on Grand Lake for the weekend and was just getting back. Charlie opened the back door of the car and began taking out the bags piled on the seat. His arrival had initiated a chain reaction. After opening the garage door, Joe had picked up the phone and dialled the number for the front office. "Hulse is in the building," he barked into the receiver.

Everyone was then on full alert, just as if a call had come into a fire station. Charlie walked over to Joe and handed him the car keys. "Hello, Joe," he said.

"Good day, sir."

"It is a good day. Now, I'll be leaving again in an hour, could you please wash my car?"

"Of course," Joe replied.

With that, Charlie picked up his bags and started inside. That's when he saw me.

"And who might you be?" he asked.

Joe walked over to introduce us. "This is Brian McGarry, sir. It's his first day. Not a bad car washer, either."

Charlie studied me for a moment, then put down one of the bags he was carrying and extended his hand. "That's right, you're the young man from

Wakefield. Welcome to the business."

I shook his hand. "Thank you, sir," I replied.

He bent over to pick up his bag. "Now, Brian," he continued. "Here's a little advice for your first day. Don't forget where you came from, and I'll show you how far you can go."

And with that, he was off. It was kind of an anticlimactic meeting after everything I'd heard about him, but those words have stuck with me ever since.

Charlie was a bit of an introvert. Not shy exactly, but reserved. Keith Playfair, on the other hand, was much more outgoing and less formal. At times, Mr. Hulse could seem aloof and difficult to approach. He didn't have a personality that you could warm up to immediately, but he had a keen business sense. Mr. Playfair was more approachable and welcoming. The combination of the two personalities worked well for the firm.

Mr. Playfair loved to be at the front door to greet people as they walked in. He had a way of making people feel comfortable as soon as they arrived at the funeral home. A good idea, since many people feel overwhelmed when they arrive and are already on the edge, emotionally speaking.

Playfair was a tall and imposing man who looked more like a football player than a funeral director, and when he shook your hand, you knew it. He had a wonderful, big booming voice that went along with his stature.

Charlie would usually come down from his apartment, say a few quiet "Good mornings" on his way to his office, and get right to work.

Keith and Charlie may have had contrasting personalities, but they always got along well, and they only ever had one falling out that I know of. Both men were working on a funeral at a local cemetery. After the interment was over, they were getting ready to drive back to the funeral home in the car reserved for the clergy; Keith was driving. Usually the clergy would sit in the front seat next to the driver, but since Charlie was also there, he and the clergy took the back seat so they could chat. Just before they were about to drive off, Charlie leaned forward and said, "Home, James!"

I'm sure it was a joke, and Charlie didn't think anything of it until after they dropped the clergyman off at his rectory and were about to start back to the office. Mr. Playfair was furious. He pulled the car over and turned to face the back seat so he could look Charlie right in the eye. With barely restrained anger he said, "I am *not* your driver."

Charlie told me years later that they had a real spat over it. Mr. Hulse eventually apologized, and Keith accepted that it was only a joke, and that was the end of it. As far as I know, that was the only time the two men ever argued throughout all the years they were business partners.

Keith was known to have a short temper at times, and it was a well-known fact that you didn't want to find yourself on the wrong end of it. When he arrived at the funeral home, he always walked in through the back area where the technicians work. He would usually stop and talk to everyone on his way to the front office. One day he came through to find five guys in the flower room. He stopped and half jokingly said, "One, two, three, four, five—five people. That's a lot of salary for guys standing around not doing too much."

There were a few guffaws, and I'm sure the guys made an attempt to be a bit busier, then Keith continued on his way. A little while later he phoned down. "I've got a job for one of you. I'll be needing someone to drive my wife and me to the Château Laurier at noon."

Well, whoever answered the phone said, "Sorry, sir, but everyone is just about to leave for lunch."

Sure enough, they all left. When they returned, they were met at the door by an angry Keith Playfair, who summarily informed them that each and every one was now unemployed. Luckily for them, George Schaef had a meeting with Mr. Playfair later that afternoon. "I think we'd better sit down with these men," he suggested, "and talk to them about the lesson that can be learned here instead of firing all of them."

George never told me how much convincing he needed to do; nevertheless, everyone was working again by five o'clock. I'm sure it was a day that none of the men ever forgot, and I don't think Mr. Playfair ever had trouble finding a driver after that.

Back in those early days, part of the job of the junior staff was to act as drivers for both Keith and Charlie. They could say "Home, James," to me and I would just take them home.

One afternoon, I was driving Charlie out to the airport and we were running late. He was sitting next to me in the passenger seat. We came rolling up to a stop sign on Fifth Avenue in the Glebe and Charlie looked over at me. "Keep moving," he ordered. "There's no one around."

"But, sir, there's a stop sign . . ."

"Ahh, don't worry about it, keep going."

I followed his instructions, and wouldn't you know it, there was a police car coming down the street in the other direction. The squad car's red flashing lights went on immediately, so I pulled over. Charlie and I sat in silence, waiting for the police officer to walk up to the window, while the whole time I was thinking, "Well, Mr. Hulse will say something."

I rolled the window down, and the constable leaned over to look inside. He recognized Charlie right away. "Good afternoon, Mr. Hulse," he said warmly.

"Good afternoon, sir."

The policeman turned to me. "Son," he said sternly, "did you not see that stop sign?"

"Actually, sir, I did see the stop sign."

"Well, this should be a good one. So why didn't you stop?"

Now, this was the moment when Mr. Hulse was surely going to come to my rescue. I glanced over at him, but he was looking at me as if he also wanted to know why I went through the stop sign. I didn't know what to say. Finally the officer cleared his throat. "You know, your boss does a lot of nice things in this city. You should listen to him."

I nodded solemnly, all the while thinking, "Yeah, sure, that's why we're having this little conversation." After a short lecture on the importance of following the rules of the road, the officer was kind enough to let me off with a warning. As we drove away, I looked over at Charlie. He smiled a little and said, "A good lesson."

To this day I'm still not too sure what that lesson was.

You could say that Charlie had a unique sense of humour. He was in Kiwanis with a very nice French-Canadian man named Jack Legault. During one of their meetings, Jack took a sip of water and it went down the wrong tube, as they say, and he started coughing. The fit went on and on before stopping after a minute or so, but it was serious enough that the meeting had to be paused to make sure he was all right. A little embarrassed but no worse for wear, Jack regained his composure and the meeting continued. An hour later when everyone was on their way out, Charlie walked over to Jack. He took out one of his business cards and handed it to him, saying, "If that cough gets any worse, you're going to need this."

Charlie was never one to miss an opportunity to have a laugh.

On another occasion in late fall, Earl Canham, one of our funeral directors, arrived at the office wearing his best "Perry Como" sweater. He was pleased with himself, because Charlie had asked him to go to the golf course with him that day, and Earl was making sure that everyone knew about it. "Have any of you guys ever been invited to go golfing with Mr. Hulse?"

"No, Earl. It must be your lucky day."

Earl was very excited about spending the day on the golf course while the rest of us were busy at work. I think he really believed he was moving up in the world. I'd be lying if I said I wasn't envious that Earl seemed to be getting the day off, and I think everyone felt the same way. Later that afternoon, I bumped into Earl in the hallway; he had just come back. To my surprise, he seemed a little sheepish.

"How was your game, Earl?" I asked.

"Oh, all right," he replied.

"Just all right? How did you shoot?"

"Mr. Hulse shot very well, actually."

"Well, did you spend a lot of time in the rough?"

"I wasn't exactly playing."

"You weren't 'exactly' playing?"

"I was caddying."

I couldn't help but laugh, and I'll tell you, Earl certainly heard his share of jokes about the matter. "Say, Earl, the flowers have arrived, and would you mind passing me the nine iron?"

Of course, most of the time Charlie was quite serious, especially at work. There would be trouble if he came down from his apartment and found no one waiting at the front door to greet people. He thought this was a very important part of the job and often told us that we were the only funeral home in Ottawa that did this. He wanted people to feel welcome from the moment they walked into the building.

When we worked the night shift, we stayed in the staff quarters. Most of the employees did this unless they lived close by. Charlie would often leave the door to his apartment open so he could see us coming and going down the hall to our room; he liked to be part of everything, even after he was done work for the day. Occasionally, when his wife, Margie, was up at their cottage and Charlie was at the apartment by himself, he'd invite us in for a chat. I remember doing this on several occasions. The Hulses had this huge dining room set, much bigger than they needed, and Charlie would ask me to sit down. He'd pour a scotch for himself, a soda for me, and we'd talk. He'd ask how things were going and if I was enjoying the work, and what my plans were for the future. Charlie was always thinking about the future. He wasn't just concerned about next week, or the week after, he thought in years. The business was something he took very seriously, and he wanted you to do the same. He would ask me what my plans and goals were for the years to come, and he listened carefully to my answers, offering words of encouragement or advice. He really was a father figure to me in many ways.

There is one story about Charlie that has always stuck out in my mind. A retired construction worker passed away, and his wife, Mrs. Warner, came in to make the arrangements for his funeral. The man had lived a long life and had passed away at the age of ninety-three. Just by chance, I happened to be sitting in on the arrangement. I offered my condolences and we talked about her husband's funeral. After the details had been arranged, we began chatting, and she mentioned that her husband had worked as a labourer at our funeral home when Charlie and Keith had built the chapel in 1939. I love the history of our firm, so I was interested to hear more. She continued.

"Hubert was very proud to have helped build your chapel; he was a stonemason."

"Well, they certainly did a fine job. I know Mr. Hulse was very happy."

"My husband never forgot Charles Hulse. In fact, that's why I'm here today."

"I'm sorry. I'm not sure what you mean."

"After the chapel was built, every single worker received a personal invitation from Charles Hulse and Keith Playfair to go to a banquet at the Château Laurier Hotel. My husband was overcome with emotion. Neither of us had ever dreamed that we might get to have dinner at the nicest hotel in Ottawa. In all the years Hubert worked, no one had ever done anything like that for him and he made me promise that when he died, I would bring him to Hulse & Playfair."

And here she was, almost fifty years later, keeping her promise. It made me proud to have worked for such a fine man.

Every day for the first three months of work, Doug dropped me off at the funeral home at a quarter to seven. After the first month I was given a key, I think partly so I wouldn't wake anyone up with the doorbell. I didn't want to get an apartment in Ottawa right away, as for those first few months I was on probation and afraid that I might not last. Once my probationary period came to an end, and I was told that they were going to keep me on, I started looking around Centretown for a place to live. After viewing a couple of apartments, I finally settled on a comfortable little rooming house on Lewis Street, just off Elgin and within short walking distance of the funeral home. The building was owned by a kindly, older lady who rented out rooms primarily to young men who had moved into the city from the outlying rural areas to find work. She always wore a colourful print dress with a little cloth belt around the middle. I think it would have been referred to as a housedress back in those days. In my memories of her, she is always wearing an apron. This likely had something to do with the fact that meals were included with our rent and, with five other borders living there, she was probably always cooking.

My room was small but clean, and I was well fed. Today, this space is the laundry room in a beautiful home owned by "Myrna," whose family also owns a wonderful restaurant I frequent. We often have a good chuckle over this fact, whenever I come to dine there.

With the $40 a week I earned, I was able to pay the rent, pay for my Voyageur bus ticket to Wakefield, and have a little left over for entertainment. I worked every other weekend, and on my days off, I'd usually take the bus home.

My first job was working on the flower truck as Art Dupuis' assistant. Art was a dapper little French-Canadian fellow with a mischievous sense of humour whom Charlie had taken a liking to, but who also seemed to have a nose for trouble. Our job was to gather up the flower arrangements from the chapel after the service, along with any arrangements in the visitation room. We would quickly load the flowers into the van and bring them to the cemetery, setting them out nicely before the cortege arrived for the interment. After the graveside service was finished, the family would often ask us to take some of the arrangements to the Perley Hospital or to St. Vincent's Hospital, and that was part of our job as well. Of course the hospitals would rearrange them so they didn't look like funeral bouquets, but in recent years we've all but stopped the practice of bringing flowers to the hospitals. This is partly because they don't have the staff to spare for little details anymore, but it's also because there are far fewer flower arrangements at funerals. More often families are requesting that friends make donations to various charities and causes on behalf of the deceased. There are still some flower arrangements of course, but it's not like it used to be. Back when Art and I were working together, the visitation rooms would often be full of flowers. It wasn't uncommon to have fifty or sixty floral tributes in a room, and nowadays there might be five or six.

Working on the flower run might sound like an easy job, but sometimes there would be twelve funerals in a day, which adds up to a lot of flowers—and a lot of driving. On one occasion, Art and I loaded the van and were on our way, supposedly to Capital Memorial Gardens Cemetery. We were driving along when it occurred to me that Art seemed to be taking a strange route to get there.

"Are we taking the scenic route?" I asked.

"How do you mean?"

"Well, we're going the long way to get to Capital Memorial Gardens."

"Capital? I thought we were going to Pinecrest."

We shot each other a worried glance. As I scrambled to look for our notes, Art pulled the car over. I found the information and, sure enough, we should have been going to Capital. We had been headed in the wrong direction. Art put on the signal light and turned around.

"I don't think we're going to get there ahead of them, Art," I commented.

"No, no, we've still got time."

We sped down the road, passing cars and jerking around corners. Finally, we turned onto the Prescott highway and, sure enough, we came up behind the cortege.

"I guess they were ahead of us by a little," he observed dryly.

Luckily it was a very small funeral and there were only six cars in the group. I looked at Art who was deep in concentration.

"What are you thinking?" I asked.

He looked over at me quickly. "Only one thing to do," he said.

"What's that?"

He shrugged his shoulders. "Pass them."

"Won't they recognize the car?"

"We'll be going too fast."

I wasn't very confident in this plan, but I didn't have a better suggestion.

I checked to make sure my seat belt was secure. Art waited until we got to a straight stretch of road, then pulled out and pressed the gas pedal to the floor. It took the van a moment to get up to speed, and we seemed to crawl by the first two cars, but after that, it kicked into high gear and we moved quickly past the other vehicles. Art was driving for all he was worth, and we finally got up beside the lead car. I had forced myself to look straight ahead through the whole thing, but I couldn't help stealing a glance over. When I did, I found that I was looking straight into the eyes of Keith Campbell, vice-president of our firm. For a moment he looked puzzled, but then his eyes narrowed. Keith was a very hard worker and for a long time he was Charlie's right-hand man, eventually becoming one of his employee-partners. He was fierce in his standards, and you wouldn't want to cross him. Art and I managed to get to the cemetery with just enough time to have the flowers properly set out. Keith didn't say anything at the service, of course, but afterwards when we got back to the funeral home, we were called into the office and we got a blast. I think it would have been worse, though, if we hadn't made it in time. I've always wondered if Keith didn't secretly admire our effort that day.

For the longest time, I thought I would always be on that flower car. Art wasn't licensed as a funeral director, but he did assist in the operating room occasionally. At that time there were no crematoriums in Ottawa, and if a family requested cremation, we had to ship the body to Montreal. We would place the casket inside a shipping container and bring it to the old train station downtown. The container would be shipped to Montreal, and a couple of days later we would go back to the station to pick up the urn. One of Art's jobs was to transport the remains down to the station, and I would usually go with him to help out. We had to make sure that the remains were placed on the right train and that all the paperwork was properly completed. However, once everything was in order, Art would usually say, "Brian, I'm just going across the street to the hotel to get some cigarettes."

Off he would go, while I sat in the hearse or walked around the entrance of the train station and waited for him to get back. I can remember thinking that it would sometimes take a long time to buy those cigarettes. As it turns out, he was going into the hotel bar across the street and having a draught beer. Now, of course this is strictly forbidden, but it was usually the evening train, so I guess he thought he would just have a quick drink before going home. I had no idea that he was doing this until we became good friends. One night he went over and when he came back, he said, "Brian, I have to tell you. I always go over and have a beer if it's an evening train."

"Oh. Well, you know it's against the rules."

"I thought I might as well tell you, and I'm counting on you not to say anything to anyone. If you want to join me another time . . ."

"Art, I've got to go back to work, but you can do as you like."

I didn't let the cat out of the bag, and he continued having his evening tipple. He never got caught.

After what seemed to me to be a long time, I was put on the overnight shift. I wasn't in charge of anything, but I was there to help if we received a call and had to make a removal in the middle of the night. There were always three people working at night: a senior employee who would answer the phone or greet people at the front door, a technician, and a junior employee who was there as an assistant—me.

When it comes to handling human remains, we are very strict about procedure, and I would hope most funeral homes are the same. There is a level of respect for the dead that needs to be maintained at all times. When we arrive at a house where a death has occurred, the senior director goes in first. Normally, we have a contact person that we've spoken with over the phone, usually a family member, but sometimes the family doctor. When you arrive, you find the person you spoke with. You discreetly look at the layout of the home or apartment to find the best route to take when bringing the body out on the stretcher, making a mental note of any furniture that might have to be moved. After speaking with your contact person, you go to the room where the deceased is. If the family is still there, you sit down and chat with them about the procedure. After a few minutes, you ask them, with their permission, if you could have a few moments to do some initial preparation on the body. I always suggest that the family sit in an adjoining room while we are doing this, and most people agree, but there are some people who want to stay and see everything. The reason we ask people to leave is simply because we don't know what we're going to find under the blankets. When a person dies, they lose control of their muscles, and as a result, bodily fluids can be excreted. It's not the nicest way to see your loved one. It's not always the case, but it does happen, and those few minutes give us a chance to prepare. We place a sheet under the remains. If the blankets are soiled, we offer to take them with us to have them laundered and brought back, or disposed of.

Rigor mortis differs slightly with each person. It can set in almost immediately, or it can come hours later. It is a temporary condition that leaves the body after awhile, but sometimes it can last for several hours. We can tell by the flexibility of the body if rigor has set in, and we can also determine if it has been and gone. There is never anything gruesome about it. You see on television people dying in strange contortions, but that doesn't really happen. Nurses or home care professionals will sometimes have the body positioned at rest when we get there, hands folded and eyelids shut if they weren't already.

If the family leaves the room immediately, then you remove the body right away, but some people stay for a few minutes to talk. You never rush someone out. It is a very emotional time, and people can easily become distraught. Once the family leaves the room and we prepare the body, we move it onto a stretcher and bring it to the front door. I always insist that the deceased leave through the front door. It is the last time that person's physical presence will be leaving their house, and it's an important journey. Almost always the family will come to the door and witness the removal of the remains. Very few will let you leave without accompaniment.

I remember one circumstance that wasn't at all comfortable. A man insisted on accompanying his deceased wife in the removal vehicle. He wanted to sit beside the stretcher the whole way. We don't do this for two reasons. First, because there simply isn't room, and second, because it's not a hearse that we use for the removal, so there isn't anyplace for anyone to sit. After some gentle persuading, the man agreed to ride in the front seat with us. His daughter and son-in-law followed us in their car. I think the man just wanted to see where we were going to place his wife for the next few hours, and afterwards he went home with his daughter. We get these kinds of requests from time to time, and it's important to keep in mind that everyone handles death a little differently. People who have just experienced the death of a loved one are under a great deal of stress and sometimes aren't thinking clearly.

Before any of our staff are allowed to go into a family's home to make a removal, they must first spend a lot of time doing removals from hospitals. The family is often not there and the doctor will usually release the body right away.

One particular night we received a call to go to a nursing home in the city; one of their elderly patients had died in the middle of the night and they didn't have a morgue, so they called us. This wouldn't likely happen today, since most nursing homes are now equipped with small morgues. Earl Canham and I arrived at the hospital, and a nurse greeted us at the front door to bring us up to the room of the deceased. We went into the room, trying to be as quiet as possible, so we wouldn't wake up the three other people sleeping there. The nurse led us over to the bed that the deceased occupied, while I opened the stretcher and pulled it up beside the bed. We were about to touch what we thought was the body when suddenly the nurse said in a loud whisper, "Wait a moment. I'm sorry. This is the wrong bed."

She had made a mistake, and we were moments away from moving a live person. There is nothing humorous about it, but when something like that happens, the stress can make you laugh. Earl started to kind of chuckle, and before long, the three of us were trying hard to stifle the laughter. We had to leave the room until we were able to calm ourselves down.

My friend Bob McKinnon had a similar experience. He now owns his own funeral home, but at one time he was working for a large firm in Toronto. An elderly person was pronounced dead by the coroner, and Bob was called in to make the removal. He went to the hospital, picked up the remains, brought them to the funeral home, then moved the body into the preparation room and placed it on the operating table for embalming. That's when, to his great surprise, he noticed that the body was actually breathing. I can only imagine his shock. I'm sure if it had been a new employee, he might have run out of that room and never looked back. Luckily, Bob was experienced, and he immediately called for an ambulance. The coroner got into a lot of trouble over that, and the story made the news. The person did die, I believe, however, within hours.

People sometimes ask me about urban legends, such as a casket being exhumed and when they open it they discover scratch marks . . . on the inside. In theory, this sort of thing might have happened years ago before modern medicine and before embalming became common practice. In fact, the fear of accidentally being buried alive was very real and in the mid-to-late nineteenth century, several patents were registered for "life-detecting" devices designed to be installed in caskets. One such device patented by Theodore Schroeder of Hoboken, New Jersey, in 1871, included a long chain that was placed in the hand of the corpse. If it was pulled, a bell would ring and a signal flag was raised. An air vent would also open, allowing the occupant of the grave to breathe comfortably while waiting for rescue. As far as I know, none of these devices was ever sold, but it may have given rise to the expression "saved by the bell." I would say it would be impossible for this scenario to happen today.

From the beginning, I enjoyed working at the funeral home and I felt especially satisfied when I would be asked to go out to my hometown of Wakefield. I liked the fact that I was helping the community where I grew up. By Christmas of my first year, I was so enthralled with the work that I mentioned to one of the mid-management employees, Len Hawkins, that someday I was sure I would own the firm. We were in the preparation room at the time, and he looked over at me and started to laugh. Len called some of our co-workers into the room and said, "I want you to meet this golden-haired boy here. He just told me that he is going to own this firm some day!"

Of course there was quite a chuckle. I didn't mean it in any kind of arrogant way, but I could see that after getting to know the business, opportunities were going to arise. I knew that Charlie Hulse wanted to keep the firm locally owned, and there was talk about selling shares to employees. Sure enough, within a few months, Morris Hulse, George Schaef, and Keith Campbell were brought in as shareholders. This started a tradition that is still in place today and is the reason why, eventually, the McGarrys were able to own the firm.

I worked as an assistant helping with removals for a while, and I knew I was in the right profession. After I came to this realization, I decided to register for the funeral director's course at the University of Toronto. The Banting Institute is where I was trained, and the funeral service students share some facilities with the medical students there. Hulse & Playfair sponsored me for the two-year course. At the Institute, we travelled to nearby funeral homes to witness embalmings, and afterwards, we were shown the procedure on human remains that had been donated to science. We also spent time on grief-related matters, to help us gain an understanding of what families go through when they are dealing with a death. During the second year I became an apprentice at Hulse & Playfair.

At the end of the course, there was a practical exam, which involved embalming a body in front of an examiner who is a member of the Board of

Funeral Services. It was nerve-wracking! The course is necessarily intensive to make sure that the students are well trained before they're sent out into the workforce. After graduating from the course, I was able to move on to other jobs in the funeral home, and I think I did just about everything from setting up graves to driving the hearse and family limousine.

As a junior employee, I wasn't allowed to answer the phone unless it rang more than three times. That was a cardinal rule. Charlie and Keith wanted only the most experienced people to take calls from bereaved families. If the phone happened to ring more than three times, I was allowed to pick it up because it meant that all the senior staff members were occupied. We would often joke, "Which ring can you get? Is it the fourteenth or fifteenth?" Of course, if the phone rang fifteen times, you would probably get fired. I would listen for that fourth ring, though, waiting for my chance to talk directly to the public.

Charlie also wanted you to know who was calling. He wanted you to know the community you were serving. You had to be conscious and up to date about what was going on in the city, and this meant reading the newspaper every day and keeping your ear to the ground. Charlie would often go out in the evenings, for dinner or social functions, and when he returned to the funeral home, he usually wouldn't go upstairs to his apartment right away. He'd come in and sit down and talk to you in the front office, questioning you about how the day went and about any news, and I'll tell you, you really needed to have the answers. Of course he was doing this because he cared about the business and he wanted to make sure that his employees took their jobs as seriously as he did.

You really knew you were doing a good job if you were asked to start driving the limousine for the family of the deceased. It's a task that requires propriety and sensitivity. At first glance it might seem like a simple job, but remember that family members are in the midst of dealing with extreme emotions. There can be outbursts of anger or frustration, or the quiet resignation of sorrow. No family is perfect, and the intense emotional upheaval surrounding a death can be a time when deep-rooted issues and old feuds bubble to the surface. As the driver, you must be able to listen patiently and be empathetic.

One of the first times I was asked to drive the family car was for the funeral of the son of a university professor who had been killed in a motorcycle accident. His father was very bitter. It was a large funeral, and after the service we were on the street waiting for people to leave the chapel and make their way to their cars, so we could start the procession to the cemetery. The funeral director and I had already guided a number of the family members to the limousine, but trying to organize any group of people takes time, and you must be patient. It was a hot summer day at a time before air conditioning was prevalent in cars, so I had all the windows down in the limousine. After a few minutes, the father of the deceased leaned out of the back window and said briskly, "What's the delay?"

It was one of the first times that I had experienced this kind of anger from a family member.

"I'm sorry, sir, we'll be leaving very shortly."

"Why the hell aren't we moving?"

"We're just waiting for some of your friends to move their cars into position."

"Forget them. I want to go now."

I wasn't sure what to do. I understood that this man had just lost his son and was bitter. I knew that even though he was directing his anger at me, it was only because his world had been turned upside down and he didn't know how to handle it. I excused myself and went to talk with the funeral director. I explained the situation and said that the father of the deceased wanted to leave immediately. He nodded and said that we should start moving slowly. I walked back to the limousine, and we began moving down the street. I was driving slowly so that all the other people at the funeral wouldn't feel that we were leaving without them. I was somewhat worried that the man would lash out again because we were not moving very quickly, but the speed of the cortege was not really the issue. He just wanted to be moving, and by the time we reached the cemetery, he had regained his composure. I could tell that he was embarrassed at having lost his temper. The rest of the funeral went by without incident; however, I learned a valuable lesson that day—the job of funeral director requires patience and understanding. But sometimes you also need a thick skin.

When I first started working at the funeral home, every employee at one time or another was asked to do every job. Since that time we've become more specialized. We now have employees whose specific job is to meet with families and begin planning the funeral, and others who work as service directors. The service directors are the people who will be with the family on the actual day of the ceremony. At one time the thinking was that it was best to have continuity;

the same person would deal with a family from the planning stages of the funeral right until the reception after the interment. But there are so many choices available now, as far as timing and type of service, that it has become too difficult to maintain this kind of consistency. The funeral might happen the same day that the death occurs, or it could happen a week later. The planners meet with the family and make all the necessary arrangements and then they introduce the family to the service director. As long as the family is able to meet the person who will be in charge of the funeral, things usually go smoothly.

We also have staff who are dedicated to the prearrangement of funerals, a practice that has been steadily growing over the years. After a person prearranges their own funeral, I often hear them say that it has given them peace of mind. They can be confident that all the details surrounding their death will be taken care of, and they take comfort in the fact that their families will not be under any additional stress or financial burden at the time of their passing. Patrick McGarry and his brother Robin (both young cousins of mine) are presently very active in the prearrangement department of our funeral home. Their hard work has built this department into one of the largest in Canada for a private family firm.

Before we embalm human remains, the family needs to give their consent, and we can accept verbal permission. At one time it was understood that most people were embalmed and we would just proceed automatically, but in recent years diverse cultures and religions have brought change to Canada. Members of the Jewish faith, for example, have a tradition where a group of people from the Jewish community will prepare the remains. Their faith calls for minimal preparation, believing that the body's integrity should be maintained and that the funeral should happen as soon as possible after the death occurs. Jewish caskets are usually made out of wood with little or no metal on them, and have at least six holes cut into the bottom to let nature take its course quickly.

Embalming has been practised and refined for thousands of years by many different cultures. It is widely thought to be the first surgical procedure that human beings undertook. In the ancient world, the Egyptians were well known for their funeral practices and made the greatest advancement in the embalming arts. Although the Egyptians were not the only culture that mummified their dead—the Inca as well as other Central and South American cultures also practised this tradition—they certainly seemed to have perfected it. There is evidence that the Egyptians were embalming their kings and nobles as early as 4,000 BCE, and they continued to do so for the next 3,000 years. Their skill was such that some mummies, discovered thousands of years after they had been buried, were found to have skin on the soles of their feet that was still soft and elastic. In the Egyptian culture, embalming was closely linked to religious beliefs about the fate of the soul after death. Mummification was seen as a way of helping the soul attain the afterlife and preserving the body until it could someday be reclaimed.

Other ancient civilizations also embalmed their dead; the Persians, Scythians, Assyrians, and Jews were well known for their embalming techniques. Various methods were used. Body cavities were often filled with a mixture of herbs, balsams, and aloes, or the remains may have been immersed in honey or wax (Alexander the Great was embalmed in this way).

The custom of embalming spread from North Africa and Asia to Europe, although it was not as common there. Most notably it was practised in the Middle Ages during the time of the Crusades when noblemen fighting in the Holy Land expressed a desire to have their bodies brought home for burial. Sometimes, herbs and spices with preservative qualities were inserted into the remains through incisions before the body was wrapped in tarred or waxed sheets for the journey.

Modern embalming techniques share very little with these ancient practices. The procedures we use today can be traced back to the American Civil War. Similar to the European Crusades, the practice gained momentum when wealthier families of soldiers killed in battle wished to bring their loved ones home for a local burial. Gradually the practice became more popular. After Abraham Lincoln was embalmed so his remains could be returned to his home state for burial, the idea became well known to the greater American public.

The first modern embalming fluids were made with various combinations of arsenic, mercury, creosote, and alcohol, and were understandably very toxic. After the practice became more prevalent, there was a very real fear that embalmed remains might poison groundwater over time, so the search began to find a more suitable preserving agent. In 1866, a German chemist named August Wilhelm von Hofmann discovered formaldehyde, a preservative that was much less toxic than its predecessors. It became the foundation for the fluids that we use today.

I always recommend that if there is going to be a viewing we be allowed to embalm. I've had only one family that outright refused, and in fact, they wanted the viewing to be held in their own home. We try to accommodate most requests, as we did in this case, but if the visitation is happening in our funeral home and is going to take place over two or three days, we insist on doing a minimal amount of preparation, simply for hygienic reasons. If no preparation is done, there would be a noticeable difference in the remains after a few days.

The job of the embalmer is difficult and important. He or she helps to ensure the family will be left with a pleasant image of their loved one, and many consider this to be an important first step in the healing process.

Occasionally, a family won't like the idea of cosmetics being applied. I explain that we can do some preparation, but we don't have to apply any makeup. Again, I do recommend it if there's going to be a viewing.

It's important that the human remains we have in our care are as presentable as possible at the viewing. It's a reflection of our standards. We pride ourselves that the remains we prepare resemble the way the person was in life as closely as possible, and people do take notice and aren't afraid to comment on it.

One example of this happened with a funeral we arranged for a couple who had been murdered. In certain instances when the body is damaged, we recommend that the casket be open for the family, but closed for viewing by the public, and that's what we suggested in this particular instance. We told the family that we could prepare the remains well enough so that the caskets could be open, but we thought their family might be more comfortable if the caskets were closed during public visitation. The family insisted that they wanted to have the caskets open for the viewing.

Our technicians are all very skilled, but after a violent event, the body can swell and the features might not be what you want. I can understand the family wanting to see the body to confirm, and we won't ever prevent any family from viewing if they insist, although we will be tastefully descriptive if the remains are beyond reason to see.

On this particular occasion, our technicians prepared the remains to the best of their ability, but after they were finished, we still recommended that the caskets be closed. The family asked to see the remains, and we brought them in. They thought our technicians had accomplished excellent work and insisted the caskets be open for the public viewing. We complied with their wishes and the service went ahead.

A few days after the funeral, I received an angry call from a woman who was a close friend of one of the deceased.

"It's outrageous that you would have the caskets open," she said. "I'm going to write the newspaper about this travesty. You should be ashamed of yourselves."

After she finished, I calmly explained the circumstances to her and said that I thought it was outrageous for her to be calling and scolding me. She simply didn't know the facts. I told her that she could write the newspaper if she liked, but if she did, she was going to have to answer to the family who had insisted that the caskets be open.

"The only thing you will accomplish by bringing attention to this is embarrassing the family and yourself."

She wasn't entirely satisfied when she hung up, but she never did write to the paper.

A similar event happened to me early in my career. I was working at our West Chapel at the time and was taking care of the arrangements of a man who had been murdered a few days before. The family came to the funeral home to discuss the details. I had prepared the body, but I didn't think it was suitable to see. Therefore, as gently as I could, I explained this to them. The brother of the deceased was incensed.

"My brother's body is here?" he asked.

"Yes, sir."

"And you've prepared him?"

"Yes."

"I'm going to tell you something, Mr. McGarry. We're going to see his body, and we're going to see it right now."

"All I can do, sir, is recommend that you don't."

"I don't care what you say. I want to see my brother!"

"I will take you in, but I'd like you to talk to a senior colleague of mine first."

He agreed and I called Keith Campbell, who lived not too far from the funeral home. Keith came in and went into the preparation room. He then came out and sat down with the brother.

"Brian is right," he began. "I don't think this is the image of your brother that you want to be left with."

The man was still insistent. "I don't care what you think."

Keith looked at him for a moment, realizing that he was not going to change his mind. "All right," he said. "Come with me and when you get back you can advise the rest of your family whether they should go in."

He was understandably distraught. His brother had just been violently taken away from him, and the only thing to do was to let him have his wish. Keith led the man into the preparation room. A few minutes later he came out and recommended that the rest of his family not go in.

It's not a pleasant aspect of our work, but it is important, and the role of the technicians cannot be understated. Of course these are extreme examples and most remains are very presentable.

More often today, people are choosing cremation, and this is a big change from the custom of full burial. As the requests for cremation increased, we felt it would be more convenient for our families if the procedure could be completed by our family. Therefore, we decided to build a crematorium of our own. At that time, there was an old law on the books in Ontario that prevented funeral homes from owning crematoriums in the same province, so we found a suitable location in Chelsea, Quebec. We had the approval of the Chelsea town council, and we were ready to start building, when the permission was suddenly revoked. There are many misconceptions about crematoriums and the biggest fallacy is the belief that the air and water will be polluted around the site; this has been proven false. It is my own belief that the objections people have about crematoriums being built in their communities is that a crematorium represents death. It's a physical reminder of the fate that awaits us all. Personally, I believe that you can only really start to truly live after you've earnestly accepted that you will one day pass away. This realization makes life that much more precious. The McGarrys now have crematorium properties in Ontario and Quebec.

Since our bodies are made of more than 70 percent water, and the heat used in the crematorium is upwards of 1800°F, most of the exhaust takes the form of water vapour. It takes about four hours for the entire process to be completed, and after that, the remains are mostly made up of bone fragments. These fragments are then placed in a machine that reduces them into a fine powder, and that is what the ashes comprise. The ashes are placed into an urn or other receptacle, and can then be buried, placed in a columbarium, or scattered. Many crematoriums are located in industrial parks or in dark basements, and were never designed for families to see. However, we wanted to build crematoriums that would make people feel comfortable if they chose to be present for the cremation, to allow them to be part of the process. My brother-in-law, Barry Schwerdfeger, his son Tyler, and Colin Dolan are three of the best crematorium technicians in Canada. Barry helped us design our buildings and has played a big part in making our crematoriums the envy of many other service providers. Our buildings remain unique, constructed from post and beam by Ron Hill Construction, and have become prototypes for additional buildings.

In some cultures, cremation is an ancient tradition. In the Hindu faith, it was customary for the eldest male child to light the funeral pyre, and this practice continues. We are sometimes asked if a member of the family can initiate the process, and we fully support this tradition.

The choice of cremation does offer a certain flexibility, as your ashes can be scattered just about anywhere you want, within reason. Alternately, if you want a full burial, for instance, on the family farm, you have to apply to the province to have an area of your property defined as cemetery grounds, which can take a lot of time and effort. Cremated remains allow flexibility, with no need for a cemetery plot (the most expensive real estate a family will ever purchase).

As a side note, many of these high-profit cemeteries avoid paying municipal taxes while neighbouring properties subsidize their infrastructure (e.g., water, waste management, fire and police services, access roads). I am not referring to faith-based cemeteries, but rather such entities as, in Ottawa, Pinecrest Cemetery, Capital Memorial Gardens, and Beechwood Cemetery. Some of these cemeteries find it quite humorous, and one individual asks me frequently, "Do you still enjoy paying your taxes, Brian?" They should be ashamed of themselves, taking advantage of their tax-paying neighbours—private and corporate.

The McGarrys have lobbied long and hard to level the playing field in this regard and we (as in "the community") may win. Naturally, the concern goes well beyond Ottawa. However, while this issue has dragged on for twenty years, it is expected that the appropriate changes to provincial legislation will occur in 2012.

After our proposal to build a crematorium in Chelsea was rejected by the town council, we went searching for another location, eventually finding one just outside of my hometown of Wakefield. Our proposal was approved and construction started in the fall of 1997; it is owned by Brett and Erin McGarry, my and Sharon's son and daughter.

Construction was still underway when the Ice Storm of 1998 hit much of eastern Ontario and western Quebec, including Montreal. It was just after New Year's when the power went out and stayed out for over a week. The workers were doing what they could to continue with the construction when a man stopped by. It was Peter Jennings, the famous ABC news anchor and Ottawa native. Peter was a friend of mine and happened to be in town. He knew that we were building a new crematorium and thought he'd stop by to see how construction was coming along. He drove onto the site and found the foreman.

"Hello, there! Is McGarry around?" he asked.

The man, a nice French-Canadian fellow, replied, "*Non.*"

"That's too bad. It looks like you're working under some duress here."

"Yeah, we're having a tough time."

"Well, when you see McGarry, tell him I came by and that I'll stop by his house sometime."

"OK. What's your name?"

Always humble, Peter paused and said, "Have you got something to write on?"

The foreman checked his pockets for a piece of paper. Not finding one, he looked around and picked up a discarded wooden plank and handed it to Peter with a pencil. "Here, just write your name on this."

Peter, smiling the whole time, wrote his name down and passed it back to the foreman. "Can you tell me when you expect the construction to be finished?"

"Should be done by next fall."

"All right, tell McGarry I'll be here to open it for him when it's ready."

The foreman looked puzzled, but said he would pass along the message. With that, Peter got back in his car and drove off. I came by a few days later and the foreman walked over. "There was a man here to see you," he began. "He said something about opening the funeral home, but I'm not sure what he meant exactly."

He pulled out the plank and handed it to me. I had a good laugh when I saw Peter's name written elegantly in pencil on this little piece of scrap wood. Afterwards, I explained to the foreman who Peter was. He got a good laugh out of it as well when he realized that he had actually met a famous person.

"I can't wait to tell my wife," he said.

We opened in August of that year and, sure enough, Peter, his wife, Kayce, their two children, and Peter's sister, Sarah Jennings, were all in attendance. We also invited Ray Hnatyshyn and his wife, Gerda, dear friends of our family. Ray had just finished his tenure as governor general. It was a lovely midsummer Saturday in August and more than 500 people came out to the party. Many folks were there out of curiosity and some wanted to have a glimpse of Peter and Ray. When it came time for the official speeches, Peter got up and said, "I had a choice. I could either come up here and open this crematorium, or stay in New York and follow the Lewinsky story. I chose the crematorium."

The Monica Lewinsky scandal was just starting to break, and in fact, during the dinner, Peter leaned over and said, "Brian, I can't stay. I really do have to get back to New York to cover that story."

Sure enough, the next day I flipped on the television and there he was.

A few years later, Peter died of lung cancer. He had been a heavy smoker for years and had quit, but after the terrorist attacks of September 11, 2001, he had started up again. He told me once that the smoking helped him get through that difficult time. His funeral took place in New York City at Carnegie Hall. My wife, Joan, and I had the distinct pleasure of attending this memorable tribute to a great man, a great Canadian. Eventually, Kayce and Sarah brought Peter's cremated remains back to the Gatineau Hills, a place he always remembered fondly. A memorial service was also held at the National Arts Centre in Ottawa.

One of the wonderful things about the funeral profession is that it has introduced the McGarrys and our colleagues to such a wide spectrum of people, rich and poor, famous and unknown. Charles Hulse opened the door for me as a young man, and I think I've carried on the tradition for many of the young men and women who have worked at our funeral homes over the years. Since I began working in funeral and cremation services more than fifty years ago, more than 67,000 funerals have been conducted through our firm (more than 87,000 since the firm's founding in 1925). The range of social strata over the years has been profound—". . . from paupers to prime ministers," wrote Ken Bagnell of Toronto, our early company historian who produced a much-read booklet in 1985, entitled, *Decades and Dedication.*

The experiences I've had over all these years have been invaluable, not only for me, but for the hundreds of employees who have been a part of this Canadian institution known as Hulse, Playfair & McGarry.

The funeral of former prime minister Mackenzie King, as the casket departs from St. Andrew's Presbyterian Church to travel from Ottawa to Toronto, where the former prime minister would be interred in Mount Pleasant Cemetery. Charles Hulse, who conducted the funeral, gave each honorary bearer an engraved silver cigarette case as a memento of the occasion. 1950.

Newton Photographers.

CHAPTER 5

State Funerals

Hulse, Playfair & McGarry Funeral Homes, as well as its sister company, McGarry Family Chapels and Cremation Services, are honoured to have been chosen to be a part of state funerals since Prime Minister Mackenzie King, who died in 1950. State funerals are generally reserved for the sitting prime minister, past prime ministers, the governor general, past governors general, and the chief justice and past chief justices of the Supreme Court of Canada. State-assisted funerals, as opposed to full state funerals, are reserved for citizens who have contributed to Canada in a significant way, and who are likely to be nationally mourned. The government always asks the family of the deceased if they will accept a state ceremony, and it is ultimately up to them to decide. In 2011, Prime Minister Stephen Harper offered a state funeral for Jack Layton, Leader of the Official Opposition, who died in office, which Jack's widow, Olivia, accepted. Canadians of all political persuasions were grateful for the opportunity to recognize a great Canadian.

State funerals are governed by strict procedure, and the protocol covers every detail down to the order of mourners who file past the casket to pay their respects. When a death of national significance occurs, the prime minister, or the heritage minister if the prime minister has died in office, informs the nearest relative of the deceased of the government's desire to hold a state funeral. Condolences are formally sent to the family from the prime minister, and a message is sent to inform the reigning sovereign. Flags on all federal buildings are ordered lowered to half-mast, and they remain so until after the funeral. If the family accepts the offer of a state funeral, the director of state protocol, part of Heritage Canada, will then step in to oversee the ceremony.

The director of state protocol works with the funeral director and other government agencies to coordinate the arrangements. Meetings are held with the family to determine the date and location of the funeral, choice of honorary pallbearers, and place of burial, whether full burial with casketed remains, or burial of cremated remains following the state occasion. State funerals do not necessarily have to be held in Ottawa, and the family can choose any location they wish, although if the location is outside of Ottawa, a memorial service will usually be planned in the capital.

The lying-in-state for a prime minister or a former prime minister takes place in the Hall of Honour located in the Centre Block of the Parliament Buildings in Ottawa. When a governor general or a former governor general dies, the lying-in-state takes place in the Senate Chamber. For chief justices and former chief justices of the Supreme Court, the lying-in-state occurs in the foyer of the Supreme Court building.

One notable exception to these rules occurred in August 2005, when Sgt. Ernest Alvia "Smokey" Smith died. Mr. Smith was the last surviving Canadian recipient of the Victoria Cross, the highest military honour given in the British Commonwealth. The medal is awarded for "gallantry in the face of the enemy" and was presented to Smith after he single-handedly held off German tanks and soldiers near the small, northern Italian town of San Giorgio di Cesena in 1944. Prime Minister Paul Martin offered a state funeral to Sgt. Smith's family, and they accepted. The lying-in-state occurred in the foyer of the House of Commons; Sgt. Smith was only the ninth person to be accorded this honour outside of the usual protocol.

At state funerals, when the time comes for the viewing, the family spends a half hour in private with the deceased before the official ceremony. The first representative of the government to pay respects is the governor general, followed by the prime minister and the chief justice of the Supreme Court of Canada. Following them, former governors general, former prime ministers, and former chief justices. The official order continues through to senators, members of Parliament, and members of the diplomatic corps, and then the general public is invited in.

The history of how our firm became involved with state funerals goes back to July of 1927, when Canada was celebrating its sixtieth birthday, our Diamond Jubilee. As part of the festivities, the famous aviator Charles Lindbergh, who had only just returned from his historic flight from New York to Paris, had been invited and was set to arrive in Ottawa in his plane, *The Spirit of St. Louis*. Thousands of people went out to watch Lindbergh's arrival, and the event caused so much excitement that the city renamed the airfield to honour the famous flier. The name, Lindbergh Field, lasted for a few years; it is now known as CFB Uplands.

At the time, the Hulse Brothers had recently purchased their new ambulance. In those days, funeral homes often had ambulances and it wouldn't have been unusual for them to be involved in the furniture business as well, although Hulse was not. It was well known that the Hulse Brothers had the newest ambulance in the city, and when Prime Minister Mackenzie King decided that there should be some emergency equipment on hand at the airfield, Charlie was called and was subsequently present at the airfield for Lindbergh's arrival.

On July 2, Lindbergh had set out from Detroit, Michigan, accompanied by a twelve-plane military escort. He arrived in Ottawa and landed without incident, while his escort planes circled above. It was during that time that Lieut. J. Thad Johnson, one of the pilots in the formation, miscalculated a turn. Johnson's plane veered into the path of the aircraft beside him, and the pilot could not avoid clipping the tail of Johnson's aircraft, which was sent spiralling out of control. Lieut. Johnson, a respected airman in his own right, had been forced to bail out of planes in the past. He was able to jump clear of his machine just as it veered into a nosedive, but he didn't have enough altitude for his parachute to be effective, and he fell to his death.

Charlie was one of the first to arrive at the scene, and he recovered Johnson's body, bringing the airman's remains to the funeral home. King ordered a state ceremony to be held before the airman was sent by train to his home state of Michigan. Wanting to ensure that the American pilot was given due respect by the country where he had died, the prime minister requested that the absolute best casket be provided. Charlie didn't have the particular casket in stock, so called on other funeral homes in the city to see if anyone could help him. One of his rivals had one of the elegant caskets on hand and offered to provide it— for the price of $3,000. This was a considerable amount of money in 1927, and was out of Charlie's reach. So, instead of paying the exorbitant amount, Charlie made a phone call to the company that made the exquisite casket and talked them into providing one on credit.

Charlie went out of his way to make sure that the central train station and the funeral car that was to carry the pilot's remains were both draped in funeral colours and tastefully embellished with flowers. It was this attention to detail that so impressed King. Immediately after the ceremony, he instructed his executors ensure that when he died, it would be Charles Hulse who would look after the funeral.

Twenty-three years later, in 1950, Mackenzie King died at his estate in the Gatineau Hills, and sure enough, Charlie was called upon to take care of the arrangements. Part of this job included setting the former prime minister's features for the creation of a plaster death mask, and today there is a bronze statue of Mackenzie King in Ottawa that was moulded from that same mask. King's funeral was one of the largest of its time, and nearly 35,000 people came to Parliament Hill to pay their respects.

Our funeral home has been graciously chosen to be a part of twenty-three state-assisted funerals held in Ottawa.

The first state funeral that I witnessed as a junior employee was for Governor General Georges Vanier, who died in office in Canada's centennial year, 1967. The next state funeral that I had some involvement in was for former prime minister Lester Pearson in 1972, who coincidentally had chosen to be buried in my hometown of Wakefield. In fact, the cemetery is only about 500 metres from the house where my sister, brother, and I were raised, and where my sister, Mary-Ellen Schwerdfeger, and her husband, Barry, live to this day.

Mr. Pearson had a cottage in the area where he spent a lot of time during the summer months. Before becoming prime minister, Mr. Pearson worked for external affairs, and during that time he made a pact with two fellow cottagers and diplomats, Hume Wrong and Norman Robertson. The three men agreed that when they died, they would be buried next to each other in the little cemetery in Wakefield. The cemetery is located on a hill and is blessed with a stunning view of the Gatineau Hills. If you go there today, you'll find the graves of the three "burial buddies." The Canadian government has commemorated the site by erecting a plaque and flag at the cemetery entrance, and by building a stone path to Mr. Pearson's grave, an honour that has since been bestowed on every former prime minister's resting place.

By the time Prime Minister John Diefenbaker died in 1979, I had become a partner in the firm and was privileged to play a larger role in the ceremony. I worked closely with Cliff Lloyd, who was the president of our firm at that time and a true professional.

The first time I ever saw Mr. Diefenbaker was when I was attending the Ottawa Technical High School in the late '50s. To get to school in the mornings, I travelled with Larry Lafleur, who had a job working on Parliament Hill. Larry would park his car behind the West Block, and from there it was an easy walk over to the school. At three o'clock when school was done for the day, I made my way back to Parliament Hill to catch my ride home, but I had to wait for about an hour and a half for Larry to finish work. The entire time I attended Ottawa Tech—and to keep warm in winter!—I would go sit in the House of Commons gallery. Security wasn't as much of an issue as it is today, and as long as I left my bag at the entrance, I could walk right inside. I didn't realize it until years later, but those hours sitting in the gallery provided the best education in Canadian politics that I could have received anywhere. John Diefenbaker's Progressive Conservatives were in power at the time, and I remember watching intently as Mr. Diefenbaker and Jack Pickersgill of the Liberals debated back and forth. Both men were skilled orators and seeing them outmanoeuvre each other was like being at a fencing match—the two men lunging and parrying in verbal combat. It was a fascinating way to spend a few hours and was, by far, the best free entertainment in town. Today, behind Parliament's West Block and approximately fifteen feet from where Larry Lafleur used to park his car, stands a statue of John Diefenbaker. It's larger than life, just as he tended to be.

One story about Mr. Diefenbaker has always stuck out in my mind as a good example of why he was known as the prime minister of everyday Canadians. At the time, Maj. Gen. Gus Cloutier was the sergeant-at-arms of the House of Commons. Mr. Cloutier was walking up to his office in the Centre Block one morning, when he happened to notice an elderly gentleman stepping out of a city bus and crossing the street over to Parliament Hill. This would not normally be an unusual sight, except for the fact that the man happened to be former prime minister John Diefenbaker. Even though Dief had lost the party leadership in 1967, he retained a seat in the House of Commons for the next twelve years until his death, and he made the trek every day into work. Cloutier walked over to him.

"Pardon me, sir, but did you take the bus here today?" he asked.

"Yes, I did," Diefenbaker replied.

"With all due respect, sir, do we not provide you with a car?"

"Actually, no."

"And you take the bus?"

"Yes, usually."

The sergeant-at-arms thought that travelling by bus wasn't quite befitting a former prime minister, and made a few phone calls to see about providing some transportation for the elderly statesman. The very next day, a car was provided for Mr. Diefenbaker.

The present sergeant-at-arms (and a former RCMP officer) is Kevin Vickers, also a good friend of the McGarrys. The usher of the black rod, Kevin MacLeod, and before him Terry Christopher, became our friends through State Ceremony. These gentlemen (which they are in the truest sense of the word) are well versed in state protocol; one feels truly comfortable in their presence. Kevin MacLeod has recently taken on the added duty of Canadian Secretary to Queen Elizabeth.

John G. Diefenbaker was born in Neustadt, Ontario, but spent many of his early years in Saskatchewan. His father was a schoolteacher and a strong believer in the importance and power of literacy. It was this environment that fostered young John's love of books and his subsequent discovery of Sir Wilfred Laurier, who would become a hero for the young man. Diefenbaker attended the University of Saskatchewan, where he received an MA in political science and economics in 1916. He graduated and then served in the Canadian army during the First World War. He was sent to England, where he rose to the rank of lieutenant, but before he could be sent to the front lines in France, an irregularity was discovered in his heart, and he subsequently was discharged from service as medically unfit for duty. Back home in Canada, Diefenbaker returned to his studies at the University of Saskatchewan and completed a law degree. He was called to the bar in 1919. For many years the future prime minister worked as a defence lawyer in the town of Wakaw, near Prince Albert, Saskatchewan, where he became well known for representing poor and less fortunate clients, a reputation that would carry over into his political life. He once famously remarked, "I determined that there should be no second-class Canadians . . . I did not set out to be unjust to the powerful; they look after themselves."

Mr. Diefenbaker was a competent litigator and garnered a reputation for being somewhat unconventional in his methods. On one occasion, to illustrate how a murder was committed, Diefenbaker fell to the floor in front of the jury, clutching his throat. He succeeded in capturing the attention of every person in the courtroom that day, but his display was not meant as a gimmick; he had simply been overtaken by his own unwavering belief in his client's innocence. He went on to win the case and, in fact, out of twenty murder cases that he took on in his career, Diefenbaker only lost two.

Mr. Diefenbaker's political aspirations began in 1920, when the young lawyer was elected as an alderman to the Wakaw municipal council. He served only one term and lost his bid for re-election, but the experience ignited a passion for politics in the young man. He possessed a rare determination, running unsuccessfully in twelve elections at all levels of government before finally being elected to the Saskatchewan legislative assembly for the Conservatives in 1936. By 1940, he had moved into federal politics and was elected as an MP.

Needless to say, by 1958, when "Dief the Chief" became Canada's thirteenth prime minister, he was a seasoned political veteran. He ran his campaign on a platform that included greater development for the northern regions of Canada, as well as increased spending on social programs. Initially he was popular in Quebec as well as Western Canada, and as a result came to power with the largest majority government in Canadian history up to that time. Mr. Diefenbaker would later lose his support in Quebec after being criticized for not appointing any francophones to important cabinet positions. He never enjoyed widespread support from French-Canadians again, and the backlash from this mistake would linger even after his death when the flags on provincial buildings in Quebec were not lowered to recognize his passing. After a heated parliamentary debate, the flags were lowered on the legislative building in Quebec City, but not on any of the other provincial buildings. I personally thought this showed a lack of maturity, as death transcends all party lines. Using a symbol of mourning to take a political stand is in very poor taste.

Diefenbaker's government was hampered by economic problems as well as one of the most controversial policy decisions ever made by a Canadian prime minister—cancellation of the Avro Arrow in 1959. The Arrow was a supersonic fighter jet designed by Canadian engineers that was on the cutting edge of technological advancement at the time. The cancellation of the program, in favour of purchasing an American-made aircraft, was seen as a black day for Canadian industry. Diefenbaker's Conservatives did manage to win a narrow victory in the 1962 election, but they lost their majority. The following year, after losing two non-confidence votes, Diefenbaker's government collapsed and the Liberals came to power under the leadership of Lester B. Pearson. Diefenbaker soldiered on as leader of the Conservative Party and leader of the official opposition.

In 1964, Pearson brought in the new Canadian flag, the Maple Leaf, which Diefenbaker thought of as the "Pearson Pennant." Dief wanted to keep the old flag, the Red Ensign, and this would later cause some controversy at his funeral.

Diefenbaker's legacy has been overshadowed by the Avro Arrow, but he is also remembered as the prime minister who brought in the Canadian Bill of Rights, appointed the very first francophone governor general, Georges Vanier, extended the vote to status Native Canadians, and also for his opposition to the nuclear armament of the Canadian military. These important decisions helped shape our national identity.

The first time I met Mr. Diefenbaker was in Charlie Hulse's kitchen. I was working that evening and was on my way up to the staff quarters for a bite to eat. The door to Mr. Hulse's apartment was open as I walked by, and Charlie saw me and asked me to come in. I was stunned to see the prime minister sitting at the kitchen table. The two men were friends, and Diefenbaker would drop by from time to time for a chat. Charlie smiled and said, "Mr. Diefenbaker, I'd like you to meet one of our young employees. This is Gary . . ."

Charlie often unintentionally confused my first name with part of my last. To avoid an embarrassing moment, I decided not to correct the mistake. The prime minister extended his hand and said, "Pleased to meet you, Gary."

"It's a pleasure to meet you, sir."

I shook Mr. Diefenbaker's hand, and Charlie motioned to an empty chair at the table, saying, "Why don't you join us for a moment?"

I sat down and had a nice visit for about twenty minutes. The prime minister was very gracious and asked me several questions, patiently listening to my answers.

"Tell me, Gary," he asked, "where were you born?"

"Wakefield, sir."

"I've been through that area. It's very nice. How long have you worked for Mr. Hulse, Gary?"

"Almost a year now, sir."

He asked me a few other questions, the whole time calling me "Gary." I was too excited to care, but I couldn't help smiling every time he said the name. It wasn't until years later when I met Mr. Diefenbaker again to discuss his funeral arrangements that I told him my name was actually Brian.

Diefenbaker had his funeral organized down to the smallest of details. He was almost obsessed with the planning process and the arrangements, which he referred to as "Operation Hope-Not." This was the same code name that Sir Winston Churchill had used for his funeral plans. Diefenbaker was a great admirer of Churchill, and his funeral arrangements copied Churchill's in many ways. Even the headstone Mr. Diefenbaker chose, a modest slanted stone marker, reflected his admiration for the famous British leader.

Mr. Diefenbaker defined the casket that he wanted and the type of flowers that he liked, as well as naming the funeral directors he wanted to take care of the arrangements. There were to be four of us, two from Mr. Diefenbaker's home province of Saskatchewan, and two from Ottawa. Bob McKague and Don Newbigging were chosen from Saskatoon; Cliff Lloyd and I were honoured to be chosen as the Ottawa representatives. We became a great team. A key person in the whole process, however, was Chief of Protocol Graham Glockling from what is now known as Heritage Canada. Graham was the epitome of a true "English gentleman"—precise, polite, professional, and dignified.

Archie McQueen had spent several summers living at the Diefenbaker residence in Rockliffe Park in Ottawa. Mr. McQueen, a schoolteacher from Hamilton, Ontario, and a close friend of Mr. Diefenbaker's, had been volunteering as an assistant to the former prime minister in his later years. Mr. Diefenbaker never stopped working, and Archie was there to help him with correspondence and research.

Early in the morning on August 16, 1979, Archie came down from his bedroom to find Mr. Diefenbaker slumped over his desk in his study. Scattered across the desk were the parliamentary papers he had been reading. John G. Diefenbaker was dead at the age of eighty-three, and he had worked until the last moments of his life.

Mr. McQueen immediately informed the authorities and then he called us. Sharon and I were packing the car to go to a Kiwanis convention in Sault Ste. Marie and were just about ready to leave when the phone rang. It was Cliff Lloyd.

"Hi, Brian," he said. "I'm sorry to have to tell you this, but John Diefenbaker has just passed away. I'm on my way over to his house. Would you consider making yourself available for the next ten days or so?"

"Of course, Cliff, I'll be over as soon as I can."

As a junior partner who was focused on my career, I knew exactly what I

FROM PAUPERS TO PRIME MINISTERS

had to do, but more than that, I felt a duty to the former prime minister. I told Sharon what had happened and we started taking the luggage out of the car. Cliff would be leading the funeral, and I would be his assistant.

Mr. Diefenbaker's physician had been quick to arrive at the house and he made the pronouncement of death. We didn't phone anyone, as there is a strict protocol dictating the order of people who must be informed. The Royal Family must be contacted, then the governor general, the prime minister, and all of the lieutenant-governors and premiers of the provinces. These offices should be informed before the media, but somehow the newspapers found out about it, likely by monitoring police calls. Soon there were journalists at Mr. Diefenbaker's house. There was a touching photograph taken that morning, which later appeared in the media: a shot of Mr. Diefenbaker's dog, McAndy, who was with the prime minister at the time of his death. The picture shows the faithful dog watching as his master is being taken from the house to our hearse.

Every state funeral has a leader from the government, and we've met and worked with many over the years: Graham Glockling, Col. Georges Bernier, Jean-Paul Roy, Kevin MacLeod, CWO Paul "Smokey" Leblanc, to name a few. Without exception, these people and their dedicated staff have all been professional and very pleasant to work with. In addition to state funerals, the director of state protocol is also in charge of coordinating other national events, such as royal visits and the annual Canada Day celebrations in Ottawa.

Over the years I've noticed some things that seem to happen consistently at state funerals. There is always a great deal of discussion and some debate between the family of the deceased and the government, and inevitably the ceremony takes on the personality of the deceased.

Graham immediately called a meeting for everyone who was to be involved with the funeral. We had only just sat down when the first problem emerged. Mr. Diefenbaker had been very clear in his instructions that his casket should not be draped with the Maple Leaf flag. Instead, he wanted his casket covered with the old flag, the Red Ensign. To him, the Maple Leaf flag represented the Liberals. When the new flag was proposed, Diefenbaker had favoured a version that had a red maple leaf in the middle and two blue bars on the outside to signify the oceans on either side of the country, but it had been rejected. Now, here it was in black and white: "Do not drape my casket with the Canadian flag." This was bound to cause controversy. How do you drape the casket of a former prime minister of Canada with an outdated flag? Graham understood that the protocol must be upheld at all costs, but the executor, Mr. David Munroe, wanted to honour Mr. Diefenbaker's wishes. (Mr. Munroe was associated with the University of Saskatchewan where Mr. Diefenbaker was to be buried.) Immediately, we were in the middle of a debate.

The discussion went on for some time. It was going to be a large funeral attended by many heads of state, and the idea of having a different flag seemed inappropriate. The thought arose that perhaps we shouldn't have any flag at all, but doing so would only ensure that no one's wishes were met. After several hours, Cliff Lloyd and Graham Glockling came up with an idea.

"What about this, why don't we join the two flags—stitch them together."

David was leery at first. "That's not exactly protocol."

Graham looked at him and smiled, "Well, this is a rather unique situation, and there isn't a precedent to look to."

After several hours of discussion and considering other options, the "split flag" seemed to be the best course of action. It certainly wasn't standard procedure, but there was nothing in the rules of protocol that said it couldn't be done, and so it was decided. The two flags would be stitched together and draped over the casket, another example of a great Canadian compromise. We obtained the two flags and contacted a seamstress who worked through the night to have it ready for the lying-in-state, which was to take place the following day.

The unusual combination of flags was remarked upon, but it seemed to make sense—the Red Ensign was the flag that Mr. Diefenbaker had governed under.

Also specific was Mr. Diefenbaker's request for an open casket. Some state funerals involve an open casket for the family, but have it closed for the public. I think Dief wanted ordinary Canadians to see him one last time.

Initially, Diefenbaker wanted to be buried in Ottawa, next to his second wife, Olive, who had predeceased him several years earlier, but a couple of years before his death, he had a change of heart and decided that he wanted to be buried in Saskatoon, Saskatchewan. He also requested that Olive be disinterred from Beechwood Cemetery and moved to Saskatchewan to be next to him, a plan that he had discussed at length with her family.

I remember several occasions when Olive and John Diefenbaker came into our funeral home to pay their respects to friends and associates who had passed away. Mr. Diefenbaker loved people and would talk with everyone; it was usually up to Olive to remind him when they needed to leave the reception. She would smile at her husband and say gently, "Come on, John, we have to go now."

If she didn't say anything, Mr. Diefenbaker would likely spend the rest of the day deep in conversation. Frequently, his trusted assistant Betty Eligh would be with him. She had worked with Mr. Diefenbaker for many years and later worked with the famous Canadian photographer, Yousuf Karsh. She's a lovely woman and remains a good friend.

It was very important to us and to Olive Diefenbaker's family that the disinterment and transport of Olive's casket be done without any publicity. We accomplished this two days before the funeral, just after sunrise, to ensure that there would be no media coverage. We brought her to Saskatchewan by air. This procedure was kept very quiet, and in fact, when it came time for the funeral, many people in attendance were surprised to see two caskets at the graveside, instead of one.

Whenever there is a state funeral, the main entrance to the Centre Block is draped in mourning colours, a tradition we've borrowed from England. It gives the entry a very sombre, yet dignified atmosphere. When the hearse arrives at Parliament Hill with the casket, it is greeted by an honour guard made up of RCMP officers. The guard carries the casket into the Hall of Honour, where it remains for the duration of the lying-in-state. Four servicemen silently stand guard, one at each corner of the casket, and the room is filled with a powerful silence. It's a moving experience to see so many people in the hall without hearing any voices, the shuffling of feet and murmured prayers being the only audible sounds.

After Mr. Diefenbaker's family spent some private time with him, Governor General Ed Schreyer was shown in and he paid his respects. Mr. Schreyer was followed by Prime Minister Joe Clark, his wife, Maureen McTeer, and other dignitaries. Once the official visitation was concluded, the general public was allowed to pass by the casket.

For the next two days, 15,000 people went to say goodbye to "Dief the Chief."

When the visitation was finished, the room was cleared of people and the doors were closed. My colleague, Alex Caldwell, and I closed the casket in preparation for the procession to Christ Church Cathedral for the funeral. Unbeknown to us at the time, the "casket closing" was captured by Ottawa photographer John Evans. The active bearers from the RCMP then carried the casket out of the Hall of Honour on their shoulders, and placed it in the hearse. They were directed by my long-time friend, Sgt. Major Eric Young of the RCMP, a stickler for protocol and a true professional.

The procession set out, moving slowly through downtown streets that were lined with thousands of people waiting quietly for the cortege to pass by. It was a moment in time, the honour guard with their tall fur hats and red and white uniforms marching slowly ahead of the funeral cars. They were followed by a full military band playing a funeral march. The hearse was accompanied on both sides by marching RCMP officers in full uniform.

Twelve hundred dignitaries from all over the world attended the service, which left only a little room for ordinary Canadians inside the church, but this fact didn't deter anyone. Thousands of people gathered on the streets outside the cathedral.

Inevitably at every state funeral, no matter how much planning is done, there are little quirks and problems that come up. Three things happened in rather quick succession at Mr. Diefenbaker's funeral that gave us cause for alarm. After the cortege moved from Parliament Hill to the cathedral, we had to wait for all of the premiers to arrive before we could move the casket from the hearse into the church. Every premier was invited, and every premier was there on time, except one. We were just about ready to move the casket when I noticed a little man smoking a cigarette and sticking his head out between the honorary pallbearers who were lined up on either side of the entrance to the cathedral. Whenever I saw René Lévesque at state occasions, I don't think there was a single time when he was without a cigarette. In public settings, though, he would usually keep it hidden behind his back, which I always found quite humorous.

Mr. Lévesque looked over at me and whispered loudly, "Where should I be sitting?"

"Follow me, sir."

He took one last quick drag from his cigarette, and accompanied me into the church. I brought him over and seated him with the other premiers.

The second problem of the day arose shortly after. We had a seating area at the front of the church reserved for the active pallbearers, the RCMP officers who had carried the casket into the cathedral. Their seats had been roped off, which usually deters people from sitting there, but by the time the men got into the church and placed the casket on the carriage, the reserved seats had filled up. So, there we were, approaching the front of the church and there was no place for the officers to sit. We couldn't ask the people in the seats to leave, because the funeral was being broadcast live on national television and it would have caused a commotion. I whispered to Sgt. Maj. Young, "Quick change here, sir. Have your guys march off on either side, and we'll find other seating for them."

Young nodded, and when they got to the front of the church, he led his men down the side aisles.

We were hoping that would be the end of our troubles for the day, but as the saying goes, these things always happen in threes. The last problem that we had to deal with was far more serious. We were about to start the service when I noticed Graham Glockling walking hurriedly through the cathedral, stopping to talk to different people.

"Everyone go to your positions and hold, and have the organist play some music. I'll explain why in a moment."

Graham came over to Cliff and me, and spoke in a quiet, rushed tone, "I'm afraid someone has called in a bomb threat."

This was startling news, and not a situation that you think about, let alone prepare for. I felt a tinge of panic. "Should we evacuate?" I asked.

"The police are looking into it, but they feel the threat is minimal."

Cliff looked over and asked, "What if there is a bomb and we pay no attention to it?"

Graham nodded, "There's only one person in this room right now who can make a decision on this, and that's the prime minister."

The RCMP had already swept the church for bombs, as they do whenever the prime minister is going to make a public appearance, but Graham wanted to go right to the top, just in case. He walked over to the pew where Joe Clark was sitting and explained the situation, asking him what he thought we should do. Mr. Clark considered it for a moment and said, "Has the church been swept?"

"Yes, sir, right before the service."

"Well, I think the only person who could hurt me is in the casket, so let's carry on."

And so we did. Diefenbaker had famously joked only a few days before his death that Canada had celebrated the Year of the Child by electing Mr. Clark.

Despite this, Joe spoke very eloquently of Mr. Diefenbaker.

Sometimes, the people present at a funeral cause as much of a stir as the deceased. This was always the case whenever Pierre Trudeau was in attendance. Mr. Trudeau had been on a canoe trip when Mr. Diefenbaker died, and had returned with a full beard to attend the funeral. In typical Trudeau fashion, he had insisted on driving his own car in the state procession from Parliament Hill to the cathedral. Our funeral home provides cars for all past prime ministers, but Mr. Trudeau said, "Oh, no, I've got my own car."

It was his grey Mercedes convertible with the red interior that he loved so much. He hopped in with the top down and joined the cortege. It was a hot, humid day, and Trudeau left his car parked with the top down. As it happens sometimes when the humidity is high, a storm can arrive without warning, and that's exactly what happened during the service—it poured. This caused some problems when the casket was being carried down the steep, stone steps of the cathedral, which the rain had made quite slick. The pallbearers had to use extra caution; they did well and were able to get the casket into the hearse without incident. Mr. Trudeau, however, arrived at his car and found it soaking wet. This fact didn't seem to bother him and, without any fuss, he simply wiped off the excess water from his seat, got in, and joined the procession to the train station.

Mr. Diefenbaker loved to travel by train; that's how he did all of his campaigning throughout his long political career. He once said, "There are more opportunities to meet the people when you go by train."

So it was no surprise that Mr. Diefenbaker wanted his final journey home to his beloved Prairies to be completed by rail. A special train was commissioned for the trip from Ottawa to Saskatoon. One of the boxcars was draped in funeral colours and decorated with flowers, and this was where Mr. Diefenbaker's casket rested for the duration of the trip. Cannons were fired when the train pulled out of the central station in Ottawa, as Mr. Diefenbaker made his last departure from the National Capital.

There were to be three scheduled stops for the funeral train; platforms had been built in Thunder Bay, Winnipeg, and Prince Albert. We would stop and open the doors of the funeral car so that people across the nation could have a chance to say goodbye. The further west we travelled, the more I noticed people standing next to the tracks. Whole families had come out to watch solemnly as we passed by. The first morning, at about six o'clock, we came into a small town, and there were thousands of people waiting for us, but we were not scheduled to stop. Graham was looking out the window at all the faces and said, "We can't just go by these people."

He walked to the front of the train to talk with the conductor and, sure enough, a few moments later, the brakes came on and we came to a halt. This was the first of seven unscheduled stops that we made on our trip west, and as a result we were almost fourteen hours late arriving in Saskatoon, but I think it was the right thing to do. Mr. Diefenbaker would most certainly have wanted to stop. When we arrived in Thunder Bay, there were so many people at the train station that we stayed there most of the night. People had been lined up for hours before we even arrived.

We were two and a half days on the train, which had been properly outfitted for the journey. Cliff and I had a nice room with bunk beds. I was younger, so I offered to take the top bunk. Mr. Diefenbaker's family also travelled on the train and stayed in the governor general's car. So the train was divided into three sections: a family car, a media car, and a staff car.

The media had a great time on the train. When the trip was organized, there had been quite a discussion as to whether there should be any liquor aboard, since Mr. Diefenbaker was a lifelong teetotaller who rarely even had wine with dinner. Jean Pigott, a former Conservative member of Parliament who was working in the Prime Minister's Office at the time, made the final decision.

"If you don't have booze on the train, they'll find a way of getting it on, so we may as well have it and keep it under control." Tom Van Dusen, an accomplished journalist (like several of his children) who worked for many years for The Chief, not surprisingly agreed that booze must be available.

In 2011, we looked after Tom's funeral at St. Theresa's Roman Catholic Church in Ottawa, an event in itself. His wife, Shirley, an accomplished artist and author, along with his seven talented sons and daughters, created a celebration of Tom's life, which was attended by hundreds of friends and politicians of all stripes.

Well, I don't know how controlled the booze was. Val Sears, a Toronto journalist renowned for his study of Canadian politics, wrote an article about the trip including a colourful account of all the drinking that had gone on, mostly by the media. While it looked like everyone was having fun, Cliff and I didn't have so much as one drink on the entire journey. We felt we needed to be "on call" at all times, due to the unpredictable nature of the stops. Perhaps as a way to make his story more lively, Mr. Sears wrote in his article that even the funeral directors were drunk. He didn't name us, but you can imagine how we felt about being singled out. We wrote to the editor immediately to set the record straight and received an apology from Mr. Sears and the paper.

We actually had to deal with a death at one of our unscheduled stops. It was six o'clock in the morning when we arrived at a small prairie town, and it looked as if every member of the community had come out to greet us. Once again Graham asked the conductor to stop the train. Cliff and I got out of bed, and by the time we were dressed, the doors to the funeral car had been opened. About twenty minutes later, there was a commotion in the line of mourners. An older gentleman had collapsed. An ambulance was dispatched, and Graham Glockling and Peter Fleming (the latter has since become a lifelong friend of the McGarrys) travelled with them to the hospital, but arrived only to find the doors locked. Eventually, they were able to get inside, but not before the elderly gentleman had passed away.

People all across the country came out to see the train pass by, but the crowds increased in size the closer we got to Saskatchewan. By the time we arrived in Saskatoon, there was at least a thousand people waiting for us. The two local funeral directors chosen by Mr. Diefenbaker were waiting for us at the station, and, together with RCMP officers, we removed the casket from the funeral car and placed it into their hearse. Mr. Diefenbaker's remains were brought directly to the campus of the University of Saskatchewan, where he was to be interred. Saskatoon city council made a special order designating part of the university campus as burial grounds, which was the only way such a choice would be permitted. Olive's casket and burial vault were waiting there when we arrived, covered in a simple black drape.

After a ceremony that involved a fifty-member military guard, two military bands, and a group of native drummers who performed a mourning song, the controversial flag covering Mr. Diefenbaker's casket was removed and folded. Graham Glockling presented it to Mr. Diefenbaker's stepdaughter, Mrs. Carolyn Weir; Mr. Diefenbaker had no children of his own.

Mr. Diefenbaker had requested that he and Olive be lowered into the grave at the same time, and so, after the ceremony the two burial vaults descended slowly to their final resting place.

As soon as all the mourners had left, I saw a strange sight. Two cement trucks appeared in the distance and were rumbling down the lane toward the grave. They pulled up and proceeded to fill the grave with cement. Inevitably there were jokes that the Liberals had come up with the idea to ensure that Mr. Diefenbaker never rose from the grave, but in fact, the cement trucks had been arranged by the former prime minister himself, for reasons known only to him.

Another state funeral that looms large in my memory was for the Right Honourable Pierre Trudeau. It was late September in the year 2000, my wife, Joan Sun McGarry (by this time I was divorced from Sharon, who to this day remains as my corporate partner), and I had decided to take a vacation. The funeral home had been quite busy and this was to be our first trip in over a year. We packed up the car and were on our way to Quebec City, where we planned to spend a few days before heading up to northern Quebec. It's a beautiful time of year to travel in that part of Canada, late enough that the leaves are just starting to change, but still warm enough to walk outside comfortably.

It was late in the afternoon, and we were making our way through downtown Montreal. We hadn't gotten away as early as planned and were fighting rush-hour traffic when my car phone rang. It was Jean-Paul Roy. Mr. Roy had been Graham Glockling's right-hand man and had taken over the position of director of state protocol after Graham retired. I had worked with Mr. Roy and Col. Georges Bernier on Governor General Jules Leger's state funeral many years before, and I respected him highly.

"Jean-Paul, it's nice to hear from you."

"Hi, Brian, where exactly are you?"

"Caught in traffic in Montreal."

"That's coincidental."

"Why's that?"

"Well, I'm sorry to say that Pierre Trudeau has just died in Montreal. Can you stop until I find out what's happening?"

"Yes, of course."

I pulled the car over. I could hear Jean-Paul talking with several other people in the background, and then he came back on the line. "Brian, can you recommend a funeral home in Montreal? Mr. Trudeau passed away at home, and his remains are still at the house."

I thought about it for a moment before replying, "We've worked with Urgel Bourgie in the past, and they've always been excellent." As it turned out, the Trudeau family had the same funeral home in mind, as did Roy Heenan, Mr. Trudeau's law partner and executor.

"OK," Jean-Paul answered. "I'm just on the other line with Justin Trudeau. He's at his father's house with a physician. The family wants to make sure that the removal is done very privately."

A few years before, I'd been invited to Mr. Trudeau's home for an event. I remembered a door that opened into the garage area and was out of view. I recommended to Jean-Paul that they use that entrance when the time came to remove Mr. Trudeau's body. In the midst of all this, Jean-Paul was answering other calls, and I was going back and forth from being on hold, as Jean-Paul attempted to carry on four conversations at once. At the time, the Trudeau family hadn't decided whether they wanted a state funeral, and Mr. Trudeau, even on his deathbed, had staunchly refused to discuss any plans for his funeral. Usually, former prime ministers have arrangements made years before their passing. I think Mr. Trudeau was just too full of life to spend any time thinking about his own death; it was reflective of his personality. His family was concerned because when Pierre left office, he was not as popular as he once had been, and they were worried about how a state funeral would be received by the public.

Jean-Paul came back on the line. "Sorry, Brian, you can imagine things are hectic at the moment. I have to let you go because I need to inform Prime Minister Chrétien. But thanks for your help. We'll be getting in touch with Bourgie's funeral home."

I decided that it would be best not to intrude on what was happening in Montreal, so Joan and I continued to make our way to Quebec City. In retrospect, I should have turned the car around right then.

As we approached Quebec City, Jean-Paul phoned again. "Hello, Brian. Prime Minister Chrétien has talked to the family and expressed his wish that there be a state funeral, and they've agreed."

"All right, I'll get back to Ottawa as quickly as I can."

And that was that. We turned the car around and headed for home.

When I think of Pierre Trudeau, the images that first come to mind are of him sliding down a banister, pirouetting behind the Queen, or defiantly telling a reporter, "Just watch me," after being asked how far he was prepared to go to stop the terrorists during the October Crisis. I loved to watch Trudeau talking with the press, because all too often, by the end of the interview, he would be the one asking the questions. It was this kind of brash confidence and charisma that Trudeau was famous for, but which also got him into trouble, and many of his policy decisions had the same effect. His implementation of "official bilingualism" raised the ire of many people in Western Canada who felt that Trudeau's vision didn't extend past Quebec, although he frequently asked his fellow Quebeckers not to "fence him in" and pigeonhole him. The historian Michael Bliss summed up Trudeau as "one of the most admired and most disliked of all Canadian prime ministers."

I had the privilege of meeting Mr. Trudeau several times, and I always found him to be markedly different from the persona that the media loved so much. One memory of the former prime minister that sticks out in my mind occurred at another state funeral. When Chief Justice Bora Laskin died in office in 1984, our funeral home was called to look after the arrangements.

The funeral was held at the Jewish Memorial Chapel in downtown Ottawa. The streets around the chapel were crowded with cars, and there was a long line of people waiting to go inside. Whenever the prime minister or a former prime minister is planning on attending a funeral, the RCMP calls the funeral home to inform them and to find out exactly who will be greeting the prime minister when he arrives. In this case, I was going to meet Mr. Trudeau, and was waiting at the front door when his car pulled up. He always had a bit of flair about him in everything he did; he didn't just step out of the car, he seemed to spring out. For a moment after alighting from the car, Mr. Trudeau stood on the sidewalk appraising the line of people waiting outside the synagogue. Then, without a second thought, he walked down the street to the end of the line.

The synagogue was already filled to capacity, and there was no way he was going to get inside if he stayed in line, so I walked over to him, and said, "Excuse me, Mr. Prime Minister, but we have a place reserved for you inside. If you'll allow me, I'll show you to your seat."

"No, it's all right. I'm fine here."

"Sir, the line is quite long, and I'm afraid you won't be able to get in . . ."

After some gentle persuasion, Mr. Trudeau finally conceded, and we walked to the entrance. It was revealing that he didn't just march right up to the front door, and I always admired him for it.

One afternoon, we received a call at the funeral home from Mary Macdonald, a lovely lady who worked as Mr. Trudeau's executive assistant on Parliament Hill.

"Brian, I'm calling on behalf of a government official whose aunt has died here in Ottawa, and he wants to keep everything very quiet."

"That's fine, Mary. I'm sure we can accommodate him."

There had even been strict orders that the obituary not be published until after the funeral was over. Mary insisted that before she tell me who the family was, I promised to keep the secret.

"Well, here's a clue, his aunt's last name is Elliott."

"As in Pierre Elliott?"

"Yes. Mr. Trudeau wants to keep it as a private affair."

"I completely understand, and I'm sure it won't be a problem."

Mary went on to explain the details.

The Trudeau flair must run in the family. On the day of the funeral, we were ready to start the service, but we were still waiting for the prime minister's sister, who had not yet arrived from Montreal. I happened to look out the window of the clergy office just in time to see a Voyageur bus pull up and stop in front of the funeral home. The bus door opened and out stepped Mr. Trudeau's sister! She'd taken the bus from Montreal, and noticing that she was running late, had asked the driver if he wouldn't mind making an unscheduled stop at the funeral home, since it was on the way to the terminal. Even in an attempt to be unassuming, there was that trademark Trudeau flair.

The RCMP had been through our chapel and was on hand when Mr. Trudeau arrived in a grey limousine. I don't think he particularly liked travelling in this manner, but the car was provided by the government and besides, it was winter, and his convertible wouldn't have been a good choice. He stepped out of the car wearing a wonderful raccoon fur coat and a wedge hat. Of course, the clothes were typically stylish, but they did not make the man in Trudeau's case; it was his natural charisma.

The ceremony was small and quiet, and was followed by cremation. After the service was over, Mr. Trudeau walked toward the door of the chapel. I was standing there, and he stopped in front of me and smiled. "Mr. McGarry, can I meet some of your staff? I'd like to thank them."

FROM PAUPERS TO PRIME MINISTERS

"Of course, sir."

At that time, we had a maintenance woman named Mrs. Paquette. I had noticed her peeking into the chapel hoping to get a glimpse of the prime minister, so I motioned for her to come over. She stepped through the door a little shyly and walked over.

"Mr. Trudeau, I'd like you to meet Mrs. Paquette. She does a fine job helping to keep our building clean."

Mrs. Paquette could hardly contain herself. Mr. Trudeau shook her hand and then chatted with her for a few minutes. He asked her about her family and about how long she had worked for us, listening intently to her answers, and then he thanked her for doing such a good job.

"The building is pristine," he said.

I never forgot that gesture, and the next time I met Mr. Trudeau, he asked me how Mrs. Paquette was doing.

On the day following Mr. Trudeau's death, we had a meeting in Ottawa to discuss the funeral arrangements. Since he had not left any instructions detailing his wishes, there was a lot of planning that needed to be done quickly. The organizing committee led by Jean-Paul Roy decided that there would be two days of lying-in-state in Ottawa, followed by one day in Montreal; the casket would be closed for the duration. The funeral would take place at Montreal's Notre-Dame Basilica, after which he would be taken to a cemetery in Saint-Rémi, Quebec, for interment in the Trudeau family crypt. Earlier, Pierre's sons, Justin and Sacha, prepared a statement announcing that their father was gone, and the public responded with an immediate outpouring of grief.

Mr. Trudeau's body was prepared in Montreal by the Bourgie Funeral Home before being transported by government airbus to Ottawa. We met the flight at the airport with our hearse and transported his remains directly to Parliament Hill under police escort.

When we arrived at Parliament Hill with Mr. Trudeau's remains, there was already a crowd of people waiting. The RCMP pallbearers removed the casket from the hearse and started their slow march into the Hall of Honour.

Any worry the family had that the state ceremony would be under-attended was quickly dispelled. People actually flew from across the country to pay their respects, and every hotel in the city was booked. After the official visits were over and the public began to move past the casket, we discovered that we had a problem. As a single file, we couldn't get people through quickly enough, and the lineup was beginning to get out of control. We made an adjustment and set up a system with two lines. Originally, the visiting hours were scheduled to last until 11 p.m., but due to the numbers of people, we decided to keep the doors open until 3:30 a.m. Even at that late hour, there were still people waiting in line, but everyone was very respectful. At no time was there any jostling or irritation at the long wait to get inside, and some people were in line for hours. We provided eighty-eight large funeral books for the public to sign, and people didn't just write down their names—they often took time to write personal notes.

Our staff remained with the casket during the entire lying-in-state, and after the doors were closed for the night, we collected all the flowers and cards that people had left, which was a monumental task in itself.

It would turn out to be the largest state funeral ever held in Canada. More than 60,000 people passed by Mr. Trudeau's casket in two days. It quickly became clear that Mr. Trudeau had touched something deep inside the hearts and minds of the Canadian people, and his family was very moved by the grand display of respect. He had reached out and grasped our tenuous national identity and held it up to show us what it was and what it could be. His confidence became our confidence, his strength, our strength. Pierre Trudeau was unafraid to stand up, and equally unafraid to fall, and friend and foe alike came to honour him.

The family decided that Mr. Trudeau's body should make the two-hour journey from Ottawa to Montreal by train, and the necessary arrangements were made. Just like Diefenbaker's final journey, many people came out to watch. As we passed through the small towns and villages along the tracks, ordinary Canadians who had never met this extraordinary man came out to watch as we passed by. There were people wrapped in Canadian flags, farmers, construction workers, mothers, and businessmen, all standing together. Justin Trudeau eventually asked Jean-Paul Roy if the train could be slowed down. "All these people have come out to see my dad."

The train was stopped in Alexandria, Ontario, and Justin and Sacha leaned out and touched the hands of people there, accepting flowers and condolences. There were tears and smiles for the memory of a man and a time that was now fading into the past.

When we arrived in Montreal, a police escort was waiting to accompany us from the train station to City Hall, where Mr. Trudeau was going to lie in state for one day. There had been some debate surrounding this choice of venue. Originally the viewing was to take place downtown at the Cathédrale Marie-Reine-du-Monde, but the church had been previously booked and was unavailable. The city had stepped in and offered the use of the Hôtel de Ville. It was a controversial decision, because it was on the balcony of this same building where French president Charles de Gaulle had stood when he uttered his infamous remark, *"Vive le Québec, vive le Québec libre!"* Some people thought of it as a bad choice, but as the discussion continued, it was decided that the history of the building actually made it more suitable, that having Mr. Trudeau there would be reclaiming it in a way.

We removed the casket from the funeral train and placed it into the hearse. After a few moments, the cortege started to move onto the street. I was sitting with two RCMP officers in the lead funeral car when one of the officers took a call on his cell phone. He listened for a moment and then looked over at the driver, saying urgently, "You need to stop."

We pulled over, halting the procession, while the officer listened intently to his phone. He finally hung up and told us that we couldn't go any further; there had been a bomb threat at City Hall. Of course the idea that was on everyone's mind was that it might have something to do with the separatist movement and de Gaulle's inflammatory comment, but it could have just as easily been kids pulling a prank, or someone who was angry about a tax bill.

We weren't delayed for too long. City Hall had been under guard for most of the day and had been swept for bombs, but as a precaution, the bomb squad was called back in to ease any fears. About thirty minutes later we received a call telling us that we could proceed.

As we approached City Hall, I saw a crowd of people gathered around the building. I was still thinking about de Gaulle and wondering if anyone was going to shout, *"Vive le Québec libre!"* when we carried Mr. Trudeau's casket up the steps.

The hearse stopped in front of the building. Instead of the separatist rallying cry, however, when the RCMP removed the casket from the hearse, someone started singing "O Canada," and before long the entire crowd had joined in, singing the national anthem in both English and French.

Thousands of people came to pay their respects at City Hall and Notre-Dame Basilica the following day. I happened to be standing next to Justin Trudeau when his father's casket was being taken out of the hearse at the regal old church. Justin was holding a single red rose and he leaned over to me and said, "Mr. McGarry, could you have someone from the crowd, a young person, place this rose on Dad's casket for me?"

They were already taking the casket out of the hearse, but I told him I would find someone, and he handed me the flower. The police had erected barriers around the area where the hearse was parked, and people were lined up along them. I spotted a young girl about twelve or thirteen standing with her parents, and I walked over to her. They were quite excited about the idea. The young lady's mother and I lifted her over the barrier, and I helped her to the entrance of the church where the casket carriage was waiting. I crouched down and said, "Now, when the RCMP place the casket on this carriage, Justin wants you to put this rose on top of it as it goes by. You can do that?"

She nodded shyly. We waited as the honour guard slowly marched to the entrance with the casket on their shoulders. I thought the young lady might be nervous, but she seemed very calm. A few minutes later, the officers placed the casket on the carriage, the little flower girl looked up at me, and I smiled and motioned for her to go ahead. She walked over, placed the rose gently on the casket, and then walked back. Later that night I turned on the news and there she was being interviewed on national television—a few minutes of fame for a delightful young girl.

Many notable Canadians attended the funeral, as well as dignitaries from all over the world. Prince Andrew was there on behalf of the Royal Family, former president Jimmy Carter was the official representative of the United States, and there were many others. One of the most interesting and talked-about leaders who attended was Cuba's Fidel Castro, famous for the cool relationship he and his country have had with the Americans since the 1960s. It was also a well-known fact that he rarely left his island home. Seeing Fidel Castro and Jimmy Carter in the same room together was quite something.

Justin Trudeau gave a beautiful eulogy for his father. He spoke of the tolerance he had learned from him, and the need to respect every person, regardless of race or language. He ended by paraphrasing lines from a Robert Frost poem:

The woods are lovely dark and deep
He has kept his promises and earned his sleep.

He paused and then looking toward his father's casket, and with a shaky voice he said, *"Je t'aime, Papa."*

That was the moment we all realized that, while Pierre Trudeau was very much a public figure who had earned his place in the history books, he was also (and maybe more importantly) a father. When Margaret Trudeau was asked about Pierre's legacy, she answered without pause, "Pierre's true legacy is the love of his children."

The most personal state funeral for the McGarry family was for the Rt. Hon. Ramon Hnatyshyn in 2002. Ray was a former governor general, and both he and his wife Gerda were long-time friends. Sharon McGarry knew Ray from the time they were colleagues at Gowlings law firm.

Even though it was Christmas at the time of Ray's death, Gerda insisted that the festive decorations on Parliament Hill not be removed for his lying-in-state. This is the type of person she is—straight-on, kind, and considerate.

Ray had a delightful sense of humour. Peter Mansbridge of CBC mentioned the same during the eulogy at Christ Church Anglican Cathedral in Ottawa. My wife, Joan, our daughter, Sheetza, and I were once the butt of Ray's humour while dining at the Chez Piggy Restaurant in Kingston, soon after Ray and Gerda left Government House. Ray and Gerda had been sailing with friends on Lake Ontario. He spotted Joan, Sheetza, and me enjoying our meal while they were waiting for a seat in the restaurant courtyard.

"Do you see that couple and their daughter," Ray said to the hostess, pointing to our table. "Would you go over and suggest to them that they might well eat a little faster. They are holding up the line."

A little embarrassed, the young hostess came to our table, apologized, and said, "The former governor general feels you are too slow . . ."

Looking up, we saw Ray laughing with Gerda as she gave him a gentle nudge.

I believe that Prime Minister Brian Mulroney knew that Ray would be a man for all Canadians when he appointed him as Canada's twenty-fourth governor general in 1990. Brian tells the story when he invited Ray to Harrington Lake, the prime minister's summer residence, to tell him of the appointment, Ray became quite choked up. Brian offered Ray a glass of water and asked if he was all right. Ray replied that if his father were alive, he wouldn't believe that his son was about to become governor general. Brian commented that if his father were alive, he wouldn't believe that his son would be in a position to offer the position!

Brian asked Ray not to tell a soul about the appointment, until he had shared his choice with Cabinet. As Ray was leaving, Brian noticed Ray's car stop, then back up, coming to a halt at the cottage entrance. Ray, with his trademark sense of humour, then shouted from the car window, "Brian, if something happens to me on the way home, could you tell Gerda I was going to be governor general?"

Would you believe that a fifteen-year anniversary for the state funeral
of John Diefenbaker was held in the Centre Block on Parliament Hill?
Rare is a funeral anniversary ever celebrated, but Dief's funeral was
special, meriting a film by the National Film Board of Canada.

Diefenbaker's funeral was one of the most complicated in Canada's history,
involving transport by train and plane, and the disinterment of his wife's remains
from Beechwood Cemetery in Ottawa, which were reburied alongside him on the
grounds of the University of Saskatchewan, Saskatoon. Hundreds of friends and
funeral organizers came from across Canada for the 1994 reunion. From left to
right: Brian McGarry; Sharon McGarry, President of Hulse, Playfair & McGarry;
former prime minister Joe Clark; and Chief of Protocol, Graham Glockling.

Barry Schwerdfeger.

CHAPTER 6

Quirky Stories

I've met all kinds of people through my profession as a funeral director. Rich and poor, famous and unknown, young and old—we all face the great adventure of death at some point. While part of the job of a funeral director is to help prepare the physical remains of those who have died, an equally important aspect of our work is to help those who have been left behind and who must come to terms with the empty space that is now present in their lives.

The rituals we have surrounding death help us recognize the passing of a life; they are the first steps toward healing. It is a time of sadness, as we feel the loss of someone we loved, but there is also room for joy and celebration supported by the fond memories that remain. I think one of the most important lessons I've learned is that everyone deals with death in their own way, and it's important to keep an open mind.

One afternoon I was working at our West Chapel when I received a call from a German lady named Mrs. Andrews.

"Oh, hello, Mr. McGarry, I'm afraid to say that my kid, Sasha, has died."

I found it a little bit odd that she would refer to her child this way, but it's not my job to judge anyone so I carried on. "I'm sorry to hear that, Mrs. Andrews. Would you like to make the arrangements with us?"

"Yes, thank you."

"When would you like to come into the office to see us?"

"Well, I only just live down the street from you, so anytime, I suppose."

"Do you want to come by this afternoon?"

"Yes, that will be fine."

A few hours later she arrived. I invited her into my office and offered her a cup of tea before we began arranging the ceremony.

"What type of funeral would you like to have for Sasha?"

"Oh, nothing too elaborate."

"That's fine, we can keep the arrangements very simple. How old was she?"

"Almost sixteen."

This caught me by surprise. I would never have guessed she had a child that young, but then I realized that it may have been her granddaughter. I was about to ask when she continued, "Sixteen is a ripe old age, I suppose, and she did have a good life with me."

At this point I was starting to wonder if Mrs. Andrews was so distraught that she was still in shock.

"I'm very sorry," I said.

"Well, she hadn't been eating the last few days, and then this morning I found her under the kitchen table and moved her to the porch."

It isn't often that I'm at a loss for words, but this was one of those times. It was the middle of winter, and I can't tell you what was going through my mind.

"You moved your daughter onto the porch?" I asked.

She paused for a moment and then looked at me curiously. "My daughter? Sasha was my cat."

"I'm sorry, did you say your cat?"

"Yes, she was a tabby."

Only then did I realize my mistake. I am deaf in one ear, and since we don't usually take calls about pets, when she said that her "cat" had died, I thought she had said that her "kid" had died. She had put her pet out on the porch as a way of preserving her until the funeral arrangements could be made.

"She's like this . . ." Mrs. Andrews brought up her hands and tilted her head to illustrate the position her cat was in. "She's very stiff."

I wasn't exactly sure what to do. I had misheard her on the phone and because I hadn't asked her to clarify, she was now sitting in my office. It was clear that she cared very much for her pet and I didn't want to offend her or make light of the situation, but at the same time we had never held a funeral for a cat.

"I'm afraid we don't normally look after animals, but let's talk about what we can do."

"Well, I'd just like something small."

"Would you like to have a service for her?"

"That would be lovely."

So, that was that. I went over to Mrs. Andrews' apartment, removed her cat's remains from the porch, and brought them back to the funeral home. It had been so cold outside that we had to let Sasha thaw out a bit, but then we placed her gently in a small child's casket, which we decided to provide at no charge. We couldn't have the cat in our visitation room, but we let Mrs. Andrews have one of the smaller meeting rooms, so she could spend some private time saying goodbye before the cremation at a pet care service provider. Mrs. Andrews was grateful for this; her cat was just as important to her as any human being.

One day early in my career we received a call from a young man I'll call "Kevin." He calmly explained that he had discovered his mother dead in the bathtub. The police had already been to the apartment, and after they and her physician had left, he phoned us. I wasn't going to be arranging the funeral, but I was sent over to help with the removal. Cliff Lloyd and I went to the house and brought the woman's remains to the funeral home. I remember feeling a strange sense of uneasiness as we were making the removal. The following day, Kevin came in and met with Cliff to make preliminary arrangements for the funeral.

Afterwards, Cliff came to me and asked if I would drive the young man to a local cemetery so he could choose a plot for his mother, since he had taken the bus to get to the funeral home. During the drive to the cemetery, there were moments when he seemed to fall into a deep depression, while at other times he was almost manic, talking a mile a minute. I found his behaviour strange, and I felt a sense of concern about the whole thing. Even though I could identify no reason, I had experienced enough to know that people can become irrational when dealing with the death of someone close.

We arrived at the cemetery, and I waited outside while he purchased a plot. Afterwards, we got back in the car and I brought him home. Once again, the drive was punctuated with his off-putting sense of nervousness. When someone is going through a loss, there are no rules for how they are supposed to react, so it's important to be as accepting as possible at all times.

We arrived at his mother's house, which the two of them had been sharing, and I accepted his invitation to come inside. He told me he didn't have a lot of friends in the city and didn't want to be alone, just yet. Once inside, he continued to act erratically, bouncing from one topic to the next and from one emotion to another. He put the kettle on and paced around the living room, talking the whole time. At one point he asked me to accompany him to the bathroom where his mother had died. Again, I found this to be an unusual request, but I went anyway. We stood in the doorway for several minutes looking at the tub, and for the first time since we had left the funeral home, he was silent.

After a cup of tea, I said that I needed to get back to the funeral home, but he should feel free to call us if there was anything we could do for him.

Back in the car, I reflected on how odd the whole experience had been. It wasn't anything specific—more of a strange feeling. As it turned out I wasn't the only person who felt this tension, and later that day I found out that the police had ordered an autopsy on the woman.

Sure enough, a week later, Kevin was arrested on suspicion of murder and was later found guilty. It still sends shivers down my spine when I think that I was standing at the scene of a murder, sipping a cup of tea that the murderer had made for me.

On another occasion, I was actually able to help the police solve a case.

One hot July day, a young cousin of mine in Wakefield told his mother he was going for a drive. He subsequently got into his car and vanished. We were related on my father's side of the family, and as he was quite a bit younger than me, we were not close.

After his disappearance, there was some discussion about the fact that he had recently been hanging around with a bad crowd, and after a couple of days with no word from him, the police were called in. After two weeks of searching, he hadn't turned up and the police didn't have any leads. Around this time I happened to be in Wakefield visiting my mom, who was filling me in on the latest news about the mysterious disappearance. At one point she said, "You know it's the strangest thing. I saw him the same day he went missing. He was parked on a vacant lot on the outskirts of town. I think he was working on his car."

"That's interesting," I replied.

"I waved at him and he waved back."

I asked her where the lot was located and then I called up my brother-in-law, Barry Schwerdfeger, who works at our funeral home in Wakefield. He came over, and the two of us drove down to the vacant lot to have a look around. The grass was quite long, but as we were walking about, Barry noticed that if you stood in one particular spot, you could just make out two tire tracks leading to the back of the property, where a steep embankment plunged into the river. We made the rocky climb down to the water's edge and near the bottom of the embankment we discovered a licence plate.

In the province of Quebec, you are not required to have a front licence plate on your car, but often people will have one for fun, and the one we found had a fleur-de-lis and a maple leaf on it to symbolize Canadian unity. It also had a jagged piece of plastic on the back, as if it had been torn off whatever car it had been on.

The water in that part of the river is quite deep, and we couldn't see the bottom. Barry and I went to the young man's house and talked with his mother. I showed her the licence plate, and asked, "Does this plate look familiar?"

"Yes," she replied. "That's the plate that he had on the front of the car."

We called the police from her house.

A diver was brought in, and after a quick search, the car was discovered at the bottom of the river, with my cousin's body inside. The police are not sure exactly what happened, although it looked like he might have been backing the car up for some reason and had gone a little too far, sending the vehicle sliding down the embankment, where the front plate had been torn off by one of the rocks before it plunged into the water.

It was a series of lucky coincidences that had allowed us to help solve the mystery. First, that my mother had seen the boy at the vacant lot; second, that Barry was able to see the tracks in the grass; and third, the fact that the plate had been ripped off and was visible. It's still a mystery as to how the car found its way into the river, and it was certainly a bittersweet discovery for the family. It was heart wrenching that the young man had died, but there was also a sense of relief that his remains had been recovered and could be given a proper burial, allowing his family to mourn and start the healing process.

Even though people sometimes refer to Ottawa as "the big city with the small town feel," there are still a few underworld figures in our city, and since death doesn't discriminate, some of these folks have come through our doors. On one occasion there was a traffic accident that took the life of a man who was a member of a large motorcycle gang; André Robert, one of our partner funeral directors, was looking after the arrangements. There was some trepidation about the funeral, because some bikers have a dangerous reputation, and everyone at the funeral home was quietly wondering if there were going to be any problems.

On the day of the funeral, all you could hear was the roar of Harley-Davidson motorcycles growling down the street and pulling up to the funeral home, every machine mounted by a tough-looking gentleman. At one point I looked out of the office window and saw that there must have been at least one hundred bikes lining the parking area, from one side to the other. The police were aware of this funeral, and there were a couple of patrol cars circling around the block every once in a while, making their presence known.

Needless to say, there was some tension that day at the funeral home, but any worries we had were quickly dispelled. All of the bikers were very respectful, and there was no trouble at all. Most of them wore their usual attire—metal-studded leather vests, jeans, and heavy black boots—making them seem imposing, but they were there to honour one of their own.

It was an occasion they took seriously, but it wasn't without its eccentricities. I watched one fellow walking across the street toward the front door, and as he heaved something onto his shoulder, I looked a little closer and saw that it was a case of beer! I wondered how far he was going to get with it and who was going to stop him. André, a very good-natured fellow, opened the front door to let the man in, and saw the case of beer.

"Excuse me, sir," he said politely, but firmly, "but I'm afraid we can't allow alcoholic beverages into the service."

"Oh, no? Well, that's not too cool."

"I'm sorry, but you'll have to leave it outside, or, if you prefer, we can keep it for you in the office."

"Well, if that's the rule, I guess you can take it for now."

He handed André the beer and continued inside. That was the closest we came to having any kind of problem that day, as the service was quiet and reflective with several gang members getting up to speak on behalf of their friend. When the service was over, they held their own reception in the parking lot. We couldn't allow them to drink in the chapel, but no one was going to stop them from having a few beers outside; it was a compromise we could live with. We kept an eye on things and even went out and socialized a bit. The police cruised by a few times, but no one seemed to notice. The gang was having a good time exchanging stories about their friend, which I'm sure is exactly what he would have wanted them to do.

Everyone began to make their way to the cemetery. Within a few minutes, the whole group was rumbling slowly down the street behind the hearse, the sound of their procession remaining audible long after they were out of sight.

We had to spend some time afterwards picking up the odd beer bottle that had found its way onto the lawn, but there was no real harm done, certainly nothing compared to some of the scenarios that had run through everyone's mind earlier in the day.

There is a beautiful road in Ottawa that winds along the banks of the Ottawa River, just west of the downtown core. Driving along this scenic route, it seems an unlikely spot for a cloak-and-dagger style murder, but that's exactly what happened here in the early 1980s.

A group of Armenian terrorists had been attacking and killing Turkish diplomats around the world, and in 1982, this violence found its way to Canada's capital. In April, a Turkish diplomat had been targeted and seriously injured when a group of gunmen opened fire on his car as he was driving into the underground parking lot of his apartment building. The victim was not killed in the attack, but was left with serious injuries.

Later that same year in August, Col. Atilla Alkikat, the military attaché at the Turkish embassy in Ottawa, was driving his car down the Parkway when he stopped at a red light. The terrorists must have been following him for some time, waiting for the right moment to strike. At this point, they slowly pulled off into the right-hand turning lane. One of the men then got out of the car and walked toward Col. Alkikat's stopped vehicle, coming around from behind, up to the driver's side. At that moment, he drew out a handgun and fired nine shots through the window at point-plank range, killing Col. Alkikat instantly. The assassin then threw the gun into the car, and hurried back to the waiting car. The back door opened, the gunman got in, and the car sped off.

It took several moments for people in the surrounding vehicles to realize what had happened. It was like a scene from a movie, not what you would ever dream of seeing on a quiet street in Ottawa. The assassination became an international news story and Prime Minister Trudeau condemned the act.

The Turkish community held the visitation at our funeral home, which received full protection from the RCMP and the Canadian Armed Forces. For two days, it felt as if we had wandered into an armed camp—there were uniformed soldiers posted at the front door with machine guns. The concern was that the terrorists might strike again during the visitation, or on the way to the airport as the diplomat's remains were transported back to Turkey. Sharon thought about taking our young son up to the cottage as a precaution. It was all very dramatic and made for a tense few days.

When the time came to transport Col. Alkikat's casket to the airport, the armed forces asked us if we wanted to have their soldiers drive the hearse in the cortege, in addition to providing an escort. We declined the drivers, but accepted their escort, along with that from Ottawa Police Services. We're very familiar with the layout of Hangar 11, the special gate where foreign and Canadian dignitaries are received, and we felt confident that everything would be all right. It was quite a procession, but luckily there were no further incidents. The assassins were never caught, and to this day, Col. Alkikat's murder remains an unsolved crime, a fact that must be terribly frustrating for Col. Alkikat's widow and two sons.

Occasionally we receive unusual requests from families. We try to accommodate everyone and will do everything we can to meet people's requests, as long as it's legal and in good taste.

On one occasion, a man died and his wife asked if she could have the visitation at their home. In days gone by, this was done more often than it is today and we had no problems obliging her. We brought the casket out to the house along with all the equipment we use: a carriage for the casket to sit on, a table for the book of condolences, and flower stands. Upon arriving at the house, we asked where we should place the carriage. The woman led us into a large room with a circular rug on the floor, and said, "This is the room I'd like to use. You can just put the casket on the rug."

"You'd like us to put the casket on the floor?"

"Yes."

It was a pine casket with a flat top, and we placed it on the circular rug in the centre of the room. It seemed a little bit odd, but that was what she wanted. A few days later, we returned to the house to remove the casket for the funeral. We had with us the clergyman, as there was going to be a prayer at the house before the remains were taken to the church for the service. As we approached the house, I asked the priest, "Were you at the house yesterday?"

"No, I haven't been able to get over, yet, but I want to spend a little time before going to the church."

"Well, when you go into the house, don't sit on the coffee table that looks like a casket."

"How do you mean?"

I explained that the widow had insisted we place the casket on the floor.

"You're kidding. Well, I'm glad you told me; I might have mistaken it for a bench."

I was prearranging a funeral for a scoutmaster, and he told me that he wanted to be cremated in his sailboat. At first I thought he wanted the cremation to happen on the water, Viking style, but he explained that the boat would be on land, and we would just have to ignite it. There are very strict regulations dealing with the cremation of human remains, and this approach to sailing into eternity would have been illegal.

"I'm sorry, sir, but we just can't do that."

"I'm sure you can."

"No, I'm sure we can't. I know in India they still have funeral pyres, but we can't do that in the Gatineau Hills. What we can do, however, is have you cremated and then your ashes could be brought home and placed on the boat, which, I suppose, your family could then light on fire."

This seemed to suit him fine, although I'm not sure why anyone would want to burn a perfectly good boat, but it's not my job to judge anyone's request.

We did have one occasion where we almost had an unintentional cremation in our funeral home. Laird Barclay, our senior vice-president, was at our West Chapel early on a Tuesday afternoon. There was a visitation scheduled for two o'clock, and he was upstairs having lunch before the family arrived when he smelled smoke. He rushed down from the staff area to discover that one whole wall of the visitation room was on fire. He tried frantically to put out the flames himself, but soon realized he was fighting a losing battle. He ran to the nearest phone and dialled 9-1-1. The fire department was on hand within minutes and was able to get the blaze under control.

Afterwards, Laird went in to survey the damage. Before the fire had been doused, it had reached the fabric skirt attached to the carriage that the casket rests on, and subsequently made its way to the casket itself. The mahogany finish was quick to light and, as Laird soon discovered, the body was damaged. It was at that moment that the family arrived at the front door. He ushered them into another room, and called me at the Central Chapel. I had to ask him to repeat himself, because I couldn't believe what I was hearing. I got off the phone and found Doug Kennedy, also a senior partner; he and I hopped into a car and rushed over to the West Chapel.

Laird was sitting with the family explaining what had happened. It wasn't immediately apparent how the fire started, but an investigation later revealed that an electrical outlet had short-circuited. The fire had travelled up a lamp cord plugged into it and spread from there.

When Doug and I arrived, I noticed one of our competitors slowly driving by, taking in the scene. There were still fire trucks around the building. I think if it had been me, I would have stopped to ask if there was anything I could do, but he didn't stop. At any rate, that was the least of our worries. Because the cause of the fire was not immediately obvious, the fire marshal had to investigate, cordoning off part of the room. We were permitted to move the casket.

Amazingly, the family was very understanding.

We had a record of every flower that was in the room, and went to a local florist to have the flowers replaced.

The body had some damage, which our technicians repaired; however, even though the family thought they were very professional, it was decided to have the casket closed. We offered them any casket they wanted from our selection room as a replacement, and of course there would be no charge for the funeral.

By six o'clock that night we were able to have a visitation in another room. There was some black humour. At one point the son of the deceased, trying to inject a little levity into the situation, said, "You know, Dad was going to be cremated, and I guess it just happened a little sooner than we planned."

The family had a chuckle.

The funeral went ahead a day later and the cremation was completed. The following morning at home, I picked up the newspaper to discover an article about the fire. In those days, the *Ottawa Citizen* published three editions, and the article on the fire appeared in the early first edition. I was surprised and annoyed to see the byline, "A little black humour." We hadn't been contacted by anyone from the newspaper, but then I remembered seeing our competitor. I immediately called the publisher. He hadn't read the paper yet that morning, so I explained the situation to him.

"You know, there's nothing humorous about this at all. The family has just suffered a loss, and they won't find this article funny, so why does the newspaper find it humorous?"

"Let me take a look at the article and I'll call you back."

A few minutes later my phone rang.

"I completely agree with you, Brian," the publisher said. "This story is inappropriate. I'll make sure it's removed from the later editions."

I thanked him, then phoned the family. I wanted to be the one to tell them about the article and to assure them that none of the information had come from us. They hadn't seen the article as yet, but suggested we get together later that afternoon for a meeting.

Although I had prepared myself for the worst, right away they put me at ease.

"Mr. McGarry, we know that you're very concerned about this. We didn't like the article coming out and we appreciate the fact that you were able to have it removed from the later editions. We understand the fire was an accident and that you have done everything possible to find a solution. If you're at all concerned about any repercussions from our family, you don't have to be."

I didn't know what to say, but it renewed my confidence that there are some very fine people in this world.

There have been two incidents where jewellery has been taken from human remains under our care. The first time it happened, a very sharp receptionist recognized the ring a mourner was wearing to be the same as the one she had seen on the finger of the deceased. We were able to stop the man as he was walking out the door and got the ring back. I can tell you he wasn't invited to the reception. The second incident was much stranger, although I suppose it goes without saying that you have to be a peculiar individual to steal from the dead; however, even though we knew who the culprit was, we were never able to retrieve the lost jewellery.

There was a boy of about twelve who used to spend some of his free time at the funeral home; I'll call him "Thomas." He lived only a few blocks away, and his interest had been sparked after attending a funeral with his family. Thomas was an inquisitive boy, and very bright, but there was an oddness about him that I could never identify. After several visits, he knew our funeral home well and was always asking questions, which our staff was more than happy to answer. At the time we had an alarm system on all the doors, so that whenever someone walked in, a buzzer would sound. This was particularly useful on quiet days where there might only be one person working in the building. Therefore, if you happened to be upstairs when someone arrived, the buzzer would alert you, and you could go down to greet them.

One afternoon I walked downstairs after taking a break between visitations and was surprised to find Thomas wandering around.

"Thomas, what are you doing here?" I asked.

"Oh, I just came in to see you."

"When did you arrive?"

"Just now."

"That's strange. I didn't hear the buzzer go off."

I thought that perhaps I had forgotten to turn the alarm system on, so I went to the office and checked the switch—it was alarmed. I went back and found Thomas.

"How were you able to get in without setting off the buzzer?"

"I guess the door didn't open far enough."

"Oh, I see."

He had discovered that the door had to be opened a certain width in order for the buzzer to sound, and because he was so small, he was able to slip in without setting it off. I found it a little odd, and didn't think anything of it at the time, but later the same day we discovered a ring had gone missing from the hand of the woman in our visitation room. One of our staff members remembered the ring being on the deceased's hand after the first visitation, and since that time only two people had been in the building—myself and Thomas. This, combined with the fact that he had snuck in, regrettably pointed to the young man as the culprit.

I went to see his parents and explained the situation to them. I didn't want to accuse their son, but it was just too suspicious not to discuss it with them. Thomas's parents listened as I told them how he had discovered a way to enter the funeral home unnoticed, and while they didn't like the idea that their son might be the culprit, they admitted that it did sound suspicious enough to warrant confronting him about it. They brought Thomas into the kitchen and asked him if he had taken the ring. He said repeatedly that he hadn't taken it. After about twenty minutes of questioning, I realized that we were not going to get the jewellery back. There was nothing left to do at that point except call the family of the deceased and tell them what had happened. They were disappointed but quite understanding. It was the ring's sentimental value that was most important to them, not its dollar value, and they had wanted to keep the ring in their family so it could be passed on to the next generation. We offered to compensate them for the value of the ring; the family refused. We made a charitable donation in memory of their mother, which pleased this very understanding family. Thomas stopped coming by the funeral home.

We used to stay open until 10:00 p.m. Our Centretown chapel is not a modern building, so at the end of the day we have to go through the building and turn off every light individually. One night I counted the light switches and found that there were seventy-eight that needed to be attended to. To get the job done quickly, we would divide the building into sections and everyone would be responsible for turning the lights off in one part of the funeral home.

One night our receptionist, Jackie, said that she would turn off everything downstairs in the lounge and the casket selection room. She went into the selection room first, but froze as soon as she walked through the door. There, lying in a casket, was a young man about twenty-five years old. The shock of this would normally be enough to cause a scare, but then Jackie noticed something else—the man was nude! He had removed all of his clothes and piled them neatly on the floor next to the casket. Jackie reacted quite well. She very calmly pulled the door shut and hurried upstairs to tell us what she had discovered. We phoned the police and then four employees went to investigate. They walked into the room and, sure enough, the young man was still in the casket without a stitch of clothing on. At least there was no worry that he was carrying a concealed weapon.

"Hello, what are you doing in there?"

He didn't answer, and barely acknowledged that we were in the room at all. Not that we needed much more evidence of this, but it was quickly obvious that the young man was not mentally sound.

"You'd better get up and get dressed. We'll help you out."

There had been a visitation earlier in the night, and I don't know if he had come in for that purpose, or if he had just walked in at the same time and found his way downstairs. The police soon arrived and took the troubled young man to get some help.

Since that time, we have installed locks on every door that opens onto a public corridor so as to prevent people from getting into a room where they don't belong. Jackie has since retired, but to this day we tease her about our "visitor." It certainly made for an unforgettable day.

Family dynamics play a big role whenever there is a funeral. I often overhear people talking about the fact that they haven't seen each other in years and that it's too bad it's taken the death of a family member to bring everyone together. I choose to look at the fact that people have been brought together as a positive outcome. Sometimes there will be a family feud, or two people who have gone through a painful divorce and relationships are awkward. But it's always best to try and put away whatever problems and arguments you have, so that everyone can have a chance to celebrate the life of a family member who died.

We had one funeral where a member of the family was completely estranged, and the family had forbidden her from attending both the visitation and the ceremony. I don't know all the circumstances or the reasons behind their decision, but obviously there was a serious issue with this woman and something terrible must have happened for the family to be so adamant about keeping her away. We didn't want to pry into a situation that was none of our business; however, we did suggest that alienating anyone from a funeral is a difficult decision and will almost always cause problems. I further explained that our funeral home is a public building, and it is nearly impossible for us to refuse entrance to anyone. They understood our position, but they had made up their minds, and decided to take the matter into their own hands.

Sure enough, the woman arrived for the visitation, and sure enough, there were problems.

For security reasons, we keep only the front door unlocked; all of the other doors are equipped with buzzers you can press to be let in. The woman had arrived at the back of the building and had automatically assumed that the door had been locked to keep her out. This sent her into a rage, and she broke the glass in the window of the door with her bare hands, cutting herself badly in the process. Staff hurried to the back door to discover a group of angry family members yelling at this woman who was standing in shards of broken glass and bleeding profusely. We called an ambulance and the police right away. A couple of our staff members tried to calm down the distressed woman, but between the injury and the emotion of the situation, she was in shock. The paramedics soon arrived and took her to hospital.

When people are dealing with death, it often puts them into uncharted emotional territory, which can have serious consequences.

One spring day, we were out at a country cemetery for a burial. It had been raining the night before, and the ground was still quite wet. This particular cemetery is quite small, and they don't have the same equipment that a larger cemetery might, so the grave had been dug by hand. Therefore, between the frost coming out of the ground and the rain, the grave had caved in slightly. This is not unusual, and whenever it rains, we always take the precaution of placing extra planking around the grave to stabilize it.

Before the service, Laird Barclay, who was the director of the funeral, made sure to warn the clergy of the ground's condition. As part of the committal service in a Christian burial, the clergy or the funeral director will place a handful of earth onto the casket before it's lowered into the grave. When the moment arrived, the clergy stepped off the planks to reach the casket a little easier. Almost immediately, he lost his footing and slipped straight into the grave. He must have been about six-foot-one, because he landed on his feet and all you could see was the top of his head. A couple of our staff members ran over and helped to pull the embarrassed, but otherwise unhurt clergyman out of the ground, and he carried on with the service.

On another occasion, we arrived at a cemetery and found that they had set up their own graveside equipment, including a device for lowering the casket. It's made up of a system of rollers and strapping, and is designed so that pressure from the weight of the casket keeps tension on the strapping, allowing the casket to be lowered slowly. Unfortunately, whoever set up the equipment had made a mistake and had placed the strapping under the rollers improperly. When it came time to lower the casket, there was no tension on the rollers, and the strapping slipped through, causing the casket to drop to the bottom of the grave with a noticeable thud.

There was a pause. I looked at the clergy and he looked at me, then he carried on with the ceremony. As soon as the service was finished, I stepped over to the family and apologized. I told them I would find out what the cause was and make sure the casket wasn't damaged.

After the family left, we raised the casket. This took some effort, because we had to first remove the straps, get them out from under the casket, then put them through the rollers properly. When we finally got the casket out of the grave, we brought it over to the hearse and examined it. Thankfully, there was no damage at all. I phoned the family and explained what had happened and apologized again. I also had the cemetery call and do the same. To compensate, the cemetery didn't charge for the opening of the grave or the equipment. The family was very understanding.

One of the strangest and most interesting experiences I've ever had, during my more than fifty-year career, involved my relationship with a man I'll call "Jack." Jack's mother died at home in her bedroom, and he called us. We sent two of our staff over, whom Jack greeted at the front door. He is a very large man, obese and quite tall. Jack mentioned that the doctor had already been and gone and handed our staff some papers. The trouble was, instead of a medical certificate, he gave them a statement of death, which is something different and has nothing to do with a doctor. (Before we can make a removal, we must receive a medical certificate of death signed by a doctor or coroner.) The men asked Jack if they could use his phone to call the funeral home, and he led them into a bedroom. A senior director answered the phone at the office.

"We've got an odd situation here . . ."

We found out later that Jack was listening in on the conversation on another line.

I became involved by cell phone and advised them that we could not remove the body without the doctor's certificate. Our two employees returned to the living room to speak with Jack, who had heard the entire conversation.

"Sir, with respect, we can't remove your mother's remains. This isn't the right document."

"Oh, no, you see, the doctor signed it right here." He pointed to an illegible signature on the paper.

"Well, that may be, but it's not the correct form."

It appeared to be an innocent enough mistake, easy for a sleep-deprived doctor to make. In the meantime, we called the physician and asked him to come back and fill out the proper paperwork. I was a little suspicious, partly because most doctors are well aware of the protocol surrounding a death, and also because I had never heard of this particular doctor before. I don't know every family doctor in the city, but I have met most of them over time. To ease my concern, I did some research and discovered the man was indeed a registered physician. The doctor returned to the house and signed the proper papers, and we were able to remove Jack's mother and bring her to the funeral home. That was just the beginning, but it foreshadowed what was to come.

There was something that didn't feel right about the removal, nothing you could pinpoint, just a general oddness. As a precaution, we asked the coroner to examine the woman's body, but he found nothing out of the ordinary. Jack's mother was a very intelligent lady, who had held a number of degrees from the University of Ottawa. Jack was also very bright—almost to a fault.

A few days after the removal, Jack came in to make the funeral arrangements. Right away he said that he wanted the best casket available. He had already done some research, and knew exactly which model he wanted. Jack had visited the website of Batesville, a casket company in Indiana, and found this particular casket made of solid copper. I knew the model, and it stood out because the price was astronomical.

"That's a very expensive casket, Jack. Are you sure you want to spend that kind of money?" I asked.

"Oh, yes, I'm absolutely certain. Mother should have nothing but the best."

"All right. We don't carry that particular model, but we can have one sent from a Montreal warehouse. Are you sure you wouldn't like to look at some of the caskets we have here?"

"No, that's the one I want."

The casket retailed in the United States for $22,000. I called Batesville's representative in Montreal, placed the order, and we went to pick up the casket. When our staff returned, I called Jack to tell him that we had the casket (the same model used for singer/dancer Michael Jackson in 2010).

"Well, that's good, but I've decided that I might look at a few others after all."

I wasn't overly surprised by his change of heart; $22,000 is a lot of money to spend.

"That's fine, just let me know what you decide upon."

"Sure, but I should tell you that I've decided not to have the funeral for a while, not for a week."

Again, this is not out of the ordinary. It can take a person time to get mentally prepared for the funeral. I phoned Jack early the following week. Consequently, we had prepared his mother's remains accordingly, and kept her in a cooled area in our preparation room designed for this very purpose.

"No, I'm not ready yet. I need another week."

Three weeks went by and I didn't hear from him, so I called him again. This time, he was able to commit to a date for the funeral—11 o'clock the following Wednesday. He had also changed his mind again and decided to keep the copper casket after all. I got off the phone and made all the necessary arrangements, confirming a clergyperson, and talking with the folks at the cemetery.

The day of the funeral arrived, and I was waiting in the office. By 10 o'clock, the clergyperson had arrived, but there was no sign of Jack. Eleven o'clock came and went, and Jack still hadn't made an appearance. As a few mourners had come in and were sitting in the chapel, I went in to apologize for the delay. After calling Jack's phone several times and getting no answer, we started to worry that something may have happened to him. It's almost unheard of that someone will miss his mother's funeral, especially if they've arranged it themselves. Eventually, we decided to cancel the service, the mourners went home, and we returned Jack's mother to the preparation room.

After several hours without hearing anything, we decided to get the authorities involved. That's when I discovered that the police were already familiar with Jack.

"We're not sure where you'll find him. He and his mother tend to move around."

As it turned out, they had moved several times in the past year to various apartments around town. This got me thinking about some of Jack's other eccentricities, like the fact that every time I had met with him he made a point of flashing a lot of money—a big roll of hundreds, fifties, and twenties, which he would retrieve from the inside pocket of his coat. He also carried around a briefcase, which he would open from time to time, but didn't like anyone to see what was inside. I had just assumed he was eccentric, but after finding out that he was known to the police (although they never explained why), I started to rethink the entire situation.

Two days later Jack called me.

"Hi, Brian."

"Jack, you didn't show up at your mom's funeral."

"No, no, no, I'm not ready yet."

"Well, you really should have called us to let us know how you were feeling."

"I'm sorry, I was just too upset."

In the following week, Jack came to the funeral home several times. He told me that he wanted to meet every staff member. It was an odd request, but I didn't see the harm in it, so I introduced him around. A few days later, Jack began calling employees at home and asking questions that became more and more personal in nature as he went on. I received several complaints about this, so I called Jack to put a stop to it.

"Jack, you're making some of our staff members uncomfortable with your calls."

"Oh. I just want to be sure that you have good people working for you. It's important that there are good people looking after my mother."

"All right, but please stop. I can assure you that all of our staff are quite competent. How are you feeling about having a funeral for your mom?"

"I'm not quite ready, yet, maybe next week."

I was starting to think that he was infatuated with death and he just couldn't let his mother go. Another week went by. Then two. Then four. During this time, Jack had changed his mind again about the copper casket and had settled on one made of steel.

Jack would occasionally arrive at the funeral home unannounced and ask to see his mother. After this happened a few times, I told him that he needed to start letting us know in advance before he came in. We try to accommodate people's needs as much as we can, and we are aware that it can be very difficult to let go of a loved one, but Jack's behaviour was excessive.

When he came in, we would place his mother in a visitation room, so he could spend some time with her. Every staff member was nice to him. He would arrive, and we would comfort him and get him a cup of coffee. I think part of the problem was that he was just very lonely, and we all felt badly for him. One time, he came in and gave me a great big bear hug, lifting me right off the ground.

"I can't tell you how much I appreciate your staff," he said.

My feet were dangling. "Jack, put me down!"

He did, and I continued, "Come into my office and we'll have a chat."

As soon as anyone started talking to him about his mother's funeral, he would act as though we were rushing him. That's when he started visiting other funeral homes. He didn't tell me this right away, but he went around to several other places asking for prices, telling them he wanted the same copper casket that we had just returned. One day he even brought some books to show me a line of caskets that one of our competitors was carrying.

"Have you seen these?" he asked.

"No, I haven't seen them. I don't need to see them."

"Well, they're quite interesting . . ."

We later received a call from the other funeral home, looking for their books. Apparently, Jack hadn't returned them. All I could do was give them his phone number.

Jack started making a point of coming in to tell me what he liked and didn't like about these other funeral homes. After going down the list, he'd then say, "Well, Brian, your place here is still number one."

"I'm glad you think so, Jack."

I guess if another funeral home didn't offer him coffee right away, or didn't appear to be listening closely enough, he would make a mental note.

"That's all fine and good, Jack. I'm glad we're serving you well, but let's focus on your mom's service."

"OK. But maybe I should see Mother first."

Sometimes in the middle of a conversation, for no apparent reason, he would click open his briefcase, fidget around inside, then close it again without saying a word. I started to worry that he was going to pull out a weapon.

"So, Jack, let's talk about a date for the serv . . ."

Snap, snap, up comes the lid and he's shuffling paper. Other times he would pull out the roll of money from his pocket and count through some of the bills, as if he was adding something up in his mind, then stuff the roll back into his pocket.

He was different, to say the least, but he was also very smart. I could name any topic, and he'd have an interesting fact or some detailed information about it. One day we were talking about politics, and he mentioned that he had recently met with Paul Martin, who was prime minister at the time. I was thinking that this was just an exaggeration, but sure enough he opened up his briefcase and pulled out a glossy picture of himself standing with Paul Martin. He would mix up these tidbits of fact and insight with other ideas that seemed strange and out of place. One day he saw a picture of my daughter on my desk.

"Isn't she a beautiful girl?"

"Yes, Jack, she is beautiful, but she's just a little girl."

"Well, I know, but she's very beautiful."

Now I was starting to get nervous around him. I also found that I had to watch every single word I said. Jack was very perceptive, and he remembered the smallest details. He didn't hesitate to correct you if you happened to make a mistake.

Jack travelled everywhere by taxi and often had a car wait for him outside when he came into the funeral home. One time, he was here for several hours before the taxi driver finally walked in and demanded to be paid.

Weeks turned into months and still there was no funeral. We were getting more than a little anxious to have this matter resolved. Luckily, we have excellent technicians working for us, and Jack's mother's remains were well prepared, but still, we couldn't go on like this forever.

One day, Jack called to say he was coming in, and my cousin Patrick McGarry was there when I answered the phone. Patrick could hear the frustration in my voice. After I got off the phone, he said, "I have an idea. I think you spend too much time with him, Brian."

"Well, that I know, but how do we get his mother into her grave?"

"I'll do it. You have to be firm with this guy."

I wasn't sure about his strategy, but I was coming to my wits' end and was willing to let Patrick give it a shot.

Jack arrived and was brought into an office. Patrick and I walked in together.

"Hi, Jack," I greeted him. "I've got a conflicting meeting today, so Patrick is going to be talking with you."

"That's fine," he replied.

It didn't seem to bother him, so I left the two of them together and closed the door on my way out. Patrick got right to the point. "Jack, I've got fifteen minutes and in those fifteen minutes we're going to decide when your mother's funeral will be."

Well, that's all it took to send Jack into a rage, and he rushed out of the office to find me. I had barely made it down the hall.

"You need to do a better job training your staff about respect!"

He went on and on, until I was finally able to calm him down and get him a coffee. It had been six months since his mother had been brought into our funeral home, and I was running out of patience. After Jack left, I called the Chief Coroner of Ontario in Toronto and explained the situation. He was very understanding.

"Well, you certainly can't go on like that."

"You're right, but can you order her buried?"

"I probably can, but let's get her out of your funeral home first."

"How are we going to do that?"

"You can send her to my office in Toronto."

"Sure, but you don't know this guy, he's not going to like that very much."

"It doesn't matter. I'll look after it."

So that's exactly what we did. We placed Jack's mother into a hearse and brought her to Toronto.

I called Jack the next day and asked him to come into the funeral home for a meeting. When he arrived later that afternoon, I asked him to sit down, saying that we needed to talk. As a precaution, I had asked a couple of the guys to wait outside the door, just in case things went terribly wrong.

"I want to see Mom," Jack demanded.

"Your mom's not here," I replied.

"What do you mean she's not here?"

"She's at the Chief Coroner's office in Toronto."

"What?"

He jumped up, pounded his fists on the desk, and yelled at me. I let this go on for a minute or so, then finally said, "Sit down, Jack. It's been six months. Your mother's remains are going to become a health problem soon. The Chief Coroner ordered her brought to his office."

"I'll sue you!"

"Do whatever you want, but your mom is going to be buried. She's not coming back to Ottawa, until the grave is open and you are at the graveside. If you don't comply with this, the coroner will order your mom to be cremated in Toronto, and I'm afraid there's nothing you can do about it."

The meeting went on for another thirty minutes. Finally, Jack said he was going to see his lawyer and stormed out of my office. True to his word, later that day I received a call from his attorney.

"You can't cremate his mother without his permission."

"Yes, we can. You need to talk to the Chief Coroner."

Jack's lawyer made the call and the coroner confirmed what I had said.

"Without question I can order this woman cremated, and I'm about ready to do it, too."

In the meantime, Pierre Trudeau died and we were busy looking after his funeral. Afterwards, Jack called to tell me what a fine service he thought it had been. He had been on Parliament Hill watching the proceedings and complimented us on our involvement. Then he said the words I had been waiting so long to hear, "I've decided to bury Mom."

I sighed, "That's good, Jack."

"But I have one request."

At this point I was willing to do just about anything. "What is it?"

"I'd like you to use the same hearse that was used for Mr. Trudeau."

"We will if you promise you'll be there."

His lawyer had smartly advised him not to pursue a legal fight. Along with the Trudeau hearse, Jack also wanted the same people who had worked on Trudeau's funeral to be involved with his mother's service. He had also prepared a list of people that he didn't want to be at the service, including staff members he didn't like for various reasons.

The day of the funeral finally arrived. It was to take place in a Roman Catholic church of Jack's choosing, and there were about fifteen people gathered there for the service. Jack stood up at the front of the church and made a very nice speech honouring his mom. He also made a point of thanking our funeral home and saying he was sorry for causing so much trouble.

After the service finished, we went to a cemetery owned by the Roman Catholic diocese. Jack had insisted on a steel casket in a metal vault. After almost eight months, Jack's mother was lowered into her final resting place. Jack stayed afterwards and watched the grave being filled in. I stood with him and realized that we had become friends in a strange way. I think his mom was probably his closest friend, and the whole affair seemed somewhat sad in a way. He just didn't want to let his mom go.

For all of our trouble, we never received a single penny for the funeral. Months later, I ran into Jack on the street, downtown.

"Hello, Jack. Are you planning on coming in to see us about making a payment?" I asked.

"Oh, don't worry about that," he said.

"Well, I am worried about it."

"I'm going to come in soon."

"Soon?"

"Yes. Why don't you come and have a hamburger with me?"

Jack led me into a fast food restaurant, where we sat down and ordered. We ate and talked about local, national, and international politics. The bill came and he pulled out his big roll of hundreds, twenties, and fifties, all mixed up.

"I'll buy you lunch," he offered.

I smiled and let him pay the bill, the whole time thinking, "There really is no such thing as a free lunch."

My final quirky story. Two brothers arrived at our office on a hot summer afternoon, dressed in farm clothes. They told senior partner George Schaef that their brother had died two hours ago. When George asked where their brother had died, they replied, "in the field behind our farm house. He was forking hay onto our wagon, being pulled by [horses] Prince and Dick."

"Where is your brother now?" asked George.

"In the car," replied one.

"Where is the car?"

"In your parking lot."

Holy cow, thought George. "Did you have a coroner come to your field?"

"No. We knew he was dead."

We had the brothers drive their car into our garage and called a coroner, who found the whole situation a bit humorous, but natural enough for a couple of down-to-earth, rural lads.

The funeral was arranged and that was that.

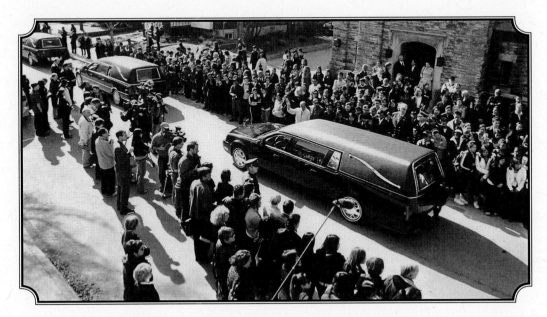

In 2005, five members of the Thach family died in a house fire.
Brian's wife, Joan Sun McGarry, who was born in China and advises Hulse,
Playfair & McGarry on Asian funeral traditions, directed the funeral.

Unknown / Courtesy of the McGarry Family Archives.

CHAPTER 7

Difficult Situations

There are often times when funeral directors must deal with especially tragic circumstances. Whenever a person dies, it is understandably painful for family and friends. But when an accident takes someone in the prime of their life, when a child dies, or when you imagine the hopelessness experienced by the person who commits suicide, the emotions and empathy surrounding these events can be overwhelming. Dealing with mortality on a daily basis reveals death as a natural part of life, but sometimes even this understanding cannot prepare you for some of the experiences you must face, and some of the tragedies you must see.

When I was president of the Funeral Association of Canada, a radio commentator once asked me during an interview, "Does it ever bother you that you make a living from death?"

I think what he really wanted to ask was, "Does it bother you that you're swindling people?" He didn't word it that way, but I sensed that was the underlying feeling.

A perception does exist among some that funeral directors are taking advantage of people at their most vulnerable. Occasionally, we must deal with people who are somewhat hostile toward us, because of their grief, and it's an aspect of our work for which we receive training. It's also a fact that some clients resent that we charge for what we do. Perhaps they've seen a movie or read a criticism that portrayed funeral directors as unethical, so they come in convinced that we're going to overcharge them.

I know the image of funeral directors has improved over the years, but I also believe that perceptions exist for a reason. While the majority of people who work in the funeral profession are very good, there have been some unscrupulous funeral directors over the years—just as in all other professions. However, these bad actors don't usually survive very long, for when a family realizes they have been mistreated, word gets out, and a funeral home's reputation can be quickly destroyed. Regardless, these dishonest few cause problems for everyone else.

The truth is, people experiencing the death of a family member are often very grateful for the service we provide. The reward of this profession is not monetary; instead, it comes from the understanding that we have helped someone get through a very difficult time in their lives.

So, this is how I answered that interviewer's question: "Do you think it bothers physicians that they make their living from sickness? It shouldn't bother them and it doesn't bother me."

However, dealing with tragedy is an aspect of our work that you never really get used to. I have seen a pregnant woman and her infant daughter killed in an accident—three lives lost in an instant and devastation for the husband left behind. There have been murder-suicides, parents who have killed their children, the anguish of sudden infant death syndrome, and the senselessness of multiple murders. The experience of dealing with these tragedies stays with you long after you've gone home for the day, and some memories stay with you for the rest of your life.

There are times when we must deal with difficult people. Sometimes, these difficulties stem from personality conflicts, or sometimes they are related to grief; but there are also times when we encounter people who, for whatever reason, distrust the funeral profession.

One Sunday morning, a young man and his uncle came into the funeral home unannounced. While not extraordinary, usually families will call first, which gives us a chance to prepare and make sure that we have a funeral director available to speak with them, but we would never turn anyone away. The young man's father, his uncle's brother, had died, and they had come in to make the arrangements. It quickly became clear that the young man was convinced funeral homes existed for the sole purpose of taking advantage of bereaved families. Perhaps he was grief-stricken, but he had made up his mind well before arriving that all funeral directors were dishonest.

"If I have to deal with someone, it might as well be you."

That's the way the meeting started. He had selected us seemingly because he thought we were the best of the worst.

Alex Caldwell, partner and vice-president of our firm, was looking after them. He's a wonderful, experienced man, but everything he suggested was immediately dismissed as outrageous and overpriced. I don't think it would have mattered if Alex had told them that the cost was $5 or $500; in the young man's mind, it was little better than theft. The uncle, meanwhile, seemed nice, but hardly spoke at all. The meeting went on for quite a while, until a break occurred when Alex got up to get the two men some coffee. I met him as he was walking out of the office.

"Brian," Alex said, "I don't know if I'm going to make it through this meeting."

He got the coffee and returned to the office. The young man decided that he didn't want the funeral for a few days, which was fine, but Alex informed him that we needed permission to do at least some minimum preparation of his dad's remains. It wouldn't have to be a complete embalming; just the necessary work for sanitary reasons.

"How much is that going to cost?"

"Very little. It's just a matter of proper hygiene. We can keep your dad's remains in our cooling area for a long time, but once we bring his body into a public space, there are certain precautions we must take."

"That's an absolute rip-off and I won't have it. I won't do it."

There was silence for a moment. Alex had presented the son with all of the options, to no avail, and he was at a loss. The young man finally broke the silence. "Here's what I'm going to do," he said. "I'm going to take Dad home."

Alex was confused by this. "I'm sorry, I'm not quite sure what you mean . . ."

"We have a big freezer in the basement, and I'll put him in there, and we'll have you come and pick him up on the day of the service."

Alex looked at him for a moment to see if he was joking, but the young man looked serious.

"I'm sorry, but we just won't do that."

"Why not? It's the same idea isn't . . ."

At last the uncle spoke up, interrupting his nephew. "Steven, Mr. Caldwell is trying to help us. I think he's a good man, and if you take my brother home to your freezer, I will have no part of this funeral. You need to make up your mind right now to accept one of the offers that Mr. Caldwell has presented to us."

They came to an agreement. This is an extreme example, but one that shows exactly how distraught people can be.

A few years ago we decided to build an addition to our downtown chapel. As a result, we were under construction for the better part of six months, an inconvenience that was unfortunate, but unavoidable. During those six months, we held about five hundred funerals at our Central Chapel, and of all those families, only one left us over the complications.

We were very busy at the time when this particular family came in to arrange a funeral. They didn't have a problem with the construction, but they did want a particular room, one of the larger rooms that we have. We checked our files and, as it happened, the room was already promised to another family.

Earlier in the week a man had come in to see me. His nephew had been involved in criminal activity in the city and had been murdered over a drug deal gone wrong. The boy's parents were not well-off, so he had come in to make the arrangements for his nephew's funeral.

"Even though my nephew had lost his way in life, I think it's important that he have a proper burial."

Love is an amazing thing. It's easy to love someone when there are no troubles, but when the person you love is hurting you or hurting himself, that's when real, unconditional love shines through.

"Was your nephew on social assistance?"

"Yes."

"Let me make a call to the social services department."

Sure enough, the young man was entitled to a social service funeral. In situations like this, the government provides a small allowance to the funeral home to cover the basic costs of the service. It's up to the funeral home whether they choose to perform the ceremony or not. I called the uncle back and told him that social services would cover the costs of the funeral, and that we would be honoured to serve his family. He was noticeably relieved, but there was one other issue that he brought up. "There's going to be a lot of people at this funeral. The boy was well known and has a large family . . . I think we're going to need a big room."

I checked our records and found that our largest room was still available.

"We can provide you with a large enough room."

In the meantime, the other aforementioned family had come in and had specifically asked for the same room, saying that if we couldn't provide it for them, they would leave. I asked them to come into my office.

"With great respect, I'm going to explain why that room is being used . . ."

They weren't in the mood to hear the reasons.

"No, Mr. McGarry, you either give us that room or we'll go somewhere else."

"I'm sorry, but the room has been previously offered to another family."

"Our dad is in your preparation room."

"I know."

"So what do we do?"

"Well, if you really feel that you must leave, you can choose another funeral home and I'll call them and make the arrangements."

"What do we owe you?"

"You owe us nothing. Let me give you some time to think about it."

I left the office, and they had a family conference. A few minutes later I returned.

"We've decided to go somewhere else," they announced.

"All right, I'll take care of it."

People are equal in death, and it's not our place to judge one life as more or less worthy than another. The boy on social services who had made some bad decisions was just as deserving of respect as anyone else. We literally do serve the full range of our nation's social strata . . . from paupers to prime ministers.

It is always best to deal with problems as soon as they come up. Most things can be solved quickly if the lines of communication are open, and if both parties involved are willing to listen to each other.

On one occasion, Doug Kennedy, who had worked with us for many years, left to work for one of the best and largest funeral providers in Canada, Turner and Porter in Toronto, which is also family-owned. We were sad to see him go, but we remained good friends.

"We just received a call from the Ontario Board of Funeral Services," he said. There had been a complaint lodged against the branch funeral home Doug managed for us in the early 1990s, some fifteen years after the fact.

"Wow, Doug, that was quite a long time ago."

"Fifteen years, to be exact . . ."

The Board of Funeral Services is the regulatory body that ensures industry standards are maintained in Ontario. Whenever they receive a complaint, they are obliged to look into it. In the half-century that I've been working here, I think we've had two complaints. So, you have to wonder what kind of issue would percolate for that long.

"Do you even remember the funeral, Doug?"

"I'm having difficulty recalling any details," he replied.

The complaint stated that we held a visitation when there was a request that there be none. I knew Doug would never have allowed this to happen, and I was interested to see the record of the funeral.

We keep a record of every funeral, detailing the name of the funeral director and the executor, but also commenting on any extraordinary events that occur. So we looked through our files and, sure enough, there was a difference of opinion between the family of the deceased and his widow. The bereaved woman had requested that there be absolutely no public visitation. From what I could gather, the executor of the estate gave permission for a grandson of the deceased to spend a private moment with his grandfather. It was not anything that was open to the public. Eventually, it surfaced that one family member had some private time with the deceased, feelings were hurt, and now, fifteen years later, people were trying to put the pieces together. It was eventually determined by the Board that our funeral home was not at fault, but it shows you how strong and long-lasting people's emotions can be.

I am a former chairman of the Ontario Board of Funeral Services. The Board does not receive many complaints. There have been a few instances in Ontario where prepaid funds have been stolen, but this is usually a case of a funeral home getting into financial trouble and dipping into their trusts. It's not easy to accomplish this kind of fraud, as the funeral home must produce false records; banks won't release any funds without proof that a death has occurred. It's a serious crime, but fortunately it doesn't happen very often. However, when something like this occurs, the family who has made prearrangements doesn't lose their money.

Years ago, funeral homes voluntarily set up a trust fund in order to provide compensation for any wrongdoing. We all pay into the fund annually; it has rarely been drawn upon.

When I was chairman of the board, we received about sixty or seventy complaints a year for all of Ontario, a low number if you consider there are approximately 80,000 deaths a year in the province. Thirty to forty percent of the complaints we received involved one funeral home complaining about the practices of another.

One of the more frequent, family-related complaints involves the release of cremated remains to the wrong person. In one instance, a funeral director released the remains to the common-law spouse of the deceased. It looked legitimate to the funeral director—common-law spouses have legal rights—so he signed the remains over to her and off she went with the urn. A few weeks later, some of the deceased's family members arrived at the funeral home and asked if they could collect their father's urn. When they were told that the remains were not available, it caused a serious problem.

The funeral director attempted to retrieve the remains from the common-law spouse, only to discover that she had already scattered them at a local racetrack (the deceased had been a car racing enthusiast). There had been a few races since the ashes were scattered and they were nowhere to be found.

When the family found out what happened, they were furious. They immediately lodged a complaint with the board and threatened to sue the funeral home. The board eventually determined that the common-law spouse did have legal rights, but that, ultimately, the executor should have been responsible for collecting the remains.

It is very important that the funeral director make sure they are dealing with the family member who has been given the authority to make these kinds of important decisions. I've seen circumstances where, with the family's permission, the cremated remains have been divided, so that each family member could have a portion to scatter in a way he or she felt was appropriate. If the remains have not been cremated, and there is an argument about where the deceased is to be buried, all we can do is wait patiently for the family to come to a consensus. On occasion, we've had to delay a funeral until the family could resolve a dispute about where the body was to be buried.

At the other end of the spectrum, every funeral home has cremated remains that have never been picked up. We had a family who simply refused to come and pick up their dad, and it took several years before the issue was resolved. I recall one phone conversation, in particular, with the son of the deceased. Maurice Hulse, Charles's brother, approached the situation with his usual diplomacy.

"Please, we need you to come in and pick up your dad's remains."

"Can't you just take care of it for us?"

"Well, what would you have us do?"

He seemed irritated by the question. "Just flush them down the toilet."

"I'm sorry, sir, but we will do no such thing."

Maurice could see that he wasn't going to get anywhere with the son, so that was the end of the conversation. Consequently, Maurice arranged for the urn to be interred in a common ground area of a local cemetery. As the interment has been recorded, the urn could be retrieved if necessary.

This scenario happens more often than you might think, and over the years storage space can become a problem. We try to be as patient as possible, but at a certain point we must be politely assertive. After a certain length of time, if the remains have not been claimed, we have the legal right to bury them.

I know of one funeral home that kept a cremated remains for twenty-five years, before deciding it was time to bury the ashes. Sure enough, Murphy's Law kicked in and no sooner had they interred the urn than a member of the family arrived, wanting to pick up the remains. The family member was angry when they found out that the ashes were not there, and lodged a complaint to the Board of Funeral Services. The board investigated and determined that the funeral home had not been negligent.

Why do people let years go by before they come in to pick up cremated remains? For some people, helping their loved one take that last journey becomes an unbearable duty; they simply cannot bring themselves to say goodbye for the last time. What they don't realize is that by doing so, they are also delaying the healing process. Most people take some comfort in burying or scattering the ashes of a loved one. They might take the remains up to the cottage and have a committal service, or scatter the ashes at a favourite spot of the deceased. These private ceremonies can provide a great deal of closure.

There are no strict regulations dealing with the disposal of cremated remains, so it really comes down to good taste and sensitivity to others. One does not have to spend a lot of money purchasing a plot at a cemetery.

Once every couple of years, someone arrives at our door with cremated remains or a tag that says "McGarry Crematorium" with a name next to it. We always identify cremated remains with one of these tags. On one occasion, a man was scuba diving in the Ottawa River and spotted a box on the river bed. When he brought it up to the surface, he opened it to discover one of our identification tags. He brought it to us thinking that perhaps it had been stolen and thrown into the river. From the tag we were able to trace the remains to a family, and after contacting them, we discovered that they had placed the remains in the river themselves.

On one occasion, having this identification tag with the remains proved to be invaluable. I arrived at work one morning to discover that a family was already waiting for me in the office. I walked in and noticed there was an urn sitting on my desk. I turned to the family and asked, "Good morning, folks, how can we help you?"

"We don't think these are Dad's remains."

There was no time for niceties. This was an issue that had clearly been on their minds for some time. I retrieved the file and discovered that in this particular instance, the family had signed a waiver saying they refused to identify the remains before the cremation took place. We understand that the identification process can be perceived as difficult, and if family members cannot bring themselves to identify the remains, they can have a friend act on their behalf. If no one can make the identification, we ask the family to sign a waiver stating that they have refused to do so. However, we strongly suggest that identification be made at the time of death, otherwise, it can weigh heavily on a person's mind, and that's exactly what happened in this case. Tom Flood, our senior vice-president and a compassionate man with many years of experience, sat down with the family and told them about the identity tag that we include in every urn.

"With your permission, I'll remove the cremated remains here and see if the tag is inside."

They agreed. It was tense, because there's always a chance, however unlikely, that there was a mistake made at the time of the cremation, meaning we would find ourselves in a lot of trouble. One of the transfer companies in Ottawa did exactly that—cremated the wrong remains. Not owning or operating their own crematorium, they had contracted the cremation to another firm.

Tom went into our preparation room and returned with a temporary receptacle, which I placed on the desk next to the urn. Tom began to pour the remains into the temporary receptacle. It took the longest time for the tag to come out, but at last it appeared. The next step was to check the identification number and compare it to the matching tag, which we keep in the file. Tom retrieved the file, and we were relieved to discover the identification numbers matched. This gave the family complete satisfaction, and us, a sense of relief. Employing exacting standards is important.

I think it's important that the family be part of the burial or scattering of the ashes. It brings a sense of closure and can even be therapeutic. In some traditions, there is direct involvement. In the Jewish faith, for instance, the family and friends of the deceased fill in the grave at the end of the interment ceremony for casketed remains.

I remember a funeral service for a young father. The clergy performing the service didn't believe in lowering the casket in front of the family, as he felt it was too traumatic. Therefore, at the end of the ceremony at the cemetery, the clergy placed a handful of earth on the casket and said one final prayer. The family members began walking back to their cars; however, the son of the deceased, a ten-year-old boy, stayed behind. He walked over to me and tugged on the sleeve of my coat.

"Mr. McGarry, what happens to my daddy now?" he asked.

I knelt down to reply. "Well, you see that device over there?" I said. "That mechanism that will lower your dad into the grave."

"Can I watch?"

I thought, now what do I do.

"Come with me for a minute."

I led him over to where the clergy was standing. "This young man would like to see his father's casket lowered into the grave."

The boy nodded. The clergy looked at me and then at the young man. "Well, all right," he said.

The three of us walked to the side of the grave and stood there as I engaged the lever, lowering the casket slowly into the ground. The boy watched quietly, and when it was done, he said, "OK, I can go now."

I took him over to his family, who had been watching us from the cars. After we said goodbye to the family, I gave the clergy a lift back to his rectory. We sat quietly in the car for a moment and then he turned to me, "Well, that was a lesson."

I understood why he had not wanted the family to witness the casket being lowered—in his mind, to protect them from undue trauma—but if we try and make it too easy for people, the ceremony is in danger of becoming artificial. Losing a loved one is a painful ordeal and, unfortunately, the only way to move on is by truly accepting the loss. Unless a family has an objection, I always recommend that they stay and witness the casket being lowered.

The other side of this coin involves families who want little or no ceremony at all for their loved one.

One morning, I received a phone call from a man whose wife had just passed away at a local hospital.

"I want you to remove her body," he said, "cremate her, and then you can just bring the urn to my home."

"All right, we can do that, but I need to meet with you so we can take care of some paperwork."

He seemed adamant that this was what he wanted, but when he was in the office signing the papers, I decided to ask him about it. "Are you absolutely sure this is the way you want the arrangements to be completed?"

"Yes, I don't want to have any fuss at all."

"That's fine, but if you change your mind, the cremation won't take place until tomorrow. If you or your family want to spend any time with her, just let me know."

"Thank you, but I won't change my mind."

We followed his directions and in this circumstance, it turned out to be a wrong decision for the family. People often do not know how to deal with the death of someone they're close to. While it's not something we're taught in schools or most institutions, other than mortuary science colleges, quite often we are asked to address schools, social workers, medical personnel, and police, for example. Sometimes people think that by moving quickly through the funeral, it will speed up the healing process, but this can actually have the opposite effect.

A few months later the man came in to see me.

"Hi, Brian. My family isn't happy with the way I handled my wife's passing. I'm afraid I made a mistake . . ."

"Well, we can still have a memorial service for your wife. Would you like to do that?"

"That sounds fine."

I booked the chapel for the following week and contacted a clergyperson. The man and his family had a private gathering, and I think it brought some closure. I don't think that every family should necessarily have a full service with two days' visitation, but it's important to have some kind of formal recognition of a life lived.

There have been two instances over the years where a family has asked us to have an empty urn or an empty casket present at a visitation or a funeral. In one case, the deceased was overseas, and due to a mechanical problem with the aircraft, the remains were still in transit and would not arrive in time for the visitation, which had already been advertised through an obituary in the newspaper. They came to us and requested that we place an empty casket in the visitation room.

"I'm sorry, but we will not do that."

"Yes, you have to do it. No one will know the difference."

"Firstly, we will know. And secondly, we certainly do not have to do it. People coming into that room will believe that your father's remains are in that casket. It's dishonest, plain and simple."

I don't think the man had thought it through, and once he did, he realized that it would be an unethical thing to do. We proceeded with the visitation without the casket and scheduled a second visitation when the remains arrived the following day.

The other occasion involved cremated remains. Again, there was a problem with the shipment, and the urn was lost for several days, causing a delay.

"Just put an empty urn in the chapel . . ."

In instances like this, there are alternatives. A table can be set up with a display of photos, flowers, and memory pieces, but we cannot deceive people into thinking that the deceased is in the room, when, in fact, he or she is not. We try our best to accommodate everybody's wishes, but there are certain circumstances where we are morally obligated to be absolutely transparent.

Over the years, new trends have emerged in funerals. Cremation, especially, has become more common, reflecting a change in society's values. When Tom Flood, who along with his experience has a good sense of humour, was asked recently how high the percentage of funerals ending in cremation will rise, he replied, "It will never go over 100 percent." Some funerals today are casket-less, which means the family can rent a casket if there is to be a viewing; otherwise there is only a container for cremation. Charlie Hulse could never accept the rental casket concept. When we introduced it in our funeral home, he said, "Brian, why would you do that? There's a big selection of containers without having a rental unit . . . isn't that a bit phony?"

I actually prefer the term ceremonial casket, to rental.

"No. It's for people who can't afford an oak casket, or object to cremating a fine piece of mahogany, but still want to have the appearance of a nice casket in the room without cremating the wood casket selected."

Charlie couldn't grasp the concept, which is partly a reflection of his own life. He was quite a man about town, and while he didn't live flamboyantly, he lived well. Renting a casket didn't jibe with his sense of values. Charlie and I did discuss the idea of offering ceremonial caskets on several occasions, but these conversations always ended up the same.

"Do it if you have to, but I've got to say, I don't necessarily want to rub shoulders with everybody when I'm alive, so why would I want to when I'm dead?"

"You have to understand, sir, there are two containers. The inside container that holds the body is removed after the service, so you're not really rubbing shoulders with anybody."

Charlie was from a different era. As it turns out, the ceremonial casket is a good option for a lot of people. There are people who, for aesthetic and/or environmental reasons, don't want to destroy a beautiful piece of wood. We use the ceremonial casket for the chapel or church service, then we respectfully remove the simpler, inner container for the actual cremation.

I've heard people criticize cremation because they feel that it is just another way for us to distance ourselves from the reality of what happens to the body in death; I see it differently. Fire is a natural element, which means that the natural process is reduced to three hours as opposed to several years. Some faiths object to cremation, such as the Orthodox Jewish faith, so of course their reasons must be respected.

While the majority of people now choose cremation, misconceptions remain. We had to deal with the public's misconceptions in this regard firsthand after we decided to build a new crematorium in Cumberland, just east of Ottawa.

We already had the necessary permits and had satisfied all the zoning regulations, but then someone distributed a flyer with the title: "Do you really want a crematorium in your neighbourhood?" We then began to receive phone calls from distressed members of the community. To try to alleviate people's fears, we offered to host a community meeting. We set up a panel with the health authorities who issue the permits, the local municipal councillor, and an expert in crematoriums that we brought up from Florida. I also asked some of our senior staff and technicians to come out for the meeting as well. We picked a date and reserved the community hall, which also happened to be attached to the local hockey arena. I drove to the meeting with my friend Bernie Mason, a retired scientist, who wanted to come along. When we arrived at the hall, the parking lot was jammed with cars. I turned to Bernie and said, "There better be a big hockey game here tonight, because if there isn't, we're in trouble."

On the way into the arena, I noticed that it was in darkness. There was no hockey game that night, but there were about 200 people inside the community centre waiting for the meeting to start. We got underway. People voiced their concerns, and we answered all the questions as best we could. I think we were able to convince many of the folks who were there, but there will always be a few who will disagree with the idea despite the evidence.

We offered a tour of our crematorium in Wakefield, which some folks accepted. One fellow who came on the tour was a doctor who was about to build a home in the area. His main concern was pollution, and this is one of the biggest misconceptions about crematoriums. The truth is, our bodies are made up largely of water, and with the intense heat, the remains essentially evaporate during the process, meaning there is very little emission. After the tour, the doctor said that he had no reservations about the crematorium anymore. This is usually the case, if people take the time to learn about the process.

One winter afternoon I was at the Château Laurier attending a political rally for Jean Chrétien. After the speeches were finished, a man came over to see me and introduced himself as a freelance writer who had gone to school with my sister-in-law, Kilby McGarry. His name was vaguely familiar to me. Unfortunately, he hadn't come over just to chat. He soon informed me of the fact that he lived in an apartment building across the street from our Central Chapel and that he had a bone to pick with me.

"You've got to quit that snowplowing at night."

His statement caught me off guard, so it took me a few moments to realize that he was referring to the snow removal service we hired to keep our parking lot cleared during the winter.

"Quit snowplowing? We're a twenty-four-hour operation. Our vehicles come and go all night, and if there's a storm, we have to be able to get in and out of our building."

"If you don't stop that snowplowing, I'm going to get you."

I thought at first he was joking, but it quickly became apparent that he was quite angry.

"I'm sorry you're upset, but I'm not sure how I can help you."

"Stop the snowplowing, and there won't be a problem," he stated, then walked away.

After rolling his name around in my mind at bit, I finally realized where I had heard of him. He sometimes wrote stories for a morning radio show I listened to on occasion. His stories were always a little offbeat and quirky, and now I knew why. Regardless, we continued snowplowing whenever we needed to, and I didn't think about his comments much more until a few weeks later when he arrived at the funeral home and asked to see me. I invited him into my office, and he immediately turned on a tape recorder that he had brought with him.

"I'm doing a story on your firm," he said.

"What kind of story is that?" I asked.

"How you've taken advantage of a certain gentleman."

"Oh, how's that?"

"One of your employees has been overcharging people."

I listened closely as he went on to explain his story. The employee in question was one of our senior funeral directors, a man who had been with us for years and whose integrity I trusted without reservation. I looked at him across the desk, and said, "We don't overcharge anyone here. If we did, we wouldn't have lasted all of these years."

"Well, that's not what my source claims."

He went on to say there was a man (I'll call him Mr. Smith), who had come to the radio station with a story about a family that had been mistreated by us. "Mr. Smith" had been the executor of the estate, and he said that he was appalled at the amount of money we had charged for the funeral. I asked for the name of the family, then told him I would look into it and get back to him.

I found the file. The funeral had been several months before and, sure enough, "Mr. Smith" was the executor. Upon closer examination, I noticed that there had been some changes to the original document, which showed that the deceased had prearranged and prepaid for the funeral himself about ten years prior to his death. The original document showed arrangements for a traditional funeral involving a rental casket, followed by cremation. It was a relatively inexpensive funeral.

I called the reporter back. "The deceased had prepaid for his own funeral years before he died, so it must have been what he wanted."

"It was too expensive."

"How do you mean too expensive? He chose his funeral and he paid for it. He wasn't under any duress, because it was done ten years before he died."

I didn't understand where the problem was, so I went to talk with the funeral director who had made the arrangements. He remembered the family and, sure enough, the executor had changed the funeral arrangements, choosing a casket that was less expensive than the ceremonial one we use; both options, however, were quite modest in price.

I called the reporter again. "Can I speak to the executor?" I asked.

"I guess you can, but I'm still going to do a story on you."

"This doesn't happen to have anything to do with the snowplowing by chance?"

"No, no," he assured me.

I reminded him that he had said he would "get me."

"Oh, I was just pulling your leg."

I got off the phone and called the executor. He was less than cordial. "I have nothing to say to you," he said.

An idea then struck me. "You didn't happen to be a beneficiary of the estate?"

The question didn't make him very happy, and he refused to answer.

In the end, the reporter went ahead with his story, and I heard it a few days later on the radio. Needless to say, it wasn't very positive. I submitted a written complaint to the radio station and went in for a meeting with the producer. I brought all the files with me. He agreed that the story was inappropriate, and we subsequently received an apology. I don't know if the reporter was disciplined or not, but I never saw him again and never received another complaint about the snow removal from our parking lot.

Although it was Malak Karsh who became noted for photographing Ottawa's
famous tulips, which are a gift each year from the people of the Netherlands
in thanks for the city giving refuge to the Dutch royal family during the
Second World War, it is the grave of his brother Yousuf in Notre Dame
Cemetery that is adorned with a sculptured tulip. Both men made Ottawa
their adopted home and became world famous for their photography.

Lynn Ball / Ottawa Citizen.

CHAPTER 8

Death and Beauty

Several years ago, we decided that for every funeral we looked after, we would plant a tree in memory of the deceased. With the assistance of the Rideau Valley Conservation Authority, we have now planted thousands of trees in the Ottawa area. We feel this is a way of creating a living memory for those who have died, and a reminder that when one life comes to an end, another begins. I truly believe that we could not appreciate the good in the world if there were no tragedy in contrast. Sadness and death possess their own beauty, if you allow yourself to see it.

Brian Smith was born and raised in Ottawa. Hockey was a constant in his early life; his father played for the Boston Bruins in the National Hockey League and was part of the team that won the Stanley Cup in 1941. Talent seemed to run in the family, as Brian and his older brother Gary both followed in their father's footsteps. Gary was nicknamed "Suitcase," because he played for so many teams in the league. By the late '60s, Brian had also been drafted and went on to play for the Los Angeles Kings and the Minnesota North Stars. When his hockey career came to an end in 1973, Brian returned to Ottawa and, after taking some time to reflect about his future, he decided to go into television broadcasting. He was soon hired by CJOH, a popular local television station, where he became the sports anchor. It was a job tailor-made for him, and he took to it immediately. Over the years, Brian became a local celebrity and well known as a good-natured and kind person. He loved his community and often donated his time and energy to local charity events.

On August 1, 1995, Brian was in a rush after his six o'clock newscast had finished to get to a charity auction he had agreed to emcee for the Children's Wish Foundation. However, as he walked out the front door of the CJOH building into the parking lot, the unthinkable happened. He was shot and killed.

Jeffery Arenburg was a mentally ill patient with a history of violent behaviour. At one time, he had been a scallop fisherman in Nova Scotia, but had left the Maritimes after being charged by police for attacking a radio station manager. When he was later arrested, he told police he thought the radio station was broadcasting messages through his teeth. He left the province before his case went to trial and found his way to Ottawa. Unfortunately, the delusions he suffered from weren't as easy to outrun as his charges, and before long, Arenburg believed that CJOH was sending messages directly into his head.

On that fateful night, Arenburg took a hunting rifle and drove to the CJOH parking lot. Brian was not Arenburg's intended target, but he was the first person to walk out of the building that the gunman recognized. Arenburg took up the rifle and fired two shots, one of which hit Brian. He then drove away, leaving the sportscaster lying on the asphalt. Brian was rushed to hospital, but succumbed to his injuries eighteen hours later. Jeffery Arenburg turned himself in the following day.

In all my years as a funeral director, I have never seen such an outpouring of emotion and support for a private citizen. The community that Brian loved so much was deeply wounded by his senseless murder. The death of such a kind and giving person had touched something inside the hearts and minds of Ottawa citizens.

Alana Kainz, Brian's wife, phoned us directly to tell us the news that Brian had died, and we made the arrangements immediately. The number of people who came to pay their respects was amazing. For two days leading up to the ceremony, thousands of people waited in a line that went out the front door of our funeral home and stretched around the block. It was likely the largest funeral for a private citizen ever held in Ottawa. CJOH's Max Keeping and his colleagues were of invaluable assistance in arranging this tribute.

Before the service, Alana spoke to me about an idea she had been mulling over. She'd been told that on the day of the funeral, the Rough Riders, Ottawa's professional football team, were going to honour Brian with a moment of silence before their game at Lansdowne Park.

"I know it's not the normal thing to do, but rather than having a minute of silence, I wonder if they could have a minute of applause instead. I just think it would be what Brian would have wanted."

Alana had one other request. "Please don't tell anyone, but at the start of the football game, I'll be jogging along the canal by Lansdowne Park."

Mutual friends contacted the Rough Riders office, which was already in the process of arranging a tribute, and they thought it was a wonderful idea. I attended the game, and there were only a few who knew that Alana was outside at the time. The announcement was made, and all the players on the field raised their helmets in a salute to Brian, and with that, the entire crowd broke into applause. But it didn't last for the traditional one minute; people clapped and cheered for several minutes. It was a powerful gesture, and when the ovation finally ended, many people in the stadium were in tears. It was unconventional, but I think Alana wanted it to be a transition for the people of Ottawa. The mourning of Brian's death was over; this was a loud and exuberant celebration of his life.

Dominic D'Arcy is known in Ottawa as "the singing policeman." He's now retired from the police force, but still sings at various charity functions around the city. He and I are in the Kiwanis Club of Ottawa together, and one day he called me up.

"I know a young man who is dying of multiple sclerosis," he said. "I go and sing for him every Thursday afternoon, but I'm afraid he's not going to live very much longer. His family isn't well off financially, and they're worried that they won't be able to afford to give him a proper funeral. Maybe we could ask our Kiwanis club to help with the costs," he suggested.

This is a heartbreaking situation; a family that has to accept the death of their son and are also burdened with the worry that they won't be able to afford his funeral arrangements when the time comes. Families like this often fall into a grey area in our society—hard-working people who make enough money to survive, but have little left over for anything else.

"We should first find out what the family wants as far as a service is concerned," I said.

"I'm going over to their place this Thursday; would you consider coming with me to talk to them about it?" Dominic asked.

"Sure," I agreed.

Dominic arranged a meeting, so that Thursday, Dominic picked me up at the funeral home and we drove over to their home. The young man was very sick. The disease had confined him to bed, but he was still able to speak. Dominic introduced me to the family, and I quickly realized their son was a remarkable young man. He was in good spirits, and it seemed that he had fully accepted his own death. He was aware that his time was short, but he was very calm. For someone so young he seemed to have a very old soul.

I prearranged his funeral and listened to him talk about the things in life that he cherished, the things that brought a smile to his face and captured his imagination. Meanwhile, I could tell that the family was a little nervous about the cost. They didn't say so, but I could see the concern on their faces. I wanted to put them at ease, and after spending some time with the young man, I went into the other room with his parents.

"Now, what kind of funeral would you want to have if money were not a factor?"

You really find out what's important to people when you take money out of the equation, and you'll often be surprised by what people will tell you. For this family, it was music. Their son loved music, and they felt that it was important to have a service with lots of singing. Dominic had already agreed to perform and was taking care of all the details in that regard. I could see that the very act of talking about the arrangements was alleviating some stress for them.

After a while, Dominic and I said our goodbyes to this delightful family. While driving away, Dominic turned to me and said, "Let's go talk to Kiwanis about the costs."

I had already made a decision.

"You know what? Kiwanis would probably pay for it, but we're both members of the club, and you've already dedicated a lot of your time to this young man."

Dominic had been going to see him for about two years.

"I think it's my turn to give something. We don't need to go to Kiwanis. The family just needs to know that there is no cost."

A few weeks later the boy died. We held the service in our chapel and filled it with joyful music and pictures. It was every bit as satisfying to me and my colleagues as any state funeral we have ever done. As for Dominic, he sang at the funeral, as he did for my mom's service, and many, many others. If anyone deserves the Order of Canada, it is surely Dominic D'Arcy.

I enrolled at Carleton University in my late twenties, but I didn't complete my degree. Halfway through my studies I was invited to become a partner at the funeral home, and consequently became too busy to ever go back and finish. However, I did enjoy the time I spent at the school, especially one particular course, a wonderful class on Canadian federalism taught by Eugene Forsey.

Mr. Forsey was a Rhodes scholar and an expert on the Canadian Constitution who became a thorn in the side of many politicians, a reputation he earned by publicly pointing out constitutional misinterpretations and gaffes. You could often find Forsey's letters published in the *Globe and Mail* and the *Ottawa Citizen*, correcting individuals on constitutional matters. It was a source of pride for him. During the 1972 federal election when Pierre Trudeau and Robert Stanfield were leaders of the Liberals and Conservatives, respectively, there was a moment on election night when it looked as though the Conservatives were going to win by two seats. Forsey called the Liberal headquarters and got a message through to Trudeau telling him not to give up on his government, yet. As it turned out, when the overseas votes came in, Trudeau picked up enough seats to win the election.

Mr. Forsey enjoyed a long career as a lecturer at McGill and Carleton Universities and was later appointed to the Senate. I loved Mr. Forsey's class; he was a vibrant man with a brilliant mind, but he also had a wonderful sense of humour. His class was popular, and I remember asking him if he found it difficult to mark all the papers. He looked at me quite seriously and said, "Oh, I don't mark any of them. I stand at the top of the stairs and throw them all down. Whichever one lands on top gets the highest mark and whichever one is on the bottom gets the lowest mark."

I thought about this grading method for a moment, imagining ways that I could somehow make my assignments lighter in weight, and then he smiled, "Well, don't think too much about it, Mr. McGarry. The truth is that I've got these wonderful people called teaching assistants, who help to mark the papers, and I look over their work to make sure that everything is up to par."

A few years later, Mr. Forsey retired and I had the pleasure of meeting him again. He had some concerns about his health and decided to stop by the funeral home to put a few thoughts on paper about the prearrangement of his funeral. Several months later, he called me to say that he was going to be spending the summer in Victoria, British Columbia.

"Brian, I don't know if I'll ever be back to Ottawa, unless it's in a box."

"Oh, come on, sir . . ."

"Well, I'm just not so sure. When I get out West, I'll be staying with a friend, and I'll tell her to call you if I happen to die."

I don't know if he had a premonition, or just knew that he wasn't as well as he should be, but sure enough, I was at home one evening when I received a call from a delightful woman in Victoria, named Betty, who informed me that Mr. Forsey had just passed away in her home. She explained that as soon as he had arrived in Victoria he instructed her that if he should happen to die, she should contact us and we would look after everything.

He wanted to be buried in Ottawa, so we made the arrangements to bring him back East. The service was held in a French-language United Church, which is unique in itself. Mr. Forsey had a lot of francophone friends, and he requested that most of the service be held in French.

After the funeral, Betty sent us a nice letter thanking us for looking after the arrangements and wondering how Mr. Forsey could have possibly known that his time had come. She wrote:

> Senator Eugene Forsey's funeral and memorial service are now past and they will always be a memorable part of my life. Several days before Eugene passed away, he said to me, "Betty, I am sure I will go when I'm in Victoria with you, should this happen contact Mr. McGarry at Hulse, Playfair and McGarry, he has all my directions and will take care of everything." This you did adequately and Eugene can rest knowing that his wishes were most certainly fulfilled.

Another Canadian senator, Marjory LeBreton, lost two of her family members in a terrible car accident in 1992. Her daughter and grandson were killed by a drunk driver with a lengthy police record for driving under the influence; because of her position as a senator, the tragedy became a national story. Often when people are faced with this kind of senseless loss, it leaves them feeling helpless, but Marjory decided that the best thing she could do was to use the tragedy to bring awareness to the problem of drunk driving. Nothing could ever bring back her daughter and grandson, but perhaps she could help to prevent similar tragedies in the future.

Marjory became very active in the Canadian chapter of Mothers Against Drunk Driving (MADD). Founded in Texas in 1980, MADD had only existed in Canada for two years at this time. However, her experience brought attention to the problem of drunk driving and caused it to become a major issue. Since then, many new laws have been created to stop drunk drivers from getting behind the wheel, penalties have been made more severe, and drinking and driving has become more socially unacceptable. There is no doubt that these changes have saved lives, and Marjory can take some comfort in the fact that she helped to bring them about. Senator LeBreton continues as the vice-chair of the Canadian chapter of MADD, working toward the day when mothers will not have to bury their children for such indefensible and preventable reasons.

Bill Mason was known as "the patron saint of canoeing," and he had a lifelong passion for the wilderness areas of Canada and the United States. A well-known artist, author, filmmaker, and naturalist, Bill embodied what some might call the true Canadian identity—our natural heritage. Bill spent his life trying to preserve these special wild places and conveying through his art the rapture he felt whenever his paddle sliced into a river or lake. Unfortunately, at the age of fifty-nine, Bill developed cancer. The disease swept through his body, and a few months later, he was gone.

I received the call with the bad news from his wife, Joyce. I'd known Bill, and finding out that he had died was a sad moment. As I was getting ready to go to the Masons' home in the Gatineau Hills to make the removal, I thought of my son, Brett, who had met the famous naturalist on several occasions. I asked Brett if he would like to come with me, and he did.

What an experience for a young man of nine. Some people might think it macabre, but death is very natural, and for Brett, who had lived his whole life in the apartment above the funeral home, it was nothing out of the ordinary.

Brett and I arrived at the house with another attendant. Joyce had just put on the kettle to make a pot of tea and asked us if we wanted to join her for a cup. We sat around the kitchen table and talked about the funeral and reminisced about Bill's life. After a while, the attendant and I went into the bedroom where Bill had died and moved his body onto the stretcher.

Bill's funeral was a reflection of his life, and everything was very natural. One of Bill's neighbours was a woodworker, and he had fashioned a pine casket for his friend, which we picked up and brought back to the funeral home. The visitation room was filled with Bill's paintings and photographs, so even in death he was surrounded by the natural splendour that he loved so much.

There's a great little diner in Ottawa called the Newport Restaurant, and it's famous around town for being the home of the Elvis Sighting Society. I've been going there for years and was often served by a friendly woman named Heather Crowe, who was originally from Nova Scotia, but had been living and working in Ottawa for many years. It was always nice to see her face; she had a way of making you feel at home as soon as you walked into the restaurant.

One day in 2002, she discovered a couple of lumps on her neck. She was in her late fifties, but had always been in good health and rarely missed a day of work. She assumed she had picked up an infection somewhere. She went to see her doctor who, thinking that it might be something more serious, sent her to have X-rays done. The X-rays pointed to lung cancer, and a biopsy confirmed it. It turned out to be a type of cancer that is most commonly associated with smoking, but Heather hadn't smoked a day in her life. After she got the biopsy results, one of her regular customers asked her how she was doing. Fatefully, this customer happened to be an assistant deputy minister for Health Canada and was in charge of the government's national anti-smoking campaign. He asked her on the spot if she would consider being in a television commercial and she accepted.

Anti-smoking groups had been commissioning studies to try and bring attention to the dangers of second-hand smoke, but they were finding it difficult to convince people simply with graphs and statistics. The issue always came down to the rights of smokers versus non-smokers. Heather's story was different. This was the first time anyone had looked at the issue from the point of view of those who worked in places where smoking was permitted.

The commercial was quite simple—just a shot of Heather telling her story— but it was sincere and it was poignant. Here was a woman, a single mother and grandmother working as a waitress for forty years, who was dying of cancer because she worked in an environment often filled with cigarette smoke. Heather was someone that every Canadian could relate to.

For the next four years, Heather worked hard travelling across the country talking with politicians at every level of government. She also spoke to community groups and high school students, lobbying for a ban on smoking in public places. She often said that she wanted to be the last Canadian to die of second-hand smoke. Throughout it all, however, she never lost her sense of humour. After we helped her prearrange her funeral, she remarked to journalists, "I was standing there holding my new urn and thought to myself, this is 'Freedom Fifty-Five' for the unprotected worker."

Heather fought to have smoking banned in the workplace right up to the end of her life. The cancer eventually spread through much of her body, and she was finally admitted to the hospital for the last time. However, even though she was very ill, she made one final plea for a nationwide ban on cigarette smoking in public spaces. She died a few days later, yet four days after her death, tough new anti-smoking legislation came into effect in Ontario, with much credit to local MPP Jim Watson (since 2011, mayor of Ottawa). Since then, just about every province and municipality in Canada has gone smoke-free, an amazing change in public policy. Heather would have referred to herself as just another ordinary Canadian, but to many, she has become a true hero.

The McGarrys are co-founders of the Ottawa Chapter of Dialogue Canada, an organization that provides Canadians with opportunities to know each other better and to acknowledge their differences, to share their respective concerns, and to exchange their vision of the country's future. 1993.

QMI Agency.

CHAPTER 9

Staring Down the Giants

At one time, a funeral home wouldn't be put up for sale until the owner of the establishment died. If the business hadn't been left to a family member, another funeral home in the city might come forward and offer to take over the operation. There was still competition between businesses in the city, but all the owners knew each other, and the atmosphere was quite neighbourly. The most important aspect of the job was always to help people in need.

A conglomerate, in the simplest terms, is a large company that owns many branches, at many levels of a particular industry. By operating in this way, a company can have full control over processing, marketing, distribution, and other areas, because they own the businesses that provide these services. If you're a conglomerate that builds houses, you might have a subsidiary company that handles the architecture and design, another that provides the bricks and mortar, and a third that carries out the actual construction. Since jobs like accounting and management can be consolidated for all the subsidiaries, you may proclaim to lower costs for the consumer; profits certainly increase, in any event.

The conglomerate idea is not new and has arguably been around since the first tea and sugar barons ruled over their respective industries, but the business model was perfected in North America after the Second World War when interest rates began to drop. By the late '50s and early '60s, some businesses began making use of the inexpensive loans to buy up their competitors and "branch out."

There are definite financial advantages by expanding in this way. As a single, independent firm, suppliers will charge you a set price, but if you can bring those same suppliers the business generated by ten firms, then you're in a position to negotiate a lower price, thereby most certainly increasing profits for all your branches. With the conglomerate business model, the bigger you are, the greater the profit.

Conglomerates have been very successful over the years, and have found their way into just about every kind of business imaginable; however, one of the problems I see with this business model is that when the services are centralized, so is the profit. When a locally owned business generates a profit, that money stays in the community where the business is located. If the owner decides to build an addition, he or she will call contractors they know in the community first. When one of the branches of a conglomerate builds an addition or purchases new cars, they may have a contract with a company in another city who supplies all the branches. Likewise, when that branch office makes a profit, the money leaves the community and goes to the head office, which may not even be in the same country, let alone the same city.

Another problem may be the quality of service that the customer receives. A small, family-run business will most likely have the owner in the store—he or she may even be your neighbour. In this scenario, the owner has a vested interest in making sure that you're happy when you leave their store. Obviously, it would be impossible for the owners of a conglomerate to live in every community where they have a branch; in fact, it's likely that the employees at your local branch have never met the people they work for. Furthermore, the employees know that they're not likely to rise to the top of the company, and owning it is out of the question. I believe these factors create dissociation between the company and the community where it does business. I don't want to imply that conglomerates are entirely wrong in the way they do business, but it is an approach different from that of a local, family-run enterprise that has a vested interest in the community.

In the early 1980s, the conglomerate business model began to emerge among funeral service providers in Canada. The formula was essentially the same: buy up small, family-owned funeral homes and reduce overhead costs by sharing and consolidating resources. For instance, embalming for all the branch funeral homes in one city might be done at a central location, and all their caskets might be purchased from one supplier. As an example, Arbor Memorial Services Inc., the largest funeral service conglomerate in Canada (and present owners of Kelly Funeral Homes in Ottawa), purchases 90 percent of their caskets from the United States. However, when a conglomerate buys a family-run business, it also makes sure to buy the family's name, which it continues to use on the funeral home. This is done to try and preserve a "personal" image, instead of imposing a corporate one.

Arbor and the McGarrys have an issue of transparency (or non-transparency) in this regard, which ended up before an Ontario tribunal with the McGarrys winning. In an appeal by Arbor (also known as Trillium Funeral Services Corporation, the actual appellant) to Divisional Court, the appeal was granted on technicalities related to the Tribunal. However, the Tribunal's ruling was replaced with an even more severe interpretation of transparency.

In brief, if the public can read "Kelly Funeral Homes," for example, on the signage, then the public must also be able to read as clearly the disclosure as to who actually owns the funeral home, i.e., Trillium Funeral Services Corporation.

Service Corporation International (SCI) was founded in 1962 by Robert L. Waltrip and is currently the largest funeral home conglomerate in the world. Based in Houston, Texas, they own funeral homes all across North America and in Puerto Rico. In Ottawa, SCI currently owns Racine, Robert & Gauthier; McEvoy-Shields; and First Memorial, as well as several other funeral homes in Gatineau and the surrounding area.

I don't believe that funeral service fits naturally into a conglomerate business model. Conglomerates were created as a way of increasing profit, and when you take the same approach and apply it to a business that involves helping people through a painful time in their lives, the two ideas clash. Visit the websites of any of the big funeral conglomerates and you will find stock prices and other business news next to information on "how to find a provider." They treat their prepaid funeral funds as commodities, using them as leverage to finance the purchase of other funeral homes and even other conglomerates (and their prepaid funds). For example, SCI at one time owned more than 60 percent of Arbor, of which it eventually sold off portions to J.C. Clarke of Toronto and others.

Distasteful practices have evolved, in my opinion, such as paying commission on the sale of caskets and other services at the time of a death and encouraging funeral home employees to "push" the most expensive caskets as a way of making more money for themselves. High-pressure sales tactics are the last thing anyone needs to encounter when they're dealing with the death of a family member.

There have also been several cases involving questionable advertising. One billboard campaign in particular, which Arbor used, and which we successfully fought to have taken down in Ottawa, had a picture of a casket with the phrase,

"Think outside the box." I heard many complaints from families we were working with at that time, as the advertisement was making every funeral provider in Ottawa look callous.

Several factors helped the conglomerates gain a foothold in the funeral business, and this was partly due to a generational change. By the 1980s, the owners of many independent funeral homes in North America had reached retirement age. As a result, an unprecedented number of small, family-run firms went up for sale. Many of these funeral homes had been established in city centres, and over the years, the value of the land on which these homes stood had appreciated considerably. Therefore, anyone who might be interested in buying would need to have extensive resources. There was also speculation that the "death care" industry would eventually be a growth market, because of the aging population. The conglomerates saw an opportunity to expand, and had the necessary capital to invest. I sometimes wonder if they ever looked beyond these two factors.

Charlie Hulse and Keith Playfair decided that there must be a better way. They had not founded their business on the cornerstone of independent ownership just to watch it be taken over by a faceless corporation. They felt they owed it to the community that had been supporting them for forty years. Therefore, Charlie and Keith developed a formula that would keep the funeral home locally owned, even with the high cost of land.

Some smaller, family-run businesses had been selling to their employees, but it was unheard of at the time for a larger business to do so. Charlie and Keith were recognized as the first bigger business owners to perfect this formula, and when they sold to their employees, it was in newspapers all across Canada. Their combination of imagination and willingness allowed Hulse and Playfair to retire with the knowledge that their funeral home would remain locally owned.

The first funeral home in Ottawa (and one of the first in Canada) to be bought by a conglomerate was Racine, Robert & Gauthier. Horace Racine and Marcel Robert were both accomplished and well-known funeral directors in the city. I always thought of them as the Charlie Hulse and Keith Playfair of the French-Canadian community. Horace and Marcel were leaders, and had built up a sizeable firm, which had been faithfully serving the French community in the Ottawa area for decades. This was in a time, since gone by, when citizens associated funeral homes with various religious beliefs. Hulse & Playfair were thought of as a Protestant business, while Racine, Robert & Gauthier were primarily Roman Catholic. Thankfully, society has evolved to a point where these sorts of distinctions are not real to most people anymore.

In the 1960s, SCI offered to buy out Horace and Marcel, and they accepted the offer. A few years after the sale, I ran into Mr. Racine at a charity function at the Château Laurier Hotel, and he said something I've never forgotten.

"Brian, I have to tell you, I made a mistake by selling. I got stock options and a good chunk of money, but my firm has never been the same. Charlie Hulse and Keith Playfair have it right."

After Racine, Robert & Gauthier sold, the business started having troubles, and the number of their funerals fell dramatically. The French-Canadian community didn't seem to accept the American conglomerate.

The funeral industry was shocked when Arbor (Trillium) was able to gain a foothold in our firm. Just about everyone working in funeral service knew Charlie Hulse's thoughts about large corporations making their way into the funeral business, and my opinions were no secret, either. If the primary focus is to make the greatest return for the shareholder, I'm certainly not the chief executive officer that you want. When it comes to choosing between making a greater profit and providing a greater service, we provide service every time, and that's why we have lasted since 1925. While everyone has to eat, and there are high costs associated with running a twenty-four-hour service industry, the return on investment we earn doesn't wind up in Texas or Toronto; it stays in our community.

As soon as Tricky Dickie, my new partner of seven months, sold his shares to Arbor, the local media saw an opportunity to make it into a story. Charlie Greenwell called me from CTV.

"You've been promoting family ownership all these years," he began, "and here you are in bed with a conglomerate."

"I'm still promoting family ownership."

"All right, Brian, but you've got to tell me, do they own the whole thing?"

"No, the McGarrys are majority owners."

I can't remember how many times I had this same conversation with other reporters, or with families and inquisitive friends.

Dealing with Arbor was challenging to say the least. We clashed almost immediately and continued to do so for the entire time we were partners. A few weeks after our partnership was finalized, we found ourselves on opposite sides of a Select Committee at Queen's Park in Toronto. The committee had been set up to look into the practice of telephone solicitation and door-to-door sales, which some funeral service providers had been using. Arbor had been employing this practice themselves, and I found it completely distasteful as some of the telephone solicitation had been aimed at elderly citizens in seniors' residences. We had a petition signed by community leaders in Ottawa (including Maureen McTeer, lawyer, long-time friend, and spouse of former prime minister Joe Clark), and we were invited by the Select Committee to present our case; representatives from Arbor were there arguing to continue the practice. At one point, one of the MPPs sitting nearby looked down at the file and made the connection.

"Aren't you guys partners?" she asked.

"Well, they're minority shareholders in our firm, but we have differing opinions."

"How is that going to go over?"

"I guess we'll find out."

In the end, we were able to stop the telephone solicitation, but it certainly set the tone for what would become a long and difficult relationship.

There were always three of us on the Hulse, Playfair & McGarry Board: Sharon McGarry, myself, and a revolving door of representatives from Arbor. Any debates were decided by a vote, and it must have been frustrating for the folks from Arbor, because more often than not the decision would be two-to-one in our favour. For the first few years our corporate partners didn't send a funeral director as their representative; they sent one of their financial officers, and this spoke volumes about their focus.

The first representative they sent was a pleasant fellow. He would come down every few months, and we'd have meetings, go over the books, and look at the business in general. Arbor's man was a good-natured guy and after a while we became friends. I think he looked forward to his visits to Ottawa, even though whenever we had a vote, the decision usually went against him. He never let the differences we had in business carry over into our personal relationship; this is something I have always respected in good businesspeople. He had worked with us for a couple of years when, one day, he called me from Toronto quite upset.

"Brian, I walked into the office this morning and found my door locked. I've been dismissed."

"What happened?"

"I really don't know, but I'm gone. I have to pack up my office and they're going to walk me out . . ."

I remember wondering if it had anything to do with the fact that we had become friends. I never found out, but that's the way the corporate world works sometimes.

Arbor replaced their financial man with a funeral director. I was hoping that he might be more willing to see our firm from a non-corporate perspective, but his background seemed to make very little difference. Except for the odd minor detail, the decisions were still two votes to one in our favour. I think Arbor's strategy was to wait us out, perhaps thinking that they would eventually wear us down and force us into selling.

Every so often I'd get a call from Arbor's head office. "So, Brian, you're a year older now, are you ready to sell?"

"No, no, I've got lots of life in me, yet!"

"I know how cold those winters are up there in Ottawa, wouldn't you prefer to be in Florida?"

"That's awfully considerate of you, but I don't think we'll be going anywhere for quite some time."

"Well, just making sure you know that the door is still open."

There wasn't an overt animosity between Arbor and us, but there were constant differences, due mainly to the fact that they had placed their emphasis on profit. We have always judged our employees by the number of thank-you letters they receive, as opposed to what kind of sales figures they have. We have to make a living, but we're careful to make sure that a family doesn't overbuy. We do have bonuses, and we'll sometimes send an employee and their family to a nearby resort for a weekend, if he or she has worked hard and gone beyond what is required. We don't give bonuses, however, based on how many expensive caskets a person has sold. Our focus, which goes back to the days of Charlie Hulse and Keith Playfair, is all about service. We maintain that the families we deal with purchase funerals and cremations from us; we don't sell to them, and I think people appreciate that there is no pressure to buy above their means.

Arbor would call me from Toronto and when I picked up the phone they'd say, "It's head office calling."

"Head office of what, exactly?"

There would be a pause, and they would say, "Arbor."

"You might be the head office of Arbor, but you're now talking to Hulse, Playfair & McGarry, and our head office is here in Ottawa, on McLeod Street."

Now, of course, we were just one of a hundred funeral homes that Arbor had an interest in, and this poor person had to call every month to "get our numbers." I would tease the rep, and eventually that person stopped saying "head office."

Being in partnership with a conglomerate did give us an opportunity to work with funeral homes in other parts of the country that were also part of their organization, but I soon found that I didn't particularly want to work with some of their branches. If a death occurred in another city and we were asked to bring the remains back to Ottawa, I found myself oftentimes contacting an independent firm in that city to help us instead of the Arbor branch. Arbor didn't like this policy, but I refused to deal with a funeral home simply based on a financial arrangement. I would always choose the people I thought would best serve our families, funeral homes we had previously worked and had established a good rapport with.

I don't think the conglomerates are wrong in everything they do, but their approach is very different from ours. When our partnership with Arbor started, there were only two other funeral homes in Canada where they held minority ownership, and it wasn't long before they were able to secure a majority—we were the lone holdouts. I believe Arbor thought it would only be a matter of time before we sold to them; they had the resources and were prepared to wait for us to tire of the arrangement. It was frustrating, because the prices being paid for funeral homes continued to climb to the point where I thought we would never be able to afford to buy them out. I had to resign myself to the idea that if Arbor ever did sell, it would probably be to another conglomerate. It looked like we were stuck with a corporate partner in one form or another, but they were also stuck with us.

The entire process, from the time Tricky Dickie came on board to "help" me, until the partnership with Arbor was formalized, was stressful for everyone at our funeral home. One of my former partners was angry that I had "allowed" a conglomerate in, but of course Sharon and I had no choice. Many of our staff members didn't like the new situation and they didn't like the way the arrangement had transpired; I don't blame them. Keith Shaver, former president of our firm and a true gentleman, was the first to leave, and he died not long after. I remember thinking that the situation at the funeral home may have broken his heart, as Keith had not hidden his disappointment. Laird Barclay was the next partner to retire and, finally, Alex Caldwell. Alex's last day was difficult. I watched him pace around the funeral home, and it was disquieting. He sat in the chapel for a while, then got up and walked into the clergy office and thumbed through some papers, then went back to the chapel. He seemed very anxious. Finally, I stopped him.

"Alex, you know you don't have to leave."

"Yes, I do, Brian. This arrangement with Arbor just isn't going to work."

It was upsetting because I knew Alex didn't want to go, and frustrating because there was nothing I could have done to stop Arbor from getting in. Sharon and I didn't have the necessary financial resources, nor did anyone else. Alex and I haven't been close since that time, and it's one of my greatest disappointments. We had been good friends, even vacationing together on occasion. To this day, he's still angry about it. He was in his sixties when Arbor came in and was just getting ready to retire. He saw them coming and perhaps he thought he could have kept them out by getting some resources himself. We only talked about it on a couple of occasions. One time, sitting in an office, he asked me, "Do you not think there was another way to keep them out?"

"Alex, we're talking millions of dollars. Neither you nor I have that kind of money. Sharon and I were very fortunate to get the extra 3 percent to be in a majority position, and needed a lot of help to do it."

I still see him socially, but the friendship is not what it was. My hope is that someday we can go for a beer and put it behind us.

Throughout the entire ordeal, however, I maintained that Sharon and I would never sell to Arbor, a promise we kept.

Our competition in Ottawa was only too happy to point out the fact that we were partly owned by a conglomerate and often overstated the case that we were entirely "taken-over." The very day after the partnership was signed, we found ourselves under attack. It wasn't long after Arbor came in that three of our competitors began publishing ads in the local papers denouncing what they saw as a corporate buyout. Up to that point, we had been relatively good friends with most of the other funeral homes in town. There had always been amicable competition, but as soon as Arbor was in, Andy Doyle, who owned McEvoy-Shields funeral home, got in touch with some of the board members of National Selected Morticians (they've since changed their name to Selected Independent Morticians).

NSM was an American-based association that represented independent funeral homes across North America, and both Andy's firm and ours were members. Andy called their head office in Chicago, and the following day I received a phone call from them. They got straight to the point.

"From what we can gather, you're going to have to drop your membership in our organization."

"I'm not surprised to get the call, but do you know all the details? The McGarrys are still majority owners here."

"Oh, that wasn't explained to us."

"It's a fact. It's not a huge majority, but it's still a controlling share."

As a result, we weren't kicked out of the organization, but we eventually had to resign because, technically, each city is to have only one representative funeral home. They made an exception in Ottawa, because Hulse, Playfair & McGarry and McEvoy-Shields had such a good business relationship that we were both granted memberships. However, after finding out that we still qualified as an independent funeral home and weren't going to be kicked out of the organization, Andy began to make an issue out of the one-funeral-home-per-city policy. While we had an equal claim to be the Ottawa representatives in the association, I decided that it wasn't worth all the trouble of fighting to keep our membership. I didn't want to sit at the same table with a guy who felt strongly that we shouldn't be there, so I resigned voluntarily. Ironically, only a few years later, Andy Doyle would sell his funeral home in its entirety to SCI of Houston, Texas. Racine, Robert & Gauthier had already sold to the same conglomerate, and Kelly would soon follow, by selling to Arbor (Trillium).

During the first year of our partnership with Arbor, our firm applied for membership in an organization called the Canadian Independent Group of Funeral Homes, which had been founded by Ottawa's own Lorne Kelly, of Kelly Funeral Homes. I admired Lorne. He had started this organization and built it up to more than 550 members, making it the biggest funeral service association in Canada. This tremendous growth was a testament to Lorne's unwavering commitment to fighting the corporatization of funeral service. He started the CIG as a way of developing solidarity among small, family-run funeral homes that were under attack by big conglomerates. Clearly, independent ownership was an issue that generated a lot of passion.

We were refused membership in the CIG due to our association with a conglomerate. This was a blow, since I felt as strongly as anyone about the importance of independence; the history of our firm had been guided by that very principle. However, Lorne Kelly wanted us kept out, and even went so far as changing his association's policy to do just that. Originally, as long as a funeral home was majority family-controlled, they could become a member. When we were immediately rejected, I discovered that they had recently changed the bylaws so that only those firms that were completely independent could be members. Even though I found this unfair, with an orchestrated change in bylaw, there was no recourse for appeal. We were forced to accept the association's decision. I realized then that our firm had ventured into a grey area—we weren't majority-owned by a conglomerate, yet neither were we entirely independent. We were completely on our own.

Lorne Kelly and Andy Doyle would continue to criticize us until they sold entirely to those they had complained about for years, a fact that is not without its ironies, but that was just the beginning.

McEvoy-Shields had followed our tradition of bringing on their employees as partners, one of whom was Andy Doyle. Eventually, Andy was able to buy out all his partners, making him sole owner. So, as soon as Andy and Lorne found out that Arbor had gained a foothold in our funeral home, they went after us in public. Andy took out print ads that verged on libel. I don't like conglomerates, either, but I wouldn't print what he did. The ads implied that it was the end of Hulse & Playfair and that the conglomerates had taken us over. They detailed bad experiences that some families had with other funeral homes owned by Arbor, and then stated that this could now be expected from Hulse, Playfair & McGarry. The ads were blatantly inaccurate and led people to believe that we had completely sold out to a conglomerate.

Lorne Kelly was less overt, but nevertheless criticized us on his website where he wrote that Arbor had attained a "major shareholding" in our company. This was carefully worded so that anyone who read it would assume that Arbor was the majority owner. While it was correct that Arbor was a major shareholder, it was also misleading and likely a deliberate attempt to confuse people. Several clergypeople came to tell me that Lorne had spoken with them personally and had told them that we'd been bought out. One of Lorne's staff members was telling anyone who was interested that the McGarrys were only figureheads, and that things would never be the same at Hulse & Playfair. We took out counter ads; not to attack them, but to clearly explain the situation and reiterate that at our core, we were still an independent, family-owned funeral home.

These attacks went on for years. On one particular occasion, three local funeral homes—McEvoy-Shields, Tubman's, and Whelan's—got together and took out an ad in the *Ottawa Citizen*. It was during a time when a lot of takeovers were happening; Tubman's had seen an ad in an American paper that they thought applied to the situation in Ottawa. The theme of the ad was "Isn't it too bad another independent is gone?" The three funeral homes wanted the newspaper to print the original ad, only changing the name of the American firm to Hulse & Playfair. The *Citizen* printed it, but they made a mistake. Instead of revising it, they published the original in its entirety. It looked as though these three funeral homes in Ottawa were lamenting the loss of an independent firm in the southern United States!

The morning that ad appeared, my phone rang off the hook. CBC and CFRA, a local radio station, wanted me to comment. The advertisement had already become somewhat of a joke. I hadn't read the morning paper, yet, so I picked up a copy; sure enough, there it was. Even though the advertisement was changed the next day, the damage had been already done. I thought they would just pull the ad, especially after their embarrassment, but in some ways the mix-up gave their cause more prominence. They decided to run the revised copy, which of course was also inaccurate, but for different reasons. The ad was in the paper for several weeks before I finally ran out of patience. I could have sent a lawyer on my behalf, but I decided to visit the three funeral homes myself. I made appointments at all of them for a Saturday afternoon and went to speak to each of the owners.

"If that ad appears one more time, the next meeting you'll have will be with my lawyer."

They were all surprised to see me. It's one thing to attack someone in the newspaper, but another thing to face that person at your front door. The ad was not in the paper on Monday.

In the following years there would be many other similar ads. My visits that day did nothing to stop slander from appearing on websites, and being voiced in clergy cars on the way to the cemetery. Did these attacks do us any harm? Families certainly questioned us about ownership when they came into the funeral home. We told them the truth and citizens of Ottawa were understanding of our situation, remaining loyal. This only reinforced my belief that most people value local ownership, especially when dealing with the death of a person in their care. The question arises: "Do you really want someone from Texas burying your dead?"

At one time there was a great little restaurant on Bank Street called John's. The food was good, and you never knew whom you might run into. I often went there for lunch and got to know the owner quite well. One afternoon I went by and found the restaurant closed; this was odd, since it was the middle of the week. I later found out that the owner's wife had been killed in a car accident the night before. The visitation and funeral were being held at McEvoy-Shields—Andy Doyle's funeral home—and I went over to pay my respects to the restaurateur. While there, I ran into Andy and the two of us walked out together after I offered my condolences. As we were walking down the stairs, something popped into my mind. I'd recently heard that two of Andy's good friends had sold to conglomerates in Texas. Chris Markie in Niagara had sold his family's funeral home to SCI, making him a lot of money and enabling him to retire as a young man. Soon after, John Morrison, who had inherited his dad's funeral business, the Rosar-Morrison funeral home in Toronto, also sold.

"Can you believe that John Morrison and Chris Markie sold out?" I exclaimed. "John was a member of the National Selected Morticians, and he sold to the Americans."

Andy just looked at me and didn't respond. I went home that night wondering if he was well. As it turns out, he was in the middle of negotiations with the same conglomerate, SCI, and a short time later also sold to them. I was shocked and disappointed when I found out.

Some time later, I ran into Andy at the Rideau Club. "Do you ever reflect back on the advertisements you took out against me?" I asked him.

"You know, Brian, I knew you'd get around to asking me that someday, but business is business."

"No, the trouble with business is that it's not always business. Did you ever imagine that you'd ignore your principles and sell out? You have betrayed your former business partners, who could have sold out rather than giving you the chance to buy them out."

"My employees couldn't afford to buy . . ."

"Come on, Andy, my employees could afford it and they're no different from your employees."

"Well, I did get a lot of money . . ."

"I know that, but don't you ever reflect?"

He just shrugged his shoulders and never really answered the question.

The greatest shock of my corporate life happened one day when I was at Beechwood Cemetery for a meeting with their general manager. At one point during the conversation he said, "Did you hear the news? The rumour is that Lorne Kelly is selling to Arbor."

"What!? That's ridiculous."

I didn't believe it. The idea that the founder of the Canadian Independent Group of Funeral Homes was selling his business to the very same people he had railed against for so many years . . . It was impossible for me to imagine.

Over the next few weeks the rumours of an impending sale kept bubbling up all over. I finally decided to phone Larry Kelly, Lorne's son, to find out the truth.

Larry's a nice guy, very bright and an accomplished lawyer in the city. In fact, Larry and I had met on several occasions to discuss the possibility of he and his brother purchasing their dad's business. He wasn't in his office when I called, so I left a message on his answering service, "Hi, Larry. There are rumours that your dad might be selling the funeral home. Now, I know you don't need a lot of advice from me, but if the rumours are untrue, then you might want to do something about it, because it's getting out into the community."

Larry never called me back.

Sure enough, within a couple of weeks, the rumour was confirmed. Lorne Kelly had sold all of his funeral homes in Ottawa to Arbor. Obviously, his sons didn't purchase and five senior employees weren't even given a chance to consider the idea of a Charles Hulse-Keith Playfair "formula" for employee ownership. It was a sad day for the profession. A news release from Kelly's made the ambiguous announcement that Lorne had sold to a "Canadian organization."

This was true. Arbor is a Canadian conglomerate, the same conglomerate that we had been forced to partner with, a relationship that Lorne had decried for many years. The announcement also mentioned that Lorne would be staying on at the firm. It failed to mention, however, that SCI of Houston had owned more than 60 percent of Arbor's common shares.

Lorne's actions drew criticism from the funeral service community. You can imagine the talk around the boardroom table at the Canadian Independent Group of Funeral Homes. Lorne himself was quoted as saying that he felt "a dreadful loneliness" after the sale was completed.

There is a man by the name of Harald Gunderson who lives in Calgary and publishes a magazine about the funeral business. He's a great guy and a genuine Alberta cowboy. He prints the latest news and rumours that come up in the business. If he knows something, he'll print it, especially if it has to do with the conglomerates. Gunderson and Lorne Kelly were good friends, and the news of the sale sent shock waves through the entire profession across Canada.

Gunderson dug up and reprinted an old interview he had done with Dan Scanlan, chairman of the board of Arbor Memorial Services. In that interview, there were details of a conversation between Mr. Scanlan and Lorne Kelly back in the 1970s. Lorne had promised that when he sold his funeral home, Scanlan would have the opportunity to purchase. This was another disappointment. How could Lorne have promised to sell to a conglomerate so many years ago and then go on to found an organization dedicated to independent ownership? It just didn't make any sense.

Again, Kelly's could have followed Charlie Hulse and Keith Playfair's formula by selling to senior staff. Five of their staff members had been with the funeral home for more than thirty years. They had dedicated their lives to Lorne Kelly and could certainly have purchased the firm and provided Lorne with a reasonable profit. This was never an option.

I checked Lorne's website after the sale. He had kept up all the information attacking conglomerates, including Arbor; it wasn't updated for months. Eventually, Arbor Memorial Services discovered the page on Kelly's website and removed the offending criticism.

The fact that Lorne sold out to a conglomerate had a detrimental effect on the association he had founded. Ironically, Lorne was forced to withdraw from his own creation. At one time, there were about 550 members of the Canadian

Independent Group, but after Lorne sold out, they began to lose members and the organization is now struggling.

After Kelly's was sold, one of their key employees, Peter Vallee, resigned and joined our firm. Others followed Peter to our firm, or joined various independent funeral homes in Ottawa. These were people who believed in independent ownership and were disillusioned with what they saw as a betrayal. Peter told me that their staff had been hearing the same rumours as I did leading up to the sale. They couldn't believe it, because Lorne would often preach to them about how terrible the conglomerates were, and how awful it was that they got a foothold in Hulse & Playfair. At one point, a group of Kelly's employees had considered making an offer to buy the company themselves. They knew of the formula we had used and thought they might have a chance to do the same — if they had been given the opportunity to raise enough money to purchase a majority share like we had done, it would have been better than the alternative. Lorne always said that he wanted to sell his business to the people who had helped him get to where he was, the employees who had dedicated years to the firm and whom he referred to as "family" on many occasions.

Eventually, this group of employees approached Lorne, asking if there was any truth to the gossip. When Lorne told them he was indeed selling the business, the employees immediately asked if they could buy in. That's when Lorne was forced to admit to the promise he made to Dan Scanlan in 1972. Many of his employees felt they couldn't stay on. As already mentioned, Peter Vallee joined our firm and he has since been invited to become our partner.

As soon as Arbor took over at Kelly's, things changed rapidly. One of their first steps was to take nearly every casket out of the selection rooms (i.e., Canadian-made) and replace them with their own choices, the vast majority being American products. Lorne must have found that offensive. His firm was handling 1,600 services a year, so obviously he knew the community he was serving, but Arbor didn't see it that way.

It's a well-known fact that when a conglomerate purchases a business, it often downsizes the staff. Lorne did as much as he could to protect people's jobs, but as soon as the ink was dry on the contract, a sizeable number of employees were laid off. Some of those staff members had been there for many years. Arbor also tried to get some of the senior funeral directors, people who had been working there for thirty or more years, to take on additional jobs, like mowing the lawn!

A sign was also placed in the arrangement office suggesting early payment. I was told that the day that sign went up, Lorne flew into such a rage he insisted his name be taken off the building. One of his former employees quipped dryly, "Lorne, you've sold your name."

I suspect Lorne's anger was directed mostly at himself. It's a disappointing way to end a spectacular career. He received $24 million dollars from the sale of his business, but I think he soon realized that it wasn't just the firm that was on the auction block, it was also his lifelong proclamation of the benefits of family ownership. Lorne died five years after the sale to Arbor (Trillium).

I wasn't surprised when I heard about the changes that Arbor instituted at Kelly's. They had tried a similar conversion with us. When Arbor wanted us to purchase all of our cars from a dealership they dealt with in Toronto, we replied, "Who out of Toronto is going to want to purchase a funeral from us? We want to support our neighbours."

Arbor wasn't interested in nurturing local business relationships. In fact, they wanted me to buy nearly everything from Toronto, and most of the caskets from Batesville, Indiana. It might cost more to buy locally, but isn't it worth it? We like to buy Canadian products, and we didn't care that Arbor had a deal with a casket company in the United States. We are by no means anti-American, but we have always supported our community and I wanted to continue to do so in order to support Canadian manufacturers and our way of life (e.g., health care).

These examples illustrate the corporate mentality—profit is the goal even if it means supporting companies whose proceeds leave Canada. However, this kind of policy can have serious consequences. One can appreciate supporting our American neighbours in a global economy, but there has to be a healthy economic balance. You can go broke trying to save money.

I sat on Arbor's sister board (Trillium) for several years, and it was an interesting experience. I thought that the best way to control the destiny of our company was by being proactive and trying to understand the corporate idea firsthand. One thing became clear very quickly: the constant focus on dollars. At every meeting, they would hand out all kinds of awards and plaques and cash bonuses, all related to the profit generated for the company. The idea that a funeral home's primary mission is to help families get through the death of a loved one is drowned out by the ka-ching! of a cash register. Maybe that's why things transpired the way they did.

When you're a conglomerate, you can lose track of the very basics in funeral service. You can't be everywhere at once, so efficiencies are introduced and standards can fall. I opened up the newspaper one morning to discover that Arbor was implicated in a scandal in Calgary involving Leyden's funeral home, which they had purchased several years before. Arbor had tried to control the damage by keeping the scandal as quiet as possible, hoping to deal with it as an internal matter, but it was leaked to the newspapers and quickly became a controversy of national proportions.

After a five-month investigation by the Calgary police and Alberta Government Services, charges were laid against the general manager of Leyden's and against Arbor. The scandal swirled around allegations that an employee at the funeral home had been selling cremation containers, removing the bodies at the crematorium, placing the remains on a piece of plywood, or similar, for the cremation, and then reselling the original cremation containers. There were also allegations that the funeral home had been raising their prices for members of the Asian community in Calgary. When an Asian family arrived to arrange a funeral, they would be quoted an inflated price, which would be reduced over the course of the meeting, giving the appearance of a discount. The charges were understandably serious.

A warrant was issued for the arrest of the general manager, but the problem went much deeper than the bad judgment of one employee. There was so much pressure placed on the employees to make a profit and show a return on investment that a misguided employee started to look for ways to cut costs. I don't believe that Arbor's head office in Toronto told them to do it, but they were certainly responsible for applying pressure on the funeral home to meet sales targets. In fact, during the investigation, several employees at Leyden's admitted that this was the case. In the end, the money from the switched cremation containers wasn't going into the pockets of the employees directly; so, for the most part, the employees weren't gaining financially from it.

This scandal underscored how the drive for profit can undermine the quality of service. The *Calgary Herald* followed the story closely as it wound its way through the various investigations. Mr. Leyden actually called me at one point after he sold to Arbor. He was still emotionally attached to his former business.

"Do you know what's happening at my firm?"

I later had a very revealing conversation with one of Arbor's representatives. This fellow would come up and see us occasionally, and he had the annoying habit of walking around the funeral home like he owned the place personally. One night we were going out for dinner and he said to me, "Brian, do you keep your prices high for Asian families?"

Now, that's pretty close to saying, "Raise your prices for Asian families."

"How do you mean?" I asked.

"Well, you know they buy well and they always want to bargain, so it just makes sense to keep your prices high."

"Wait a minute. First of all, my wife is Asian . . ."

I'm sure he knew this detail, but it had obviously slipped his mind.

". . . and secondly, our prices are the same for everybody."

I could tell he realized he'd made a mistake but I continued, "Isn't this what got Leyden's into trouble?"

"Well, that's exaggerated. It was blown out of proportion."

The difference was that in Calgary they allegedly said, "change the prices," whereas I was being offered a subtle suggestion that keeping the prices high might be a good idea.

I stood by Arbor during the scandal. I don't believe they ordered anyone to change caskets before cremation. At the same time, I told Arbor they should have let me know of the trouble before it got into the newspapers. I had people coming into our funeral home asking if we were associated with the business "out West" that was changing people's caskets. Our competition was only too happy to let people know of the inadvertent relationship that existed between our two firms. There were people who saw the word "Arbor" and assumed, "That's McGarry's place . . ." Of course, it had nothing to do with us.

I phoned our senior contact at Arbor. "I'll support you because no one ever asked us to replace a casket for cremation, but if the question comes up about inflating prices for the Asian community I'm not going to lie about it." Consequently, I was never called during the investigation. The suit launched by bereaved families affected in Calgary was eventually settled out of court, but not before there had been several disciplinary hearings.

It was a terrible time. Most major newspapers in the country carried a version of the story. It made all funeral homes look bad. The events in Calgary indirectly affected all funeral professionals, particularly us, because of our affiliation. The people of Ottawa stuck with us, though, and I think this has a lot to do with the fact that we have always been close to our community. People know us personally and they trust us.

The whole Calgary experience had tried my patience. I called Arbor's head office and made an appointment. I told them that I wanted to make them an offer to buy them out. A few days later I found myself in a richly decorated conference room in Arbor's Toronto headquarters. I cut to the chase.

"Look, we've had it," I said. "No one in funeral service needs this publicity. I want out."

"I'm sorry, Brian, we have plans for your firm in Ottawa . . ."

"Not with me you don't."

The discussion got heated. I was determined to find a way out. "Either I'm going or you're going. But before you answer that, you're going."

"It'll cost you big dollars."

The market was still fairly high, and I was worried that they might keep fighting for years, but the prices being paid for funeral homes had peaked a few years earlier and were starting to drop. I also knew Arbor had to settle with at least forty bereaved families over the Calgary fiasco.

"I have no idea what your settlement is in Calgary, but this sale might help you."

"Well, give us a figure."

The fact that they were even ready to negotiate gave me a little confidence.

"I'll tell you what; we'll each write out our numbers, place them in envelopes, and pass them across the table."

I knew that we couldn't go up to where the prices had been, and that my figure had to be based on the reality of our business in Ottawa. As I was writing down my figure, I was hoping they wouldn't try to double their money. We exchanged envelopes. I opened their offer and discovered that their figure was only 5 percent higher than mine. I looked across the table. "Well, you're a little high."

"Brian, you know very well we're in the ballpark."

They must have needed the money more than I thought—they wanted to sell (and likely had already decided they would purchase Kelly Funeral Homes in Ottawa).

"OK, we'll buy you out."

It was done quickly. An ordeal that had gone on for seventeen years was over in the time it takes to write a signature, although the paperwork at our lawyer's office in Ottawa covered the entire eighteen-foot length of a boardroom table. Within a few weeks, Arbor was gone and we were back to being 100-per-cent family-owned. It was quite a day in the Canadian private sector, the little guy buying out the big guy. It made the news, and we received letters and phone calls from people all over the country, congratulating us.

We didn't know it at the time, but the economic bubble that had driven up the prices of funeral homes was about to burst. In retrospect, it had to because the market had got out of control. In the late '90s, the conglomerates became extremely aggressive, creating a lot of competition to buy up as many small, family-owned businesses as they could. Consequently, the prices became inflated and the conglomerates began accumulating huge debt loads.

When Arbor bought a small funeral home, they also acquired that firm's prepayment trusts. As a result, they experienced a jump in net worth, which triggered a rise in the value of their stock price. The higher stock value increased their credit with the banks, allowing them to access bigger loans, which were used to buy more funeral homes, and so the cycle continued.

This strategy worked well partly because interest rates were so low at the time. Fuelled by technology and international trade agreements, the 1990s were a decade of unprecedented growth across the entire economy. The boom lasted until the recession of 2001, after which interest rates began to rise to combat growing inflation. Suddenly, the conglomerates' profits dropped considerably. At the peak of their buying frenzy, the conglomerates were engaged in bidding wars for funeral homes without stopping to consider that the income being generated by these businesses could never pay for the debt.

During those boom years, the conglomerates never stopped trying to buy us out. It got to the point of being ridiculous. Every so often, one of the three big corporations would send someone down to see us. The offers started at around $22 million, and went up every time. The next offer was $27 million, then $32 million, eventually peaking at $39 million!

I remember the last offer we had from Arbor. John Earle came up from Toronto and we had a meeting. John's a nice man, who has since retired, but we knew that whenever he came around, we could expect to have an offer placed in front of us. The previous offer Arbor had made had been $38 million. He came into the office and sat down with Sharon, Brett, and me and presented the latest offer: $39 million.

This is an amazing amount of money. I don't know what kind of calculator they were using at Arbor's head office, but it must have been sprinkled with fairy dust. How they ever figured they could recuperate that amount of money with the annual return on investment we generate here . . . We would have to handle every funeral in Ottawa for the next twenty years! It was simply inconceivable. The only way Arbor could have made it work financially would have been by selling off the properties and moving our Central Chapel business out to the suburbs. Hulse, Playfair & McGarry would have disappeared over time, and there was no way that I was going to watch that happen. We didn't even have to think about it.

"John, we've made up our minds. We're not selling."

I thought he might have cried. "Brian, Sharon, Brett[1] . . . are you really going to send me back to Toronto to tell the Scanlans that we put another million dollars on the table, and you're still not selling?"

"Well, as much as I like seeing you, John, you can solve that problem by not coming back up again."

He couldn't believe it. After he left, I looked at Brett and Sharon and wondered if we were making the right decision. I certainly don't want to make it look like we're saints—we had talked about selling. Sharon and I could have retired in our early fifties, and I'd be lying if I said it wasn't tempting. However, I remembered a conversation I had with John Cole. He owns a cemetery in Ottawa and hopefully is committed to independent ownership. He said, "The day you sell to Arbor or whoever else, and you've got your pockets full of money and you walk out onto McLeod Street, you're going to say to yourself, 'Who am I now?'"

We would have been wealthy, but we would also have been unhappy knowing we had betrayed the philosophy of Charles Hulse and Keith Playfair.

The economic bubble burst soon after and that kind of money isn't being offered anymore. In fact, after 2001, most of the conglomerates found themselves in financial trouble. Loewen's, once the second-largest funeral service provider in the world, is gone. They were bought out by SCI, and the story is legendary.

Ray Loewen had a ship—not just a simple boat, but a ship equipped with

---

1   Our daughter, Erin, was too young to participate.

a helicopter landing pad. (This alone illustrates just how unrealistic things became.) Mr. Loewen invited Bob Waltrip, major shareholder of SCI, on board for a party and to discuss business. Loewen wanted to buy SCI; Mr. Waltrip agreed to attend because he wanted to buy Loewen's. They were somewhere off the coast of Vancouver when, from what I understand, negotiations became heated, eventually resulting in a physical confrontation. Ray had to call in his helicopter to take Bob off the boat, and afterwards they became bitter rivals.

Unfortunately for Ray Loewen, he later got himself into some trouble in Mississippi with a funeral home he had bought. What appeared to be an inconsequential lawsuit over a seemingly small contractual obligation turned into a nightmare. The judge on the case ruled against Mr. Loewen, and the settlement was for a mind-boggling $170 million dollars! As a result, Loewen's was in huge financial trouble, and Bob Waltrip and SCI bought up most of their holdings. It must have been a bitter pill for Ray to swallow.

There is something wrong with this scenario—the buying and selling of people's prepayment funds, which aren't really assets because they're not fluid, but the banks see it as guaranteed future business. If someone prepays a funeral, they are putting that money and trust in you, and they have chosen you for a reason. It seems wrong to use people's trust as a commodity.

Of course, anyone who prearranges a funeral with you has the right to move to another funeral home at any time, but it is a process. A letter of notice must be written, and you have to get the funds transferred from one funeral home to another. Often people will decide not to bother; but if they are unhappy with the service, the next time they have a death in the family, they might very well go somewhere else. We have been experiencing this since Lorne Kelly sold to Arbor. Many families who had been dealing with Kelly's for generations have come to us since it was sold.

SCI didn't escape the economic downturn, either, and eventually were forced to file for bankruptcy protection in the United States; Arbor also had their challenges. As a result of restructuring efforts, the conglomerates had to sell off some of their properties, sometimes selling them back to the very people they had bought from.

Paperman's funeral home in Montreal is a good example of this. The Paperman family sold their business to Loewen's for a large sum of money, and then after the crash, they were able to buy it back for much less. Paperman's was well-known in Montreal's Jewish community, but after the company was sold to the conglomerate, their business dropped off. When Loewen's was looking at properties to sell, the Montreal funeral home seemed like a good candidate, because their numbers had flattened. This is not a coincidence. I believe that when a family is dealing with the death of a loved one, there are many people who prefer to go to a funeral home that is owned by someone in their community.

I don't think the trend is going to reverse completely. There will always be conglomerates in the funeral business, but the majority of funeral homes across North America are still independently owned. As well, the largest funeral homes in Edmonton, Calgary, Toronto, and now Ottawa are all family-owned. This is a fact that people are aware of and remain interested in.

I don't want to paint all the conglomerates with the same brush, but I believe service can suffer when there's no ownership presence in the city where a funeral home is located.

Even after we were forced into partnership with Arbor, other conglomerates would still make appointments to come see us. They were constantly trying to usurp each other. At a certain point I realized that it wasn't about funerals anymore; it was about one big company trying to use our funeral home as a battleground in their fight to take over a rival. It wasn't about Mrs. Brown's prearrangement and how she trusted Charlie Hulse; it had become "How can I use that trust as leverage to make more money?" Yes, the conglomerates want to please the Brown family, but they're motivated by shareholder return and the bottom line as opposed to a genuine desire to help people. All too often trust and quality service are left behind.

It was the conglomerates' single-minded focus on profit that got them into the predicament of carrying huge debt loads. To compensate, they have had to raise their prices and start pressuring their employees to make sales. In my opinion, the fiasco in Calgary was a direct result of this policy. The funeral business is not like any other business. If you find out that your daughter has been killed in a car accident, do you want to go to a big box store, or do you want to go to the people who live in your community? It's a lesson the conglomerates have been slow to learn.

Why do I want to preserve our Canadian independence? It's a feeling, an accomplishment. I see Hulse, Playfair & McGarry Funeral Homes and Cremation Centres as a Canadian institution. We've held many historical events in our chapel, and we have been an important thread in the tapestry of our nation's capital for almost nine decades. You can't put a dollar amount on the respect that we have in the community.

Preserving our independence is also about honouring the promise I made to Charles Hulse and Keith Playfair, and it's about adhering to our principles. At the end of the day, isn't that all we have?

Who knows what the future will bring. Family firms will be sold, and conglomerates will rise and fall, but one thing is certain: Hulse, Playfair & McGarry will remain independent as long as I have anything to say about it.

Hulse, Playfair & McGarry management team, with Yousuf Karsh's famous photograph of Winston Churchill overlooking our deliberations. 1990s.

Barry Schwerdfeger.

CHAPTER 10

Tricky Dickie

I was introduced to Tricky Dickie[2] by Andy Doyle, former owner of McEvoy-Shields funeral home in Ottawa; his place was sold to SCI in Houston, Texas. McEvoy-Shields had followed Hulse's model, bringing in employees as partners in order to remain independent; Andy had been given the same opportunity. Our two firms had a good history and often worked closely together, sharing cars and personnel whenever the need arose. However, McEvoy-Shields didn't do as much advertising as we did, so Mr. Shields would sometimes call up and thank us after we had placed an ad about prearrangement in the newspaper. He said it always caused a spike in his business!

Both Andy and I were members of Selective Morticians, an organization dedicated to promoting locally owned funeral homes. So even though we were competitors, we were good friends. In the early '80s, our relationship was so good that we brought our two firms together in a co-operative venture to build a new funeral home in the east end of Ottawa, on Ogilvie Road. We purchased the property from Robert Campeau, the Ottawa-based real estate developer who had bought a large department store in New York City a few months earlier. Mr. Campeau wanted to concentrate on expanding his business outside of Canada and had put some of his Ottawa holdings up for sale. Other than some isolated developments, there wasn't much on Ogilvie Road back then—mostly farms and cornfields—so we were able to get the property for a reasonable price.

Andy and I didn't really have the money to do this, and we weren't too sure how we were going to pay for it, but we signed on the dotted line anyway. So when we walked out of the realtor's office that day, we looked at each other and said, "OK, now what?"

Andy went to talk with Mr. McEvoy's widow to ask for a loan. She agreed and gave us a fair interest rate, and then we both went to our respective partners at the two funeral homes. We told them that we had purchased the property and wanted to build a funeral home on it, explaining that a partnership would help both firms. Andy and I believed in the idea so much that we were prepared to

---

2   Not his real name.

put ourselves on the line for it. Our partners decided to give the idea a chance, and over the next four years we developed a strong business relationship.

At the time, I was the youngest partner at Hulse & Playfair, with my three senior partners all in their late fifties or early sixties. There was no immediate urgency to find a solution for the problem of how we were going to fill in the gaps when the senior partners retired, but as most of the other employees at the funeral home were either not old enough, or without the necessary resources to buy into the firm as partners, I wanted to have a plan in place when the senior partners did retire.

Others were obviously thinking the same thing, so on one bright autumn day in 1987, when Andy and I were having lunch at a downtown restaurant and talking about the future, I wasn't surprised when he remarked, "Your partners are getting older, Brian, what are you going to do?"

"I'm still working on that one," I replied.

"You think you might try and buy them out on your own?"

"It's a possibility, I suppose."

"Do you have that kind of money?"

"Well, I guess I'm hopeful that the banks will help me out."

"They might . . . but they can be fickle, too. It sometimes seems that they'll only lend you money, if you prove to them that you don't need it!"

Andy was right; I couldn't be sure that any bank would take on the risk. I did have a few other options, though. There had been some discussion with a group of independent funeral homes from across Ontario who might join together and buy into Hulse & Playfair. It wasn't a bad option, but it certainly wouldn't have been my first choice. Even though all the firms involved were independent, I couldn't help feeling the arrangement wouldn't be much different from selling to corporate interests. It would just be a conglomerate of a different size. As Charlie had often said, it wasn't all about money, and my partners agreed. They were committed to independent ownership and agreed to stay on at the firm until we could find a workable solution. I just had to figure out how to make it happen.

I met with Carl Loten, an accountant friend of mine whom I knew through my membership in the Kiwanis Club. Carl was a great guy and a bean-counter if there ever was one. I asked him if he would look at the firm's partnership problem from a financial perspective, to see if there might be a way that I could buy out my partners on my own; he said he would. We got together over lunch, and I showed him all the figures. He helped me calculate what I would need as far as resources to buy the firm outright, and not surprisingly, we discovered that it would take a considerable amount of money to make the purchase happen. "Brian," he advised, considering the numbers and my finances, "if I were you, I'd stay right where you are."

"It's an option," I replied, "but I'd be taking a chance. When my partners retire, they'll have to sell to someone, and who knows who I'll end up working with?"

"True, but there is a certain amount of risk involved when you take on that kind of debt. You need to weigh your options."

I understood his perspective—buying out my partners was a risky venture— but I thought I should explore the possibility anyway. I scheduled a meeting with our bankers. They had worked on similar transactions in the past, but admitted it was risky and they would have to scrutinize the idea further before they could make a final decision. As it was, the McGarrys owned 16 percent of the operating company and none of the land. Sharon and I had our house and about $25,000 in the bank. So, from the bank's point of view, it didn't initially appear to be a safe investment.

Andy dropped in to see me after my meeting at the bank and suggested we go down to the Elgin Street Diner for lunch.

"I was hoping I wouldn't have to buy all three partners out at once," I said, "but they're all getting close to retirement."

Andy nodded, "You're in quite a bind there."

It was starting to look like I had no real options. If the bank couldn't help me, I would have to start looking outside the firm and deal with someone who might not be as dedicated to independent ownership. I would have to find someone willing to come in on a long-term basis, someone who would be willing to place our tradition of independence ahead of profit. The pressure was becoming evident. Andy and I discussed the problem at length. Finally, Andy was struck with an idea.

"You should talk to Dickie. He's put together a few deals like this across the province, and if he can't help you directly, he might have some insight on a solution."

I'd heard his name before. Dickie was well known in the funeral industry for his business acumen and his foresight. He had been only the second person in Ontario to develop a dedicated reception centre where families could meet with friends after the service. The first to do this was Gordon Glaves, who owned a funeral home in Brantford, Ontario. When Mr. Glaves started offering a space to hold a reception, many people in funeral service thought it was a ridiculous idea, insisting that no one would ever want to have a sandwich at a funeral home.

Up until that time, friends and family might go to the home of the deceased or family members after the funeral service was finished. Mr. Glaves recognized that this often meant the family had to worry about organizing a get-together in the middle of dealing with a death. He thought that if they could provide a space for families, and offer catering, then it might help to relieve some of the stress of a day that is arguably one of the most difficult a family must face. Mr. Glaves also noticed that the reception itself can have a positive effect, a time when family members can relax after the turmoil often experienced during the period between the death and the funeral. It's also a reminder for the family that their social network is still in place. In a small way, the reception represents a turning of the page.

Dickie heard about Mr. Glaves' reception room and saw the benefits right away. He went on to copy the idea for his funeral home, taking the idea one step further by building a separate facility. When the construction was finished, Dickie had built a beautiful, one-storey building, tastefully decorated throughout. He also incorporated additional office space for his funeral directors, and moved his casket selection room over. For many years afterwards, Dickie's reception centre was distinguished as the nicest in the province. This came as no surprise, as he is well known for his eye for detail and taste.

Dickie was also known for having bought, on more than one occasion, small, family-owned funeral homes, then flipping them for a profit. Although, to his credit, never selling to a conglomerate, always choosing to work with other independent businesses. At any rate, I felt his experience putting these deals together demonstrated his expertise in the matter and thought there would be no harm in at least sitting down and having a talk with him. After thinking about it for a day, I called Andy and asked him to set up a meeting between Dickie and me.

That first meeting took place at our West Chapel. Andy, Dickie, and I sat around a desk in one of the offices. I hadn't told my partners that I was getting together with Dickie, since at that time my intention was only to explore possible options.

Dickie is a portly man, and when he walked into the room, he reminded me of a bear walking on his hind legs, sort of a lumbering gait. Yet there was no hiding the fact that he was strictly business, and seemed more like a banker than a funeral director. I felt a bit uneasy around him; he was very direct and made you feel as though you were wasting his time. This aside, Andy and Dickie were close friends and their families knew each other, although in retrospect, they had never been business partners.

Dickie was already well acquainted with Hulse & Playfair. He knew quite a lot about the firm, so I don't think he ever imagined that he might one day be a partner. Our tradition of employee ownership was well known in our profession, and it was understood that I was meeting with him purely in the interest of finding a way to preserve that tradition. I needed to make an arrangement with an investor who could help carry us over until other partners could be brought up from within the firm, and I was hoping that Dickie might have some insight into how to do this.

We walked around the West Chapel. He knew our Central Chapel downtown, but hadn't seen our other funeral homes. The St. Laurent Chapel, which Andy and I had built together, was to remain separate from any deal I would make. Dickie was impressed with our facilities.

"You certainly keep your establishment in good shape," he remarked.

"Thanks. We pride ourselves on it."

"And your reputation is second-to-none." He smiled at Andy. "No offence to you, Andy."

Andy smiled back, "None taken."

I think Dickie immediately saw the possibility of his buying a share of the funeral home. As we walked, I explained the circumstances to him, stressing how important it was to me that the firm remained independent. He listened carefully, nodding his head. "As you know, Brian, I've got quite a bit of experience in situations like this, and if you let me, I think I can help you, personally."

"I'm sure you've got some great ideas, but I'd be lying if I said I wasn't concerned about the fact you've never stayed in one place very long after you've bought."

Dickie smiled warmly, "Well, Brian, Hulse & Playfair is rather special, and

I'm young enough to be able to make a commitment to you."

"I only really need about five years. By then, some of the younger staff will be able to become partners."

He thought about it for a moment. "Five years? That shouldn't be a problem."

"Well, if you can guarantee me that," I replied, "we can start talking about a partnership. I have no idea how we're going to get the banks to go with us, though."

"Just leave that to me."

Dickie had a keen mind for numbers, and after studying the company's books and looking at my finances, he knew quickly what we could handle. He was confident that we could buy out my partners, and after a couple of weeks, he came back with a plan. It looked realistic, but I wanted to take some time to consider it. A little while later, I had lunch with Andy again.

"Dickie's business plan looks good. He really seems to know what he's doing," I observed.

"He has put a lot of deals together over the years."

"What do you think, Andy?" I asked. "Should I bring him in as a partner?"

"It certainly would get you out of the bind you're in, and give you time to bring in other partners."

"That's true, but we've never had an outside investor here. I'm not sure how the senior partners are going to feel about it."

"Only one way to find out, I suppose."

Andy was right. I looked at the proposal one last time, recalculating all the numbers to the point that I finally felt it was worth bringing to my partners. There were four of us at the time—Alex Caldwell, Keith Shaver, Laird Barclay, and myself—and we were all good friends. The four of us sat down for a meeting, and I gave them each a copy of Dickie's proposal. Alex was irritated right away that I hadn't gone to him before inviting Dickie to offer a solution, but I knew he didn't have the resources to make a proposal—none of us did. We discussed it for several hours, and there was a certain amount of hesitation at first.

Dickie's reputation was a concern for all of us. One incident in particular stood out. Back in the late '70s, Dickie had bought a funeral home in a small Ontario community and soon after discovered that a large independent funeral home in Toronto wanted to expand into the same town. Dickie contacted the Toronto firm, found them very interested in buying, and without thinking twice, sold to them. What we didn't know at the time, but would discover later from his former accountant, was that whatever the selling price was, Dickie wanted to add on 25 percent. His accountant had bristled at the idea.

"There's no way that they could ever survive if they pay that kind of price," he said.

"Never mind, add it on," he ordered.

"I can't see them going for it."

"Look, they want this place badly, and I'm telling you they'll pay 25 percent over premium."

"If that's what you want to do, I can't stop you, but if I were working for them, I'd advise them not to go near it."

As it turned out, Dickie had been right, and the prospective purchaser accepted the inflated price. To me, the important part about this story was that it hadn't bothered Dickie to conduct business in this way. His motivation had nothing to do with serving families and establishing roots in the community. There was no emotional attachment at all, and his main focus had been on making money. Unfortunately, though, I didn't find out these details until it was too late.

My partners agreed to meet with Dickie, so that he could better explain his proposal. Dickie's reputation was still causing some apprehension, but they were willing to consider every option for the sake of the business.

Dickie didn't indulge in small talk. He would walk into a room, sit down, and get right to the point. At the meeting, he made a very good sales pitch. In the simplest terms, he proposed that he and I buy out my partners' operating company, and then, if possible we would also purchase the buildings. As a little guy from Wakefield, Quebec, this seemed like a daunting prospect, and hearing the proposal spoken aloud made the hair stand up on the back of my neck. The amount of money we would need to make the deal happen was overwhelming, but Dickie assured me that it could be done.

During the meeting, he also discussed other possible options, none of which was very appealing. At one point, Dickie spun the question around, asking my partners what their thoughts and plans were for the future and what possible solutions they might have. We all knew the situation; there weren't any junior partners who could step in. Doug Kennedy would have been the only one who might have been able to consider it, and he was close to my age, but as far as we knew, none of the other employees had the necessary financial resources to consider buying in, and no bank in the country would provide full financing to anyone.

Dickie had evaluated the situation and was able to articulate what we had all been thinking. My partners had been very accommodating; they hadn't put a great deal of pressure on me to find a solution because they wanted to see the firm continue in the Charles Hulse and Keith Playfair tradition. That being the case, it was painfully clear we needed a private investor, otherwise the firm would be in danger of being lost to outside interests. It was starting to look like Dickie's proposal could benefit everyone: my partners could retire comfortably and Dickie's promise of five years would give me enough time to bring up new partners from within the firm to replace them. Hulse & Playfair would remain independent, and when the time came and Dickie sold to the new partners, he would be able to make a profit and walk away. The numbers were adding up, and Dickie's experience with banks and financing was proving to be invaluable. It seemed as though everybody's interests could be accommodated.

There were still some reservations among my partners, but Dickie had clearly stated that he would remain with the company for a minimum of five years, a promise he was willing to put in writing. This was reassuring, and it seemed like he was dedicated to preserving our tradition of independent ownership. Also part of the agreement was that my partners could keep their jobs for as long as they wanted after they sold, meaning no one would feel any pressure to leave. While it wasn't perfect, it was starting to look like we had found a good solution to our dilemma.

The next stage was to bring in lawyers and accountants to look things over. My partners used the firm's accountant, while Dickie and I brought in our own advisers.

We met at the Laurentian Club to begin negotiations over the selling price. The figures from both sides were very close and took into account market value, financial history, and business projections. Dickie was concerned about Revenue Canada. When you sell a business, the government pays close attention to make sure that you are not underselling to avoid taxes. This idea wasn't a concern for me, since I knew our appraisal had been completed by an objective third party and was based on market value. Avoiding taxes was the last thing on my mind, but in retrospect, perhaps a red flag should have gone up.

We had six or seven meetings, the last one held at the Rideau Club in the Karsh Room, so called because the walls are adorned with several prints by the famous photographer. It's a beautiful space. I remember partway through the meeting looking up and seeing Karsh's portrait of Winston Churchill staring down at us, and wondering what he would have to say about all of this.

I found the whole experience fascinating; watching the deal come together was an education in business. However, even though the deal was progressing smoothly, I did have some mixed feelings. My partners, all friends I'd known for years, were suddenly on the opposite side of the table. I wanted my partners to get a good price, but at the same time I didn't want to pay too much, either. It was a surreal feeling, like a hockey player might experience the first time he plays the team that traded him. In the end, we arrived at a price acceptable to everyone and the initial paperwork was signed. It was a relief to know that we had taken that important first step toward a solution. Now all Dickie and I had to do was convince the bank that it was a good idea to lend us millions of dollars.

Dickie would probably say that I couldn't have made the deal without his help, and he would be right, but I was also trusting him to keep his word.

Soon after our last meeting with my partners, Dickie made arrangements for us to go to Toronto and talk with some of the bankers he had previously dealt with. The institutions in Ottawa wouldn't even consider getting involved; when you start talking about more than a few million dollars, you have no choice but to go to the country's financial hub.

We arrived at what was then called the Victoria & Grey Trust Company, which has since merged with the Bank of Nova Scotia. I was in my early forties, not a kid by any means, but still, I'd never seen anything like it. We walked into this massive tower in Toronto's financial district and were immediately ushered up to a lavish conference room furnished with a solid oak table five times longer than what we needed. Our hosts were waiting for us and started off by showing us all the gadgets they had installed in the room, raising and lowering the remote-control window blinds, and flicking on the video conferencing set and camera. These technologies are par for the course these days, but in the 1980s, they were quite a novelty. I found the whole building somewhat intimidating, almost oppressive, which would probably be considered a compliment to the interior decorators who had designed it. I'm sure this is the effect they were going for—a slick physical manifestation of raw financial power.

I had been nervous in the days leading up to the meeting, as it was difficult to comprehend the amount of money we were asking for, and these surroundings had not improved my state of mind. I had planned on walking in with my hat in hand, but Dickie had other ideas. Dickie had been to this office before and was not easily distracted by the technological wizardry. He wanted to cut to the chase, and it was something to watch him in action. I sat quietly at one end of the giant conference table and listened while he told the two bankers that they'd better sharpen their pencils if they wanted to be involved in such a respected Canadian institution. The window of opportunity was closing faster than the remote-control blinds, he said, making it very clear that if the bank wanted to be a part of Hulse & Playfair, they needed to act quickly. I could hardly believe his audacity, but you know what? It worked. The bankers could relate to this show of bravado; I think they saw it as a sign of confidence. They were obviously impressed, anyway.

Dickie had some resources, and I had my smaller contribution, so I was expecting a long, drawn-out process, filled with countless papers to sift through and strategies to scrutinize, but the whole transaction was completed with head-spinning speed. The bank liked the business plan and, to give them credit, had done their homework. Our books were in order. They saw that we had a good history and an impeccable business reputation, so they came on board. It was that simple. The process had not been nearly as difficult as I imagined it would be, and as we walked out into the hustle and bustle of the Toronto afternoon, I was overwhelmed. Within a matter of weeks, the paperwork was signed and Dickie and I had acquired the entire business.

Obtaining the operating company was certainly a big hurdle, but we still did not own the property or the buildings that comprised our funeral homes, and this was our next step. If you don't own the land or buildings and your landlord decides to sell, you could easily find yourself bidding against a real-estate developer, quickly forcing the price out of reach. Both Dickie and I agreed that purchasing the land holdings was a vital part of the whole plan.

Cliff Lloyd and Keith Shaver co-owned the Central Chapel and property at that time, while Isobel Jeffrey, Keith Playfair's widow, owned the West Chapel. We were able to quickly reach an agreement with Cliff and Keith. They were eager to sell to us and thought of it as a good way to further ensure the continued success of the firm. The price was high but fair, and reflected market value.

With the Central Chapel safely in our hands, we focused on the West Chapel. I knew Mrs. Jeffrey quite well, so we called to make an appointment for Dickie and me. I told her that we were interested in buying the property, and she was open to the idea.

I often went to visit Isobel after Keith Playfair died. She would put on a pot of tea, and we would chat. Isobel and Keith had met after her first husband, Mr. Walker, was thrown off a horse and killed. Mr. Walker owned a large bakery in Ottawa, and Keith and Charlie had looked after his funeral. After a year-long friendship, Keith and Isobel fell in love and were married soon after. It seems an odd way to meet your future spouse, but I suppose the heart knows no limitations. Years later, after Keith passed away, Isobel married a third time, to Dr. Fred Jeffrey. She would often laugh and say that she had married three wonderful men—a doctor, a baker, and an undertaker, which always reminded me of the rhyme, "Rub-a-dub-dub, three men in a tub, and who do you think they be? The butcher, the baker and the candlestick maker, and they all went out to sea."

Isobel was a wealthy lady and a generous philanthropist. She helped Charlie and Keith after they decided to build a new funeral home and chapel on Woodroffe Avenue, now known as our West Chapel. She purchased the land and paid for the construction of the new building; without her help, the business would not have been able to expand. The firm paid rent for the use of the building, and Mrs. Jeffrey kept ownership. It had been a good arrangement for many years, but it was a situation that could not continue indefinitely. At some point, the land and building would be passed down to her family members, and the future of the property would be uncertain. We needed to purchase the land and building from Mrs. Jeffrey to ensure that our funeral home would be able to remain on the site indefinitely.

Tricky Dickie, like some men of his generation, had a habit of treating women in business differently than their male counterparts. It was a notion left over from a different era, when chauvinism was commonplace and sexual discrimination was often accepted with a silent understanding. Of course this is a mistake in any case, but especially so in dealings with a strong, independently minded woman like Mrs. Jeffrey.

Dickie and I had several meetings with Isobel to talk about the prospect of buying the property from her, but I'll never forget our last meeting. Dickie and

I arrived at the West Chapel, and Isobel arrived shortly after. She hadn't invited any of her advisers who had been present at our other meetings, and this may have given Dickie some courage to act the way he did. The negotiations had been progressing well, Mrs. Jeffrey was interested in selling to us, and it was just a matter of reaching an agreement on price. I think Dickie believed the whole process was going to be easy.

The three of us were in an upstairs office in the West Chapel. I made a cup of tea for Mrs. Jeffrey, and after some initial pleasantries, we started the meeting in earnest. After reviewing some of the details of our latest proposal, Isobel looked across the desk and said, "All right, gentlemen, here's my price . . ."

What happened next shocked me. Dickie started into his high-power businessman's routine. "This building isn't worth anything near what you're asking. You're simply going to have to do better than that."

I couldn't believe what I was hearing. Isobel's price was fair, and not too much over the amount that we were prepared to pay, but Dickie was trying to squeeze out every last dollar. Looking back, I think he would have haggled regardless of what her price had been.

Isobel was a good friend, and I was immediately embarrassed. Dickie's speech was unnecessary and rude. There was a marked silence afterwards. Mrs. Jeffrey looked across the desk at us for a moment, collected her thoughts, then leaned forward. "Mr. Dickie, I want you to listen very carefully. I don't need to sell this building to you, now or ever. The only reason I'm sitting here with you right now is because Brian is a friend, and I have a great deal of respect for this business, but I can tell you that I would never sell to you if you were here on your own."

This time it was Dickie who looked on silently. Isobel continued, "As a matter of fact, Mr. Dickie, you've annoyed me so much that I think a funeral organization called Loewen's might be happy for the opportunity to buy this property for the price I suggested."

Loewen's was, at that time, the second-largest funeral conglomerate in the world and had been buying up properties all across North America at a fever pitch. Dickie knew as well as I did that they would have jumped at the chance to buy.

Dickie was speechless as we sat across the desk from this amazing woman. I was unhappy with Dickie's behaviour and, looking back, that was the first time

I began to feel trepidation about our partnership. It was a concern that would prove to be well founded, as I learned more about Dickie's character.

After a few awkward moments of silence, I turned to Dickie, "I think Isobel's offer is fair and worth considering. Let's talk to the bank and see if they can help us come up with the difference."

Isobel didn't wait for his response. "Well, Brian, I don't need to hear from Mr. Dickie again. Get in touch with your financiers and give me a call. Either you want this property at my price or you don't, is that understood?"

"Yes, ma'am."

Needless to say, that was the end of the meeting. Mrs. Jeffrey gathered her papers and walked confidently out of the room. Later that day I received a phone call from Isobel. "Brian, I hope I wasn't rude."

"No, Isobel, we were rude."

"Actually, it was your partner who was rude."

"Yes, and I'm sorry about that."

"Well, at any rate, I'd like to sell the building to you, but my price stands. Please let me know what you decide."

Years later, Mrs. Jeffrey would tell me that, if push had come to shove, she wouldn't have sold to Ray Loewen, but at that last meeting, she felt that Dickie needed to be put in his place.

Tricky Dickie accepted that Isobel's price was firm, so we went back to the bank. Sure enough, they thought it was a smart investment at a fair price. Walking out of the bank that last time felt good. The last piece of the puzzle was falling into place, but I was also overwhelmed. I had been so focused on putting the deal together that I hadn't had a chance to reflect. I never would have imagined that the McGarry family would one day own an acre of land in downtown Ottawa, as well as half the company I loved so much. I had mixed feelings about Dickie's approach to business, but the firm's future as an independent organization seemed to be out of danger, and Charlie's legacy was safe. I was proud that I had helped contribute to the tradition that Charlie Hulse and Keith Playfair had started so many years before. Of course, I didn't know it at the time, but my plans for the future were very much different from Tricky Dickie's.

Up to that point in my life I had had the good fortune of never being betrayed by anyone, and I suppose I was somewhat naive. The first indication that problems were fast approaching concerned the buy/sell agreement between Dickie and me. This was the part of the arrangement that ensured Tricky Dickie would stay for the five years he had promised, and it hadn't yet been signed. At first, I wasn't overly worried. I knew that with a transaction of this size, it would take time to get the paperwork in order, but by February 1988, almost everything else had been signed on the dotted line, and the sale was due to be finalized on March 1. One of the nuances of the deal was the fact that our partnership was kept separate from the actual sale; therefore, conceivably, Tricky Dickie and I could obtain joint ownership of the company without officially becoming business partners.

I had held off signing myself, due to a few clauses I was having trouble with. One was a minor issue, a disagreement regarding company expenses. Tricky Dickie felt that certain personal costs should be covered by the business, and I objected. I had already seen several bills coming in that were unrelated to our business in Ottawa—flowers for an out-of-town wedding, and gas charges for Dickie's car when he was out of town for personal reasons. When I confronted Tricky Dickie about my concerns, he insisted that, as a partner, these expenses should be covered by the company. I told him that we would cover his costs whenever he was in Ottawa, but beyond that, I didn't think the firm should be responsible.

We did agree that the firm would rent an apartment for him, since Ottawa was not his primary residence; however, Dickie also insisted that he be provided with a corporate car. More specifically, he wanted a Lincoln Continental, which struck me as excessive.

These were relatively minor issues, however, compared to the clause Tricky Dickie had introduced concerning marital status. This so-called "divorce clause" stated that if either partner were to be divorced from his spouse, his shares would immediately become available for sale to the other partner. An arbitration system would set a price, and the remaining partner would have first right of refusal. I could see the logic behind the clause, because a divorce can all too easily become ugly, resulting in one half of the business being sold off as part of a settlement. This was certainly a danger, but I was even less comfortable with the idea that if something were to happen between Sharon and me, we would automatically lose the whole business, regardless of the terms of our divorce. On the other hand, if Dickie and his wife were to divorce, and the value of the shares were appraised at a price Sharon and I couldn't afford, Tricky Dickie would then be free to sell his shares to the highest bidder, and we would have no control over who our new partner might be.

In the past, we'd had senior employees who had gone through divorces, and there had never been a problem. I also knew that, regardless of any problems that might come up in our marriage, neither Sharon nor I would want to give up our life's work.

I asked Dickie if he would be prepared to give up such a valuable asset, if he and his wife ever divorced, and he didn't answer. It was another red flag, which I chose to ignore in the interest of preserving the deal. In retrospect, I'm not sure if Tricky Dickie ever had a life's work beyond making money and, without being emotionally involved, losing the company in a divorce settlement would not have the same meaning for him.

As a result of these concerns, the final paperwork solidifying our partnership agreement remained unsigned, even though we now each owned half of the company and land.

Dickie and I clashed almost immediately after we took possession. It was becoming clear to me that his interest was focused on selling mahogany caskets, rather than providing good service to families. In all my years working for Hulse & Playfair, we had never received a single thank-you note from a family thanking us for a mahogany casket. We had, however, received many letters from people thanking us for helping them through a difficult time. Dickie knew the importance of good service, but it seemed like it was a means to an end, as opposed to a genuine desire to help people; providing good service in order to be paid, as opposed to providing good service because you believe it helps families who have come to you in a time of need.

One afternoon, just a few weeks after we became joint owners of the business, Dickie and I were on our way back to the funeral home after a service. For some reason, Tricky Dickie always seemed to spring things on me when I was driving.

"Brian, I'm going to bring my son, Mark, into the firm. He'll be a big help to you."

That was it. There was no discussion; Dickie simply didn't feel it necessary to ask my opinion on the matter. Tricky Dickie had made an executive decision, and that was just the way it was going to be. I didn't hide my sarcasm. "I'm sorry, did I miss the meeting about this?"

"No need for a meeting. Mark is very competent."

"We've never discussed this."

"Well, he's my son."

At the very least, it was ill-mannered that Dickie would hire anyone without consulting me first, but I brushed it off as a lack of social grace. It was a family member after all, and I would have probably accepted the idea if I had been asked, but it was Dickie's approach that bothered me. Sure enough, a few days later Mark arrived with a truckload of furniture, which he moved into his father's apartment.

Mark was a nice boy, twenty-one years old, and a recent graduate of Humber College's funeral director program. In addition to his studies at Humber, Mark had also taken a course in the United States, an innovative program that billed itself as the future of the funeral business. I'd met other people who had completed the program, and, as I understood it, the course concentrated on the best way to sell expensive caskets.

I had to sit down with Mark and Tricky Dickie and make clear the fact that the job of a funeral director does not involve "selling" anything. We offer a variety of options for funerals that are compatible with any budget or income level, and we've always been careful not to put any pressure on families to buy anything, or spend beyond their means. We train our funeral directors to present all available options and then give the family time to make their decision in private. When a person loses someone they love, the last thing they need is an unscrupulous funeral director who is more concerned with making a profit than meeting their needs.

I was willing to give Mark a chance at our funeral home, but I knew things were not going to work from the first moment he walked through the door. On his arrival, he immediately considered himself to be in charge, or at least second-in-command, an approach that showed his lack of experience.

"My dad wouldn't do it this way . . ." soon became a familiar refrain.

It was evident that just about everything he saw us doing at the funeral home was outdated, or contrary to what he had learned in his studies. Not surprisingly, this attitude did not endear him to the staff, and, after several complaints, I had to talk to him about it. I made it clear that if he had new ideas for the firm, that was great, but he needed to come to me with them before trying to impose them on the staff. The only thing he was accomplishing by trying to will himself into a management role was annoying everyone on staff. And since no one took his pronouncements very seriously, it must have been frustrating for him as well.

After our conversation, Mark spent less and less time around the funeral home. However, he did start announcing at meetings that, for a price, he would set up our whole computer system, a project he considered absolutely necessary. This was at a time when computer technology was just starting to become widely used, and I remember wondering if this twenty-one-year-old kid really knew what he was talking about.

I tried to tell Dickie that the situation with his son wasn't working out, but he wouldn't hear it. Nevertheless, I refused to give Mark any work to do, and never paid him. He wound up just hanging around most of the time. Eventually, it became an issue with Dickie, and he came into my office one day to discuss it.

"He's a smart boy, Brian."

"Maybe so," I replied, "but he's not on the same track that we're on here in Ottawa."

"Well, maybe *you* need to change tracks."

I don't raise my voice very often, but Dickie's comment was enough for me to lose my temper.

"Keep your boy at home!"

"Why won't you allow Mark to work?" he asked.

"For the same reason that you wouldn't allow my children to come in and work without discussing it first. This experiment is over."

Dickie didn't immediately accept the idea that his son was not a good fit at our funeral home, and the whole issue served to widen the rift that was already growing between us. After a few more discussions, Tricky Dickie could see that I was not going to change my mind about having Mark work at the funeral home. He begrudgingly accepted my position and sent his son home.

Almost immediately after Dickie arrived rumours began to circulate. I don't think a week had gone by before I heard staff members say that Tricky Dickie was talking to some of the funeral conglomerates. I also started receiving calls from friends asking if there was any truth to the stories that Dickie was entertaining offers for his share of the company. All my friends knew the firm's reputation and were concerned. Tricky Dickie hadn't mentioned anything to me about it, and as far as I knew, everything was moving along as we had planned. Regardless, I assured my friends that I would find out. The Ottawa funeral home community is quite small, and most people involved in the business know each other, so it's not unusual to hear things. More often than not, there isn't any truth to these rumours, but occasionally, these stories are based on fact. I wanted to believe that Dickie was going to remain faithful to his promise, but I needed to find out for sure. I had planned on stopping by Dickie's office one afternoon to confront him about the rumours, but as it turned out I didn't have to. Tricky Dickie walked into my office that same morning.

"We've got a meeting to go to in Toronto, Brian," he announced.

"A meeting with whom?"

"Ray Loewen would like to see us."

Mr. Loewen was the founder of the largest funeral service corporation in Canada, a company that was fast becoming one of the largest funeral conglomerates in the world.

"What's the meeting about?" I asked, even though I already knew the answer.

"Well, you're probably not going to be able to say 'no' to this, Brian; it really is an extraordinary deal . . ."

"A deal?"

"Ray wants to buy us out."

I looked at Tricky Dickie for a moment, thinking about what he had just told me. I strained to maintain my composure. "This is coming as quite a shock."

"Believe me, I was just as shocked when he came to me, but the offer is just too good to ignore."

"What's going on here? What about our five-year agreement?"

He shrugged his shoulders. "Brian, these guys are approaching me . . ."

"Come on, they've approached me for years."

"Look, it's not going to hurt us to go and hear what he has to say. It doesn't mean that we have to sell."

And with that, the meeting was over.

Against my better judgment, I accepted the invitation, and a week later, Tricky Dickie and I were on a flight to Toronto. There was a Funeral Directors meeting that weekend in Toronto, which was why Ray, who was based out of

Vancouver, was in town. Our meeting with Loewen was to take place at the Sutton Place Hotel, an old landmark popular with Queen's Park politicians and Toronto power brokers. We weren't there ten minutes before I saw Andy Doyle. Dickie and I were sitting in the little coffee shop on the ground floor of the hotel, and Tricky Dickie had just introduced me to one of Loewen's partners who had agreed to meet us before going up to our suite. Andy walked into the hotel lobby and saw the three of us sitting there. He didn't come over, but he must have found it interesting to see the company we were keeping. I wasn't overly concerned about what anyone thought, since I had nothing to hide. Anyone who knew me understood my position as far as conglomerates went. The meeting with Mr. Loewen was purely for Dickie's benefit.

Conglomerates are not evil organizations, and I have a tremendous amount of respect for Ray Loewen as a Canadian businessman, but conglomerates certainly have a different approach to funeral service. Ray got his start in the '60s, working with his father in their small family-owned funeral home in rural Manitoba. When his dad became sick, Ray took over the business. After a few years, Ray began buying up other small family-operated funeral homes and cemeteries, and his company steadily grew. His formula was simple: when he bought a new funeral home, he made sure also to buy the rights to the original family name, which he would keep on the front of the building. He also kept on the existing staff. On the outside, it would appear that nothing had changed, but internally all of the services would be centralized and the products offered would be the same in every funeral home he owned. A seemingly small change, but this way he was able to buy his products in bulk, thereby increasing his profit. His formula worked well, and by the late eighties, he had purchased ninety-eight funeral homes and five cemeteries, making his firm the second-largest funeral service corporation in the world.

The three of us took the elevator up to our suite to wait for Mr. Loewen's arrival. I was already feeling tense, and those few minutes seemed to last an eternity. Dickie, on the other hand, was in a jovial mood. Finally, there was a knock on the door. Tricky Dickie opened it and in walked Ray Loewen, flanked by a couple of his senior employees.

The meeting started with the requisite niceties as we sat down around a low, wooden coffee table. I'd met Ray before and found him to be a nice, very intelligent guy, but for this meeting he was all business.

Without much of a preamble, he clicked open his briefcase and removed a crisp piece of paper, placed it in front of him, and slid it across the table. What I saw stunned me. In front of us was a cheque for exactly double the amount of money we had just spent to buy the business and land. I had never seen a cheque that big in all my life. It would have been enough money for me to retire right then and there, and that was how the conversation started. It was like I had wandered onto the set of a movie.

The money was an amazing temptation, and I'm sure my eyes were as big as saucers, but my shock didn't last long before it quickly turned into anger. Mr. Loewen had an agreement drawn up and ready to be signed, which he placed next to the cheque. Dickie could hardly contain his excitement, even though he must have known what was coming. Ray wasn't the first person who had approached me about selling the company, and I figured I knew roughly how the meeting was going to go. Ray would say how much he respected our firm and that the only substantial change that would occur with the business would be the size of my bank account. I'd heard it all before, but to have a cheque sitting there . . .

It then occurred to me that an offer like this doesn't just materialize overnight. Tricky Dickie must have been quietly working on this deal from the first moment we discussed becoming partners, possibly even before. Our buy/sell contract remained unsigned, which meant the confidentiality agreement that went with it was also unsigned. Without that contract in place, Dickie had been free to take the firm's financial numbers and offer them to whomever he wanted. Loewen must have been privy to all the company's records. There is a certain level of prestige associated with Hulse, Playfair & McGarry; we're well known in Canada and respected internationally. So, for Loewen to buy us out would be quite the coup.

I felt my face flush. I was angry at Dickie for obvious reasons, but I was also angry at myself for not seeing the warning signs. Dickie was clearly counting on the element of surprise, confident that I would be so dazzled by the amount of money on the table that I wouldn't be able to refuse the offer.

After a few moments, Ray got straight to the point and asked me what my answer was. I glanced around the room, "That's a very generous offer, but there's one problem."

Loewen and Dickie looked at each other, then Ray spoke, "What's that?"

"The business is not for sale."

Dickie looked over at me, shocked. "Brian, do you mean that you wouldn't even consider this offer?"

"That's right."

Ray smiled at both of us and very politely spoke, "Maybe you should take some time and think about it."

"I can't do it, Ray. I have great respect for you and your organization, but I just negotiated to buy this company, and it's a great personal accomplishment. I can't imagine turning around and selling it. Everyone I've worked with for the last twenty-five years has put their trust in me."

A little desperately, Dickie said, "Look at that cheque, Brian. You can't turn that down."

My resolve grew stronger with each passing moment. "Actually I can, and I am. Ray, if you want to buy his half, be my guest."

"No, no, we want the whole thing. We've never entered into a partnership like that."

That was his one condition. Ray wasn't interested in owning half of our firm, or any firm for that matter, and it was a good thing, because if Loewen had agreed to buy Dickie's share, there would have been nothing I could have done to stop it. Had that happened, the firm would have been deadlocked. Every major decision we made from then on would likely have ended in arbitration, making the business unworkable. Perhaps he saw the same scenario playing out, because Ray seemed determined not to get into a partnership arrangement. Dickie was not happy; I could see the disgust on his face. An awkward silence filled the suite as we sat around the table looking at each other.

Finally, Ray spoke. "Why don't you take a few days to think it over, Brian?"

"With all due respect, Ray, I don't need a few days. Go ahead, Dickie, maybe they can cut the cheque in half?"

The past few moments had been tense, and my comment was an attempt to inject a little levity into what had become an uncomfortable situation, but the joke went over like the proverbial lead balloon. Tricky Dickie looked at me. He had a funny way of tilting his head and peering at you out of the corners of his eyes, or over his glasses, as if to say, "Are you that stupid?" Ray reached across the table and pulled the cheque back, placing it carefully inside his briefcase. This was done slowly for effect, as if to say, "There's still time before it slips away!"

Dickie took a deep breath and said, "Look, Ray, I'm sorry it's coming to this. Brian and I will discuss your offer and I'll get back to you."

I think Ray could sense my determination, but he tried an old sales trick anyway. "Well, the offer is available for a few days, but we do have other funeral homes we're considering."

And I thought, "Maybe so, but no place like this one."

We all stood up, and Dickie walked Ray and his entourage to the door. After they had left, Tricky Dickie turned and looked at me. He didn't lose his composure, but I could tell he was irritated. He lumbered back over to the couch and sat down, shaking his head.

"You've got to rethink this, Brian."

"There's no point in waiting a few days. I've made up my mind."

Tricky Dickie shook his head. "There's no way they'll only buy half."

"*C'est la vie.*"

I stood up and walked out of the room. Tricky Dickie and I didn't talk to each other for the rest of the convention. I called Sharon as soon as I got back to my room.

"You'll never believe what just happened . . ."

Sharon and I both agreed that we couldn't sell. Looking at it from a strictly financial point of view, we should have taken the money and run, but I suppose that's where the distinction lies between being profit-driven and being more community-minded. If you take all the dollars and cents out of the equation, you're left with the satisfaction that comes from helping people, and that's why I'm in the funeral profession. Sharon and I could have had a lot of money in the bank, but we would have traded it for a business that we loved and had worked so hard to preserve. How can you place a dollar value on that?

Dickie didn't give up easily. Over the next few days, he worked hard to convince me that I was making a big mistake, that I was throwing away a golden opportunity.

"The best thing you can do, Brian, is to sell with me," he urged.

"Are you kidding?" I responded.

"Think about the money," he reminded me.

"I'm forty-four years old, I just bought out my partners, and you want me to flip the business?"

"Brian, I don't think I can refuse that kind of offer," he said.

"What about the five years you promised me?"

"That agreement hasn't been signed."

The truth was finally out. The promise of five years was just a way to get in the door.

After Dickie realized that I wasn't going to change my mind, he started looking at other options. Loewen's was not the only funeral conglomerate, and Tricky Dickie was confident he could find one that would be interested in owning 50 percent of one of the top six funeral homes in Canada. Within weeks, there were representatives from other conglomerates knocking on the door, and Tricky Dickie was meeting with them openly.

SCI was the first. They are, by far, the largest funeral service conglomerate in the world. An American-based firm, with their head office in Houston, Texas, SCI bought Kenyon's, the prominent funeral home in London, England, famous for its long-standing relationship with the Royal Family. Of course, almost immediately after the purchase, the Royals switched to a different, independent, locally owned funeral home.

SCI tried the same sort of tactic that the Loewen Group had used, except the cheque they offered over lunch at the Rideau Club had more zeros printed on it.

The third company that approached us was Arbor Memorial Services Inc., a Canadian company. (At least at that time they were; a few years later the common shares would be 60 percent owned by SCI.) The interest in our company was such that Dickie had managed to spark a bidding war. I can only imagine what my former partners were thinking while all this was happening.

I needed to find a solution, fast. I went to the bank to see if they could help me buy Tricky Dickie out myself, but they said that they had already stretched to get Sharon and me half of the business.

I started thinking about people I knew in the funeral business in Ottawa, and the Coles came to mind. They owned the Pinecrest Cemetery and at one time we talked about a partnership. We were good friends, so I made a call and explained the situation. They were interested in the possibility of buying Dickie's shares, so I quickly set up a meeting. Tricky Dickie was listening to every offer at that point. We met at the Laurentian Club one afternoon and I was quite optimistic that the arrangement might work, and that it could even prove to be a good partnership. I made sure the Coles had a chance to look at the numbers, and they told me they would come to the meeting with their best offer. I was excited at the prospect that we might be able to solve the problem.

The meeting progressed and finally John Cole Sr. presented Tricky Dickie and me with an envelope. Tricky Dickie picked it up, took out the offer, and looked at it. Silence. After a moment, he looked into the now empty envelope before turning it upside down and shaking it, as if to say "Where's the rest of it?" I was very embarrassed. This was no way to treat anyone, especially friends of mine. Dickie looked across the table.

"This is ridiculous!" he said.

I was annoyed, but I thought Dickie might have been up to his old tricks, knowing full well it was a good offer, but playing hardball to try and wring out a few more dollars. I turned to him. "Well, what's the offer?"

He told me. I knew exactly how much he had paid, and while the Coles couldn't match the offers that the conglomerates had put forth, the offer was enough that Tricky Dickie would still make a good profit.

"It's a decent offer."

"It's not that decent."

John Cole Sr. had made many business deals throughout his life, so I think he knew the game that Dickie was playing. "We think it's a reasonable offer," he countered.

Dickie just shook his head. "I'm afraid you're going to have to do a lot better than that, John."

That was the end of the meeting. The whole proposal had fallen flat, and it left a bitter feeling in the room. After we got back to the office, I felt I needed to say something to Dickie.

"You know, the Coles are friends of mine."

"Well, they may be your friends, but they're not offering enough money."

"It was a hell of a lot more than you paid for it," I bristled.

After that meeting, I began calling other independent firms, including Turner and Porter in Toronto, and other friends who own larger funeral homes. I was hopeful that someone would be able to buy Dickie's shares. These partnerships wouldn't have been ideal, but at least they were all independently owned. The whole process was starting to move very quickly, and I sensed that it wouldn't be long before Tricky Dickie found a corporation interested enough to deal with him on his own terms.

Needless to say, my relationship with Dickie quickly deteriorated.

It was during this time that I received a call from Andy Doyle. He was concerned about the recent developments. We were still partners in the St. Laurent funeral home, and he was getting anxious about the idea that he might soon be dealing with a new partner. I knew Andy didn't want to have anything to do with the conglomerates. (His feelings would later change!) I explained the details of what was going on. The truth was that nothing had been signed, yet, but I told Andy that it was only a matter of time. One way or another, Dickie was going to leave, and I didn't know who would take his place. Andy asked for the price, but as he had recently bought out his own partners, there was no way he could come close.

Andy arranged a meeting with Dickie and me to talk about the situation, and a few days later we sat down together. Dickie came straight to the point.

"Well, Andy, if you're nervous about the future, maybe you should consider selling your interest in the St. Laurent Chapel to us."

"I'll think about that."

I knew Andy would not be happy with his new partners, if the sale went through the way Dickie wanted it to, and I didn't blame him. So it wasn't too long afterwards that Andy called back with a price; he knew the market well and his price was fair. There was some further negotiation, but the whole process happened quickly, and a few weeks later we were set to meet one last time to finalize the transaction.

Dickie and I were the first to arrive at the lawyer's office and we sat down to wait for Andy. We had used John Clarke in the past; he was well acquainted with both firms, so we hired him to negotiate the sale. The phone rang. It was Andy. John pressed a button, and Andy's voice crackled through the tiny speaker.

"I'm not too sure about this sale. I'm starting to reconsider," he said.

"You know, Andy," said Dickie, "you've got to make up your mind."

"Well, who are you going to sell to?"

Dickie couldn't give a definitive answer, because at that point he was still trying to get the conglomerates to outbid each other, but Andy could read between the lines. Dickie was going to sell to the highest bidder; whether it was an independent firm or a conglomerate made no difference. There was a long pause.

"OK," said Andy, finally, "I'm going to come over, but I don't want Dickie there. I don't want to see him or talk to him."

Of course Dickie heard this. They had been good friends at one time, but Dickie's betrayal had soured their relationship. What was remarkable was the fact that Andy's resentment didn't seem to bother Tricky Dickie at all.

After Andy hung up, Tricky Dickie turned to John and me, and said, "Give me a call when it's done."

With that he picked up his coat and walked out. All business. Andy arrived shortly after and the sale was completed. Andy shook his head as we walked out onto the street. "I can't believe it's come to this," he said.

Things between Dickie and me were not going well and it was causing a lot of stress. If Tricky Dickie sold all of his shares to a conglomerate, it would create a miserable situation. The company would be in turmoil, because every disagreement would necessitate the services of an arbitrator, essentially placing a third party in charge of the business. I had no doubt that there would be many disagreements.

The conglomerates have a very different approach to the funeral business compared to family-run organizations. It's not that they're bad people, but they are certainly more profit-oriented. When you live in the community you're serving, you are more likely to be motivated by compassion for your neighbours than making financially based decisions from an office half a continent away.

I was also worried that the bidding war Dickie had sparked had unrealistically driven up the cost of the shares. There was no way our funeral home could generate enough business to cover the debt that any buyer would have to take on to meet the offers now on the table. In a situation like that, the funeral home could be forced to shut down or relocate so that the property could be sold to service the debt. Yet Dickie had done a good job of selling the reputation that Charles Hulse, Keith Playfair, and everyone else had worked so hard to establish and maintain over the years, so the price continued to climb.

I tried to reason with Tricky Dickie, but he wouldn't listen. He was only concerned with dollar signs.

"I have no obligation to you, Brian. I can sell my shares tomorrow if I like."

More than once we were involved in heated debates. I'll never forget one particular drive Dickie and I took from the Central Chapel out to the St. Laurent Chapel. We were on the Queensway, the busy main thoroughfare that cuts through Ottawa. Dickie had just received another offer and we were yelling at each other.

"You have to take this offer, Brian. I'm not going to refuse it!"

"I'm not selling!"

"Look at the money!"

"I don't care about the damn money!"

"You're a fool."

"If keeping my word makes me a fool then so be it."

It was amazing. After everything that had happened, Dickie still thought he could convince me to sell. I realized that it was unsafe to be arguing like that while we were driving, so we spent the remainder of the trip in silence. When we arrived at the funeral home, we continued our debate under safer circumstances. It was clear that I was going to be forced into a new partnership that I did not want.

At home that night I talked things over with Sharon. We had scraped together every cent we could to buy our half of the business. We eventually decided that the only thing left to do was try to convince Dickie to sell us a few more shares, so that when he sold the rest, we would at least have a majority. This would likely be an uphill battle, since any potential buyer Dickie was negotiating with would likely not be satisfied with less than 50 percent of the firm. All the same, it was clear we would soon have a new partner, and we needed to be in the best possible position to prepare for this inevitability.

One of our senior managers, Doug Kennedy, had also expressed an interest in helping out by buying any shares that Dickie would sell to him. However, offers from the conglomerates had pushed the price of even a single share out of reach.

We did have another option. Sharon had been involved in a car accident a few years before, forcing her to spend six months in a body cast. It had been the other driver's fault, so we sought compensation. The settlement had come through, which would be enough to buy an extra 3 percent at the price we had originally paid. Sharon was willing to use her money in order to keep control of the firm. I talked it over with Doug. After looking over his finances, he concluded that he could also afford to buy an additional 3 percent. I arranged a meeting with Dickie to discuss the idea.

"Look, I can't meet the prices that are coming in, but I'll allow the sale to go smoothly if Sharon and I can buy an additional 3 percent at the original price. Doug Kennedy wants to buy 3 percent as well, also at the original price. And I want to have a say about who my new partner will be."

"I can't do that."

"You have to be reasonable. If you don't allow us this, I promise I'll blow this thing wide open. I'll make it front-page news, and we'll see where community sympathy lies."

I suppose I was connecting, because at least he was listening. "I can't stop you from selling your shares, but I can make it very difficult for you."

Tricky Dickie didn't like the idea of selling to us, as it would mean less money in his pocket, but he wasn't completely opposed to it if it meant that he could sell the rest of his shares without any problems.

I started looking at the list of conglomerates Dickie had been talking with. He agreed to let me choose who I would be partnered with, but he certainly didn't want to hear any more no's. I knew that I didn't want an American organization, so that eliminated SCI right away. The Loewen Group had started to reconsider their position on a partnership arrangement. However, although I liked Ray Loewen, his organization owned no cemeteries in Ottawa, and if I was going to have to partner with someone, it might as well be with an organization that could benefit our firm. The only company that met that requirement was Arbor, a conglomerate based out of Toronto. Arbor had a reputation of being one of Canada's better corporate employers, and they owned cemeteries across the country, including one in Ottawa. They were the best of the worst, and time was running out. We needed to make a decision quickly.

It was in the middle of all this when Charlie Hulse died. I had officially been partners with Dickie for only a few weeks. After Charlie's funeral was over, I told Dickie about my decision to go with Arbor. I think he must have been on the phone within minutes of leaving my office, because a meeting was set up for the very next day with our lawyers.

The Arbor representatives were excited, and Tricky Dickie was happy. Of course he had told them there was 50 percent up for sale.

I decided to start things off. "Both Doug Kennedy and I want to buy an additional 3 percent from Dickie at the original price, and then you can buy the rest."

They were hesitant and looked at Dickie. "We would prefer to be fifty-fifty."

"I can't stop you," I interjected, "but I'll tell you it won't be a happy partnership, and the deal won't go through without a lot of trouble. I'll engage public opinion."

The meeting split up, and we adjourned to separate rooms. Doug wasn't at the meeting, so I took this opportunity to call him.

"Doug, you're sure you've got this money?" I asked.

He said he did.

I certainly didn't want to be unreasonable, because it could turn out to be a no-win situation for everyone involved, but I was prepared to do just about anything to keep our family from losing control of the firm. I think Arbor believed that I would soon tire of the arrangement and sell to them anyway. They weighed their options and decided they could wait it out. When they came back into the meeting room, they announced they would allow us to buy the additional shares from Dickie. Tricky Dickie, realizing he could make a quick exit with his pockets full, quickly accepted.

I suppose we're a strange group for not accepting the millions, but I knew that the firm would not survive if we sold our shares to Arbor. I just couldn't watch Charlie's and Keith's long-established philosophy of independent family ownership disappear under corporate control.

By the end of the meeting we had come to an agreement. Doug and I would buy our 6 percent from Dickie at two in the afternoon at the old price, and Arbor would buy the remainder at four o'clock at the new, inflated price. We signed the agreement that day.

After the contract was finalized, Sharon and I became majority shareholders in the company, and the ordeal of working with our new corporate partner began.

The determination of the conglomerates is remarkable. SCI must have heard that we were moving forward on a sale, because the following day they called me. Much to their disappointment I told them they were too late.

Almost immediately after that phone call, two representatives from Loewen's arrived at the door. One of the fellows had even flown in from Vancouver just to talk with us. We were very busy that day with eight or nine funerals, although when I walked out of the clergy office and found them waiting for me, I could tell they hadn't come for a funeral.

"Brian, can we see you this afternoon?"

"Sure, but let me save you some time. Dickie sold to Arbor yesterday."

"Yes, we heard about that, but we also heard that you were able to obtain a majority."

"Yes, that's right."

"Well, we've rethought our position on the whole thing."

I could see exactly what they wanted to do. If they could convince me to sell to them, they would be in a position to push Arbor out. It wasn't about helping families in need or serving the community. They wanted to use our company as a corporate battleground. It would be a high-stakes game of one-upmanship.

"Guys, stop right there. It's over. Arbor is our new minority partner, and that's the way it will remain for now."

There wasn't much else to say, and as they walked out, I wondered if this was an indication as to how our new partnership was going to work with Arbor. In fact, it was the beginning of a very challenging seventeen-year partnership.

Also during this time, Joe Tubman passed away. Joe was a great man and the owner of another independent Ottawa funeral home, Tubman's. We offered to loan a car to Tubman's, knowing that with the size of Joe's funeral, an extra vehicle would likely help them. Even though we're keen competitors we can still put business aside in times of need; I know they would do the same for us. They appreciated the gesture and accepted.

Dickie and I both attended Joe's service, Dickie insisting that he be there. It was uncomfortable, because at the reception afterwards, several people came over to offer Dickie their congratulations on becoming part of Hulse & Playfair. (The sale to Arbor wasn't public knowledge, yet, and it wouldn't be official for several months.) I had to control my sense of ire; it wasn't the time or place for me to correct them. Dickie just nodded and smiled. After a while, I pulled him aside and said in a low voice, "Do you hear what these people are saying to you? Do you see now what you've done?"

He just looked at me. It was going to be an embarrassment when the news finally came out. It didn't bother Dickie one iota.

I can't say for sure if Dickie had intended to sell right from the beginning of our partnership, but I guess he must have. The businessman in him saw a golden opportunity and jumped on it. In less than seven months, Tricky Dickie had managed to double his money, while at the same time jeopardizing the firm's independence and placing everyone in an extremely stressful situation. We were now at the beginning of a new partnership that was sure to result in a clashing of values at the very heart of the company.

After seven tumultuous months, Tricky Dickie was gone. He disappeared with his millions, and I have never seen him since.

Approximately fifty of our staff welcomed Mayor Jim Watson to the opening
of our addition to the Central Chapel, 1999. While a number of our staff over
the years have moved on to bigger and better things, many have become long-
time loyal soldiers, and some even employee-partners, part of our tradition
as a family-owned and operated funeral service to the Ottawa community.

Courtesy of the City of Ottawa.

CHAPTER 11

Looking Back

There was a funeral not long after Charlie Hulse died, where we had forgotten to distribute the hymn books for the service. The clergyman was naturally upset and he said, "This place just isn't the same without Charles Hulse."

Nothing hurt me more than to hear those words. Even though Charlie had retired years before, he had been a presence in the funeral home until the end of his life, and continues to be in many ways even now. He left some very big shoes to fill. Both he and Keith Playfair were larger than life, and their absence was something of which I was acutely aware. There were times when I wondered if his employee-successors were really up to the job. I found myself constantly asking myself, "What would Charlie do?"

What the clergyman said was true, in a way. Not that our standards of service had eroded irretrievably—forgetting to put the hymn books out was a simple mistake that we quickly corrected—but there was a deeper meaning in his words.

Without Charlie and Keith, the funeral home had changed, and it could never be the same again. Everyone who works at our funeral home makes a contribution; take any person away and there will be a noticeable difference. Of course this idea goes beyond our funeral home, and you can say the same about everyone in your own life.

The deeper truth? Change is a constant in our lives; it's inevitable. In fact, if you look closely enough, you will see that everything is impermanent. Even the greatest mountain range will eventually erode away. Everything and everyone we know will slip away in time. Looking at it from this point of view, you can say that we experience little deaths throughout our lives—moving to a new city, ending a marriage, retiring. These are all changes, and while they represent the end of one thing, it is important to remember that they are also the beginning of something else.

Why should this idea apply to all the changes in our lives, but not to the change at the end of our lives? There is a great poem by Charles Mackay that sums up this sentiment beautifully:

There is no such thing as death.
In nature nothing dies.
From each sad remnant of decay
Some forms of life arise . . .

Nothing in nature ever stays the same for long, but upon closer examination, you see that nothing ever stops, either. There cannot be death without life, or life without death; the two states are inextricably entwined.

I have trouble wrestling with the concept of an afterlife. I haven't figured it out for sure, but I think there is a spirituality that survives the life of a person, and it may be as simple as the fond memories that friends and family take with them after a death. I don't know if there's a heaven or hell—I don't suppose anyone does—but one thing is certain: life springs from death. Our bodies go back to the earth. They're broken down and then take on new forms, which go on until they change again, a constant cycle of death and rebirth.

The challenge is to learn to accept these changes as a necessary part of your life. Death will come to us all, and you can spend your whole life worrying about it, which won't do you any good at all. It will only make you an unpleasant dinner guest. The alternative is to try to appreciate everything you see around you, and to nurture the relationships you have, so that when it comes time, you can let go with the knowledge that you have truly loved.

It will always be painful to let someone go that you care about, but if you live your life in love, and are willing to be open to all the experiences you have—both the joy and the pain—then you will take warm memories with you and have no regrets. I think this is one of the principal ideas at the heart of every religion.

When I was growing up in Wakefield, my mother brought my brother, sister, and me to the local United church. Every Sunday morning we attended Sunday school at 10 o'clock, and at eleven we would go upstairs for the service. This weekly routine certainly didn't do us any harm, and probably did us some good. I still go to that little church in Wakefield on occasion. I always find it comforting and I enjoy the community, but I now describe myself as bordering on agnostic. I feel more spiritual, but less attached to any one religion.

One remark has always bothered me, although it isn't stated as much now, but when there is a tragic death, occasionally someone will say, "Something good will come of this," or "God must have planned this." I'm afraid I can't accept the idea that God planned for your daughter to get hit by a car. I think of God as a positive power—the power of decency, the power of honesty, and the power of integrity. Good things can evolve from tragedy, but to think there's an omnipotent being floating around the universe moving pieces around a cosmic chess board—that has always thrown me off.

Another idea I've struggled with is the thought that each religion has its own version of God, which often gets held up above all others. Is the Muslim God more valid than the Christian God? Is the Catholic God more valid than the Protestant? I have trouble accepting these divisions, as it seems to work against the bigger principles that are promoted at the core of every religion.

I'm comfortable sitting in any church. I have observed the funeral customs of most religions, from Roman Catholic to Hindu. I find them all appealing in their own way, in particular the Jewish faith. It's interesting to see how they overlap.

I think religion plays an important role in the funeral service. I've seen the comfort that people take in their beliefs and the amazing support that comes from church communities. Spirituality can go a long way to help people get through one of the most difficult times in their lives. The clergy also have an important part in the way they are able to guide the service. I often sit in on different services, and it's always interesting to see how a person's life is reflected in their funeral.

I believe that most people have good in their hearts. Even if a person has ventured down a dark path in life, when all is said and done, most people want the same basic things—a peaceful, healthy environment in which to live, and the love of friends and family.

I suppose we're all searching for truth and meaning in our own ways.

The famous journalist and writer, Charles Lynch, was often asked to speak at the funeral of someone he knew. I always made it a point to sit in whenever he was going to be speaking. There was some spirituality in his words, but his real strength was in the art of storytelling, and it wouldn't be uncommon for the chapel to be filled with laughter during one of his tributes. It was always an interesting phenomenon to watch. At first you could see people holding in their laughter, then there might be a stifled chuckle from someone looking around to see if anyone had noticed, but Charlie's stories had a way of conveying the idea that laughter is just as natural as sorrow. All lives contain both and there is nothing wrong with remembering someone with a smile instead of a tear.

Of course, eulogies can also be poorly done, or be too much. I remember being at a particular service, where the eulogist was going on and on about the deceased, when my friend leaned over and whispered to me, "Are you sure we're at the right service?"

The fellow who had died was a bit of a maverick, but this fact wasn't apparent in the way the eulogist was speaking about him. I don't think you should include every detail about a person's life, but no one is perfect, and it's all right to acknowledge a person's faults.

I'll never forget the day I was sitting in Dr. Stewart Oake's office. The date is indelibly written in my memory: June 16, 2004. It was a sweltering afternoon, at the beginning of what would become one of the hottest summers on record. Earlier that day, I had been down at the marina launching a new motorboat Joan and I'd bought; I was looking forward to spending the summer exploring the Ottawa River with Joan and our daughter, Sheetza. Little did I know that would be the only day I would spend on the boat that year. Dr. Oake brought me into his office and asked me to sit down. A week before, I had gone into the hospital for a biopsy, where they removed a small part of my prostate for a test.

"Brian, we got the results back and I'm afraid the news isn't good. I'm sorry to have to tell you that you have prostate cancer."

The rest of the meeting seemed to take on a dreamlike quality. I could hear Dr. Oake talking about the radical surgery I was going to need, about possible radiation and other treatments. He spoke about success rates and early detection, but all I could think about at that moment was my family.

I've always been careful about my health. We urge all our employees at the funeral home to visit their doctors on a regular basis. Due to the nature of our work, we are often exposed to various chemicals and bodily fluids that are potentially dangerous, and it's a good idea to have frequent checkups as a precaution. It was on one of these routine visits that Dr. Oake decided to order a PSA (prostate-specific antigen) test, a simple blood test that looks for indicators of prostate cancer. Developed in the late 1980s, the PSA is recommended for men over the age of fifty and has saved many lives over the years. The results came back showing higher than normal levels, so I was scheduled for a biopsy.

There is a grading system that rates the severity of cancer between one and ten, ten being the worst. My cancer was rated at eight.

As a funeral director, I had dealt with mortality on a daily basis for many years, but facing my own death was still a frightening prospect. I was angry at first, which is usual, but after a few weeks I realized that this anger was draining me, so I started concentrating my energy on the things that are important to me. My life was immediately put into perspective, and I soon realized what was significant to me and what was not. I thought a lot about my wife and three children.

Sheetza was only five years old at the time, and it was awful to imagine Joan raising our little girl without me. My son, Brett, was twenty-five and my older daughter, Erin, seventeen—both with Sharon McGarry—and were well on to their way to individual successes. My world became very focused; the little annoyances and trivialities that might have previously caused concern had somehow fallen away.

As my appointment with the surgeon loomed closer, I began to let go of the anxiety I had felt at first. I suppose I was accepting my fate, whatever it might be. I was still afraid, and I wasn't about to give up fighting, but I did experience a strange sense of serenity.

We have funerals every month for people who have died of cancer. I've seen the devastation that it has caused to so many families, and it's one of the reasons our firm has been active in the Cancer Society. In fact, Charles Hulse was one of the founders of the Ottawa Cancer Society after his first wife succumbed to the disease. Joan has since been threatened by a large tumour in her spine, and my sister-in-law, Kilby McGarry, has also been treated for cancer. My diagnosis clearly defined the importance of the work I'd been doing as a funeral director and gave me a deeper perspective into what families go through when they deal with this dreadful disease.

My surgery was a success. After the operation, the doctors were able to conduct more thorough testing on the growth, and subsequently the cancer was downgraded to a seven on the scale. As a result, I didn't have to undergo radiation. I still see my doctor every six months to have my PSA checked, and although it's been more than seven years now, I won't be considered to be in remission until my levels are normal for a few more years.

Joan, Kilby, and I are very conscious of the fact that the disease could someday return. Different things are important now; my priorities have changed. No one knows how long they've got left in this life, but when you come face-to-face with your own mortality, it gives you a different perspective. I look at every day as a blessing.

The profession of funeral director never really leaves you. My life and my work have intertwined to the point where it's difficult to separate them. Our profession demands a lot of time, and when a family is in need we must be there. You can't just get up and say that you have to go because it's five o'clock. The families that walk through our doors are counting on us to be there for them, and they rely on us. We are sometimes called upon in times of terrible tragedy.

No funeral director will ever get used to dealing with the death of a child. While most of the deaths we handle are natural, and a death is always difficult for the family in some way, there is nothing you can say to a parent who has lost a child. There is a saying, "Your parents are your past, your spouse is your present, and your children are your future." When a family loses a child, they have just lost part of their future. Those are the situations that bother me most, and I think about them long after they're over.

We also see the results of murder and suicide, and you can't just go home at the end of the day after experiencing these events and turn on the television like nothing has happened. You carry these experiences with you.

Historically, funeral directors have been known for drinking heavily, and I think there is some truth to this. I remember in my early years with the firm that it wasn't uncommon at the end of the day for two of our corporate partners to go upstairs to the staff quarters and have a shot of scotch. Even Mr. Playfair would partake, and it became somewhat of a nightly ritual. I would sometimes be sent out to the liquor store; I even remember the code for the bottle, 52B. Back then all the bottles were given a code number for identification purposes, and 52B was the code for a certain brand of scotch that Mr. Playfair liked. Of course we now have strict rules about drinking when we are on duty, so you don't see this happening anymore, but I suppose that doesn't mean it's not there. We've had two or three people at the funeral home who have struggled with alcoholism, a problem I think is largely stress related.

One of our senior employees was involved in a controversy that almost brought down the firm. He was driving his car home after work and happened to hit a boy on a bicycle. He stopped to see if the young man was all right, then got back in his car and continued home. Though the boy was unhurt, our staff member should have remained at the scene until the authorities arrived. Subsequently, the police tracked him down and charged him with hit and run and leaving the scene of an accident. It was in all the local papers and was a very trying time for our firm; it shook us to our very foundation. One competitor was only too happy to broadcast the situation, embellishing the story in the process. Although our employee wasn't charged with drinking and driving, I knew that alcohol had been a factor in the accident because he'd had troubles with it in the past. He was the nicest man you would ever want to meet, but he succumbed to bad judgment. He stayed on at the funeral home and eventually the issue was resolved, but I think it represents the deeper problems that can occur whenever stress is a factor in your work or home.

How do we deal with stress? I think everyone has their own outlet. We've brought help in on occasion—psychologists and sociologists—and we've asked some of our staff to take courses to help them through difficult or extreme circumstances, or to help them to deal with substance abuse. Of course we can't say that substance abuse is a result of work-related stress, but we want to help out where we can. Back in the 1960s, bringing in a psychologist would have been considered nonsense; it's a much more acceptable idea today. Stress surrounding a tragic situation is real and can have serious effects.

There are many psychologists who specialize in bereavement, and for many years we referred people to Dr. Mary Brown. She was great, very warm and knowledgeable. She had previously been a nun until she discovered her love for helping people through psychology. Dr. Brown taught courses specifically aimed at funeral directors, doctors, and nurses. She also held bereavement seminars at St. Paul's University. I took a number of her courses and encouraged other staff members to do the same. She helped a lot of families over the years before she moved her practice to British Columbia.

We've also designed other programs to help people cope with death. Patrick McGarry, my cousin, has set up a continual care program at our funeral home.

I wasn't sure anyone would want to see a funeral director after the funeral was over, but surprisingly, many people do. For some people, seeing a funeral director trained in grief is a source of comfort. Others will come to see us because it gives them the freedom to talk about their family member. As part of the continual care program, we do all sorts of things, ranging from helping a person fill out forms for the Canada Pension Plan, to simply talking to someone who may never have been on their own before and are feeling lonely. Presently, we have a dedicated specialist, Lynda Norwell, assisting bereaved families. We call Lynda's important work "aftercare."

I suppose I have several outlets to help me deal with stress. While spending time in my rural hometown is one way, hockey is perhaps my favourite diversion; our family is a co-founder of the modern-day Ottawa Senators, along with our very good friends, the Firestones, and sixty-five additional small businesspeople.

I also have to say that I have overcome the stress of work by actually working more. At first this might not seem to make any sense, but the fact is I love my profession. So, by keeping busy, I can focus on the task at hand and not reflect too long on the difficulties and tragedies we must all deal with. In this way, working can be a form of escape. Of course, this method has its own problems, and that brings me to the one regret that I have about my life in funeral service.

After battling cancer, and the sobering effect that comes with it, I've sometimes thought about my regrets. I suppose I've wondered what might have happened if I had accepted Dr. Geggie's offer to go to medical school at McGill University and become a doctor. I've also often wished that I could speak French, but I think there may be one area that stands out more than these.

Should anyone give 100 percent of their time to their work? I think the answer is "no." It's great if you have a job that you love, but if it starts to take up all your time, then that's a problem, especially if you have a family at home. Prime Minister Stephen Harper gave an interview recently and stated that when your work starts to overtake your family, you will know it is time to quit.

There have been two incidents in our firm's history where the spouse of a senior employee has committed suicide. I don't know the full circumstances surrounding these tragedies, but I believe that the work hours and dedication to the job played a role in both cases.

In 1991, I was honoured to receive the B'nai Brith award for Citizen of the

Year. At the reception I gave a speech, during which I said it was important to set your priorities: family first, community second, and business third. This may be good advice, but I don't know if I was following it myself. Rabbi Reuven Bulka, my long-time friend, asked me if I had my priorities in the correct order.

Looking back, I would have to say that in my life, to a fault, the business has always come first. This is a fact that I believe has hurt my family. We get along well, but the fact that I was not always there for them caused problems. The profession never leaves you, and calls will inevitably come in during the middle of Sunday dinner. When you're working sixteen to eighteen hours a day, it leaves little time for anything else.

This kind of schedule eventually took its toll on my marriage to my first wife, Sharon. Somewhere in the midst of building a career and years spent dedicated to the business, the chemistry of our relationship was lost. It's hard to keep a loving relationship going when you're spending all of your time at the office.

Sharon and I had a good marriage; however, after twenty-seven years, we decided to divorce. It was a very difficult time. We had known each other since attending the same public school as kids.

There was an old wood-panelled station wagon with a sign attached to it that read "School Bus." It was used by the school to pick up students who lived too far away to take the regular bus. Sharon lived in Rupert, and I remember seeing her getting out of this funny "School Bus" in the mornings, but I didn't meet her until years later.

One night I got a call from my friends, Doug Morrison and Orval Coté (we were known as the "three musketeers"). I was still living with my mom in Wakefield. They told me that their girlfriends had a friend over for the night and asked if I would like to go over and meet her. I agreed to the triple date. Sharon and I hit it off immediately and soon fell in love. Three years later we were married. In retrospect, this seems very young (Sharon was twenty, and I was twenty-three), but it was the early '60s and times were different. Sharon went on to Willis Business School and immediately after graduating was hired by Gowling and Henderson, a well-respected law firm in Ottawa, now known as Gowlings and our corporate lawyers for decades.

Sharon stayed with Gowlings for twenty-seven years, until I invited her to come work at the funeral home. Gordon Henderson, the senior lawyer at the law firm, was not happy to see her go. At her going-away party, Mr. Henderson got up to say a few words. He spoke so well of Sharon.

Sharon is a gifted administrator and a hard worker. Her effort went a long way to help put our administration on a good course at our funeral homes and cremation centres. We have two wonderful children, Brett and Erin, whom we raised in the apartment above our downtown funeral home and which we took over after Charlie and Margie Hulse moved out. We were only the second family to live in that apartment. Brett and Erin went to the YMCA daycare before they were old enough to go to school, and as part of their day, the YMCA would take the kids out for a walk, often passing the funeral home. Whenever they did, Brett would point at the building and excitedly tell everyone that was where he lived. I can only imagine what the daycare staff thought.

Whenever a marriage breaks up, it's difficult for everyone involved. We had a number of family conferences about it. Sharon and I sat down with our children and told them that we were getting a divorce. No child likes to see their parents split up, and it caused some tension, but there was no going back.

I was the vice-president of an organization called the International Federation of Thanatologists. Thanatology is the study of death and dying. As a member of this organization, I was invited to a conference in Beijing. It was to be the first time modern funeral practices would be showcased in China. This was 1990, only a year after the Tiananmen Square massacre, and everything had to be cleared with the government. I was to give two presentations: one on state funerals in Canada, and the other on work I've done examining how children relate to the death of a family member or friend. I took Brett with me and decided to go a little early so we could fit in some sightseeing before the conference.

China has been a fairly closed society; therefore, if you're going to do any travelling around the country, the government assigns you a national tour guide. Joan Sun was our guide. Right from the beginning she was curious about my work, which I thought was unusual, because the Chinese do not naturally gravitate to the profession. At that time in China, most people in the funeral profession were army personnel due to the shortage of people who wanted to go into our line of work. Funeral service was perceived as low class in Chinese society.

Over the next three years, Joan and I kept in touch through letters and the occasional phone call. She became interested enough in the funeral business to apply to the funeral director's program at Humber College in Toronto. During that time, I began to realize that our friendship was developing into something more serious.

Divorce is never an easy experience to get through, and the fact that Sharon and I were both senior partners at the funeral home prompted many to predict that it would be the end of the firm. *Frank* magazine, a now-defunct national gossip publication, was especially harsh. Some people really thrive on the misfortune of others, and the conglomerates saw the divorce as an opportunity to divide and conquer. However, we were determined to prove them all wrong. Sharon and I worked hard to ensure that the business wouldn't be affected by our personal lives, agreeing that the company was more important than our problems. It wasn't easy, and there were certainly difficulties along the way, but we got through it.

Sharon and I remain corporate partners. Joan finished her funeral director's course at Humber, having already obtained a bachelor of commerce degree in China. She has since received both her MBA and CMA in Canada, and works part-time for our firm, a dynamic that many people find amazing. Joan has also developed her own company, CanadaChina Business Consulting, which deals mainly with environmental issues, connecting companies in Canada and China.

Great professionals, such as lawyers Ron Gravelle of Perley-Robertson and Anne Curtis of Gowlings; auditors Al McDermid (retired) of London, Ontario; Gilles Fleury of Deloitte, Tracey Pagé of Collins-Barrow, and Roméo Pilon CMA of Comptabilité Roméo Pilon, Gatineau, Quebec, have all been great assets in the success of our various family companies.

The former owner of *Frank* magazine used to live in downtown Ottawa, and I'd see him occasionally. One time I ran into him in a coffee shop and I had to ask, "Well, were you correct in predicting the end of McGarry Family Chapels?"

He just laughed.

"It's not a laughing matter, really, and we have proven you wrong."

All he said as he walked away was, "Time will tell."

And it has.

Charles Hulse often told me how important it was to give back to the community that supports you, and he led by example. As referenced earlier, he was a co-founder of the Ottawa Cancer Society, a lifelong member of the

Kiwanis Club of Ottawa (rising to the position of international vice-president), and part of a group of people instrumental in helping Carleton University grow from its modest beginnings in the Glebe to the fine school it is today. Charlie's passion for education led him to run for a seat on the Ottawa School Board, which he held for thirty-one years, spending eight years as chairman. In three decades he never lost a single election, and he worked tirelessly to improve public education in the city. In recognition of this lifelong dedication, an Ottawa school now bears his name.

Consciously or not, almost everything I've done has been in some way parallel to Charlie Hulse's life. I was on a committee to help raise money for Carleton University; joined the Kiwanis Club, eventually becoming a Kiwanis lieutenant-governor; ran for the school board, winning three terms, spending one term as chairman; and was elected to Regional Council for Ottawa–Carleton. Charlie blazed a trail and encouraged me to follow in his footsteps. This wouldn't surprise anyone who knew Mr. Hulse. He often said that his goal was to help others go as far as they could in life. I think back to his 1962 promise to me, "Always remember where you came from and I will show you how far you can go."

Charlie Hulse loved entertaining, and was well known for his parties. He'd sometimes have a hundred people up to the Hulse apartment above the funeral home, a beautiful residence that only two families have occupied—Charles Hulse and the McGarrys. Sharon McGarry lives there to this day, monitoring our largest business location. Charles would ask one of his employees to stay at the entrance to open the door for his guests. Some of the staff would groan about having to be "Charlie's doorman" for an evening, but I often volunteered because I liked meeting all the interesting people who would inevitably attend the party. You never knew who was going to arrive next. You might open the door and find Harry Belafonte standing in front of you, or the barber from down the street. From humble beginnings, I can now proudly say that I have had the privilege of meeting every Canadian prime minister, beginning with John Diefenbaker to the present.

While meeting these great people certainly has been exciting, some of the most important lessons I've learned have come from ordinary, everyday Canadians. From a young man with a terminal disease, I found out how important it is to appreciate every moment you have, and from a woman dying of cancer caused by second-hand smoke, I learned that even in the face of adversity, you must never give up. Over the years, I've come to realize that all people—rich and poor, famous and infamous, old or young—have something valid to offer this world.

Charlie certainly opened many doors for me, or more appropriately, he taught me how to open the doors of opportunity for myself, both figuratively and literally.

Joan, Sheetza, and I have become strong supporters of Stephen Harper, his wife Laureen, and their children, Ben and Rachel. Although I've not always been known as a Conservative, I believe Mr. Harper is the right person to lead our nation during difficult economic times. I ran unsuccessfully as a Conservative candidate in the 2008 general election in Ottawa Centre. "A suicide mission," many told me, as the riding traditionally voted "left." I did it for the Harpers and I have no regrets. I've lost only one election out of five in public office.

Charles Hulse had a similar relationship with Prime Minister Lester Pearson. (Charlie was a Conservative, in general terms.) Likewise with John Diefenbaker.

I am proud to call former prime ministers Jean Chrétien and Joe Clark friends.

Other political crossover friendships we valued greatly were with the late Tommy Douglas and Stanley Knowles.

Shirley Douglas, Tommy's daughter, is among my best friends. Although Shirley and I differ in our political views, when we meet in her Toronto home, together we solve the problems of the world!

David Knowles, Stanley's son, lives in Ottawa and is a hockey fan, like myself. We have discussed the highs and lows of our local team, the Senators. The Knowles family was very kind to us following the lying-in-state on Parliament Hill of Stanley Knowles. David donated to our archives the "proclamation" from his father's Order of Canada, which we display proudly.

Tommy Douglas, recognized as the Father of Medicare, would have been granted similar recognition on Parliament Hill upon his death; however, Shirley chose to have a very modest, public celebration in Dominion Chalmers United Church, in downtown Ottawa. Prime Minister Brian Mulroney attended the service and spent considerable time in conversation with the Douglas-Sutherland family. The sincerity and appreciation shown by Mr. Mulroney for

Tommy Douglas was a moment that I will always remember and convinced me even more that history will eventually treat the Mulroneys very well, in terms of Brian's visionary leadership.

Following the interment of Tommy Douglas's urn, Shirley invited the McGarrys to a local restaurant to celebrate her father's accomplished life. During the meal a young waitress was eying her son, Kiefer Sutherland. Finally the waitress asked him, "Does anyone ever comment that you have a resemblance to Kiefer Sutherland? Kiefer took it all in stride, and the waitress happily received an autographed note.

We left the restaurant having enjoyed many memories of Tommy Douglas. Tommy had lived in my hometown of Wakefield, Quebec, and we were both members of the local United Church supper club. Again, we did not always agree on current issues, but I felt privileged to have the acquaintance of such a great Canadian.

Afterwards, my brother-in-law, Barry Schwerdfeger, drove Kiefer from the restaurant to his hotel. Kiefer asked Barry if he would like to join him at the bar for a beer. For reasons Barry still cannot identify, he replied, "Better get myself home." Barry was not a block away from the hotel when asked himself, "Why did I do that? Who in hell refuses a drink with Kiefer Sutherland?"

The lesson learned: Support the individual and don't get heavily skewed by partisan politics.

A new era. The McGarrys opened their first crematorium in Wakefield, Quebec, in 1998. We continue to look for new ways that provide more green alternatives to burial in expensive cemetery grounds. One alternative is resomation, a water/alkali-based method that is both dignified and respectful. We continue to respect faith-based and community-based cemeteries, but are fiercely opposed to corporate cemeteries, where the emphasis is on sales, rather than families.

Courtesy of the McGarry Family Archives.

EPILOGUE

What does the future hold for funeral service? While I think that the conglomerates are here to stay and will continue to grow, I believe this is a business best suited for local, family-run firms. I think people are generally more comfortable with the idea of neighbours helping them through the pain of a loss, rather than a big corporation. The conglomerates do their best to try and emulate the warmth and personal approach that comes naturally to family-operated funeral homes, but the underlying principles between the two business models are different.

For starters, we've never "sold" a casket here, and this philosophy has been the foundation of our success. We place no pressure on our employees to generate a profit, so our focus remains on the most important aspect of the job—providing good service to those in need. I don't want to colour the whole corporate side of funeral service in a negative light, but it is different. I believe that somewhere between talk of stock prices and sales quotas, the quality of service is diminished.

The funeral business is changing rapidly, and here in Ontario the government may soon overturn legislation that has prevented a) cemeteries from operating their own funeral homes and b) funeral homes from owning crematoriums/cemeteries. This will create a good deal more competition in a market that has already seen a narrowing of profit margins over the last two decades. This will also spell the end for many smaller, locally run funeral homes. At present, there are only five family-owned funeral homes in the National Capital Region. Not long ago there were eighteen.

In any event, many cemeteries have become very aggressive, particularly in Ontario, sales-driven as opposed to service-oriented, in my opinion. The playing field is far from even for independent funeral homes as compared to cemeteries. The latter pays no municipal taxes (an old law that accommodated small, community-based cemeteries as far back as the nineteenth century).

Arbor/Trillium used this loophole in Ontario to build reception centres (a.k.a. funeral homes) on tax-free cemetery properties, therefore relying on their neighbours, private and corporate, to carry the tax load. Ottawa's Pinecrest and Beechwood cemeteries have followed suit, with the latter promising to welcome "all funeral homes to their site."

The loophole also allows for embalmings to be prepared off the cemetery site, a confusing situation to be sure.

The Ontario Board of Funeral Services has ignored such activity (complacent would be a mild description of the current regulatory authority), but it is an issue that the McGarrys are pursuing vigorously.

Of course, public demands have also changed, and every year more people are choosing cremation instead of burial. This trend is partly related to an ever-increasing population, which places pressure on available space. In fact, in some large metropolitan areas, cremation is the only option available now. Simply put, a time will come when we will no longer be able to bury human remains in urban areas.

In other cases, people chose cremation as they do not want to purchase an expensive cemetery plot and casket. I think this trend reflects a change in society's values.

Yet finances tell only part of the story. People are more aware of the environment, so the idea of using fine woods for caskets and interring the remains is losing favour.

Changes within religious faiths are also having an impact on burial practices. At one time, Roman Catholics could not be cremated without a letter of permission from the archbishop. The Vatican still prefers that the bodily remains be present at the funeral mass, but Catholic families now have the option of choosing cremation afterwards, if they wish.

While I believe that there will always be caskets and urns, new service options are now available.

When I started working in funeral service in the early 1960s, cremation made up about 3 percent of our services; it is now 76 percent at McGarry Family Chapels / Cremation Centres. This translates to approximately 1.5 percent growth every year. If we hadn't built our own crematoriums, I think we would be out of business by now.

Another choice gaining in popularity is having your family member's ashes inurned in a columbarium, a small stone structure fitted with compartments, which usually have enough space to hold two urns. The word columbarium is derived from the Latin word, *columba*, meaning dovecote. A dovecote is a structure for nesting doves, a bird many people associate with peace. Thus, a columbarium takes on the idea of a peaceful and safe place. Some people prefer this method instead of earth burial or scattering, often because each space has its own remembrance plaque, not unlike a cemetery plot with a monument that family members can visit any time they wish. We built our columbarium next to our crematorium in Wakefield. It's a very tranquil spot, and I've often spotted deer grazing nearby.

Carolyn McGarry-Coté, one of our valued receptionists as well as our librarian at Hulse, Playfair & McGarry, has arranged for two niches at our columbarium. She was, unfortunately, predeceased by both her son, Tim, and her husband, Orval. They are in one niche in companion urns. Carolyn has instructed that her urn will be placed in a niche beside Orval and Tim, with a portion of her ashes placed in a locket specially made for that purpose. The locket will be inside the niche with her husband and son in perpetuity

There is always going to be ceremony surrounding death. The passage of a life necessitates some form of recognition. Every culture has rituals surrounding mortality, and it's human nature to mark this important transition. The funeral service brings a sense of closure for friends and family, and opens the door for the healing process to begin. It's also a reminder that our lives are finite and that we should make the most of the time we have left.

I see the funeral as a positive experience. In a time when life seems to be moving more quickly all the time, and instant gratification is becoming second nature, the funeral provides a time for reflection—a time to pause and consider the value and fragility of life. I believe that the way a society cares for its dead is a reflection of the society itself.

My colleagues laugh every time I say I'm going to retire. I've said it many times during the last few years, but discovered that it's very difficult to leave a job that you love. I suppose I use the term "retire" somewhat loosely, as I can't see myself pulling away entirely. I may back away from the day-to-day operations of the funeral home but, like Charlie Hulse, I'll remain as an adviser, and I'll certainly sit in on the funeral arrangements for friends. This life's work is part of my DNA, and I've enjoyed every minute of it, even the challenges.

I suppose that whenever people get a little older and start thinking about retirement, it's natural for them to be concerned that the generation following will not perform the job as well as they did. They may wonder how the business will ever survive without them; however, as the American writer and philosopher Elbert Hubbard once said, "The graveyards are full of people the world could not do without."

While looking back at what the McGarrys have accomplished here, I've come to realize that I'm in the same position now that Charlie Hulse was in when he was getting ready to retire. Looking at the company, and, despite my best efforts, I worry about the future. Will the firm be able to remain independent in an increasingly competitive market? Will it uphold the same standards? I am trying to let the new generation take over, and I am trying to accept the fact that life keeps moving forward. However, while the future holds challenges, those challenges will only make the firm and the employees stronger.

Our funeral home would not be here today if it were not for Charles Hulse's vision. Even now, twenty-four years after his death, I'm sure a week doesn't go by when I don't think of him. It's important to remember our roots, and we owe it to Charlie's memory to preserve the legacy he and Keith Playfair established. That means continuing to put our families first and maintaining our standards of service. They are led by my cousin Patrick McGarry and supported by Sharon McGarry (president) along with our son Brett and daughter Erin (studying veterinary medicine). We are all equals here, and I have faith that the firm will remain in good hands for generations to come.

I'm also concerned about what I'll do with myself after retirement. The funeral home is a big part of my life and my identity; it's not going to be easy to say goodbye. To walk out the door that last time will take some courage, because I will be letting go of part of myself.

All things must come to an end, and as a funeral director, I see this lesson every day. It is the end that gives meaning to the journey, and the journey has been good.

If I had to do it over again, I'm not sure I would work as hard. While I would spend more time with my family, I can't imagine anything that would have given me more satisfaction than my career as a funeral director. I like to think that I have spent my life working to create meaningful community events that help people get through tragedy and sorrow.

I've often heard people say at funerals that it's too bad it took a death to get the family together. This is one way of looking at it, but we all have the ability to choose how we experience the events in our lives, to choose to see things as positive or negative. Today, many families are divided. I've seen instances at funerals where half-sisters and -brothers are introduced to each other, or estranged family members meet for the first time in years. The heightened emotional atmosphere of the funeral can allow people to express thoughts and feelings that may have been pent up for decades, which can result in forgiveness and greater understanding of each other.

The funeral ritual can be therapeutic. I like to call the funeral service a "celebration of life," and I think people often leave our funeral home with a lighter heart than when they arrived. Many times over the years we have received letters from people thanking us because they have been reacquainted with long-lost relatives, or because a relationship has been refreshed.

At the end of the day, the help we give to people as funeral directors is what's really important. It's why I do this work. Spending my life in the service of others has given me a satisfaction that has been more rewarding than anything I can imagine.

I attended a retirement party at Christ Church Cathedral for the Bishop of the Anglican Diocese of Ottawa, the Rt. Rev. Peter Coffin. I've worked with Peter for twenty-five years, and I really wanted to attend the party, but I was also scheduled to attend a meeting of the Cancer Foundation. After spending some time at the retirement party and offering Peter my best wishes, I hurried out to the meeting, which was being held at Rabbi Reuven Bulka's home. I was running late and when I arrived, the meeting was already underway. I tried to be as unobtrusive as possible as I made my way to the table, but as soon as Rabbi Bulka saw me, he cleared his throat loudly, smiled at me, and then announced, "Ahh, it's the *late* Brian McGarry!"

Laughter filled the room; however, since I had now been singled out, I felt that I should explain my tardiness.

"I'm sorry I'm late, everyone. I ran over here from Bishop Coffin's retirement party . . ."

And the rabbi, without missing a beat, quipped, "It figures. Wherever there's a coffin, you're sure to find McGarry!"

It's important not to lose sight of the value of humour. Once you stop laughing, you know you're really in trouble.

ABOUT THE CO-AUTHOR

 Paul Mahar is a graduate of the Dramatic Scriptwriting program at Algonquin College. He lives in Ottawa, where his one-act play, *Grass*, was showcased at the National Arts Centre's Hothouse Reading Series. *The Story—From Paupers to Prime Ministers—A Life in Death* is his first published work.

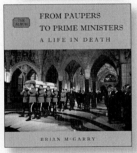

TO ORDER MORE COPIES, CONTACT:

General Store Publishing House Inc.
499 O'Brien Road, Renfrew, Ontario, Canada K7V 3Z3
Tel 1.800.465.6072 • Fax 1.613.432.7184
www.gsph.com